Y0-EEA-326

Women in Print
I

Opportunities for Women's Studies Research in Language and Literature

Edited by
Joan E. Hartman
and
Ellen Messer-Davidow

for the Commission on the Status of Women in the Profession

THE MODERN LANGUAGE ASSOCIATION of AMERICA
NEW YORK 1982

Library of Congress Cataloging in Publication Data

Main entry under title:

Women in print.

Includes bibliographical references.

Contents: 1. Opportunities for women's studies research in language and literature.

1. Women and literature—Addresses, essays, lectures. I. Hartman, Joan. II. Messer-Davidow, Ellen, 1941- . III. Modern Language Association of America. Commission on the Status of Women in the Profession.

PN481.W656 809'.89287 82-3596

ISBN 0-87352-336-9 (v. 1) AACR2

ISBN 0-87352-337-7 (pbk. : v. 1)

Published by The Modern Language Association of America

62 Fifth Avenue, New York, New York 10011

Contents

Introduction

Women in Print, the title of these two volumes sponsored by the Modern Language Association Commission on the Status of Women in the Profession, refers to the women authors who are—or should be—the subjects of our research, publication, and teaching and to ourselves as publishing scholars, critics, and teachers of women's studies in language and literature. *Women in Print I: Opportunities for Women's Studies Research in Language and Literature* assesses areas where research and publication are needed—in the fundamental tasks of scholarship, in the study of language, in the national literatures, and in the literature produced by women writers who have been neglected on grounds of class, race, and sociosexual orientation. *Women in Print II: Opportunities for Women's Studies Publication in Language and Literature* surveys ways and means to further the publication of women's studies in language and literature; it explores the nature, requirements, and resources of both establishment and alternative publishing.

When the MLA Commission on the Status of Women was established in 1969, courses in women's studies were beginning to be taught in colleges and universities throughout the United States, and then, as now, courses in literature figured prominently among them. By 1976 there were 270 women's studies programs and an estimated 15,000 courses offered at some 1,500 different institutions (Florence Howe, *Seven Years Later: Women's Studies Programs in 1976* [n.p.: National

Advisory Council on Women's Studies Programs, 1977], p. 15). Between one third and one half of these courses were offered in the humanities, and of these, half—or, at a conservative estimate, 2,500 courses—were offered in literature. By 1981 the number of women's studies programs had risen from 270 to 328 (*PMLA,* 96 [1981], 716–21) and by December 1981 there were 2,316 members of the MLA Division of Women's Studies in Language and Literature, making it the sixth largest division in MLA. The women who teach and study language and literature have contributed substantially to the development of women's studies and are substantially investing their professional energy and status in this field.

The members of the MLA Commission on the Status of Women are mindful that the charge to monitor and improve the status of women in the profession requires an advocacy not only of women as scholars, teachers, and students but also of women's literary productions and lives as subjects meriting serious and sustained inquiry. We recognize too that the work of augmenting and dispersing knowledge about women writers, of challenging their exclusion from the literary canon and the classroom, and of seeing that suitable texts are available for teaching and research can afford women opportunities for publication and for enhancing their professional reputations. That some scholars in the modern languages are doing research and writing about women authors we know from the papers they present—at national and regional MLA meetings and at women's studies conferences—as well as from what they publish: they are recording female literary history, creating feminist pedagogy, and devising feminist critiques of literature, criticism, and language. But are enough women aware of the possibilities for women's studies research, and are there sufficient opportunities for them to publish?

The commission's "Study III: Women in Modern Language Departments, 1972–73" (*PMLA,* 91 [1976], 124–36) shows, not surprisingly, that publication is a major predictor of rank, tenure, and salary in English and foreign language departments. Women do not publish as much as men, perhaps partly because of a disparity in status. A smaller percentage of women teachers than of men teachers hold Ph.D.'s, and a larger percentage of women than of men are in the lower ranks at all institutions and in all ranks at institutions where teaching loads are high. Consequently women do more than their share of the profession's teaching. But, even taking into account these imbalances, the commission felt that women could do a larger share of the profession's publishing. It suggested that publishers and editors might be less receptive to manuscripts by women than to those by men, that they might be inadequately informed about the value of and need for women's studies materials, and that, in turn, women's studies scholars might require a fuller understanding of the publishing industry.

In response to these considerations, the commission identified publishing as a promising area in which to begin working for change. Toward that end, the members planned a conference for 2 April 1976 in New York, inviting representatives from university presses, commercial publishers, and periodicals to attend a day of workshops on bibliography, scholarship, reprints, texts, anthologies and popular writings, and periodicals. Conducted jointly by editors and by women's studies scholars and teachers, the workshops aimed at an exchange of information. On the one hand, the commission wished to learn about the editors' processes of submission, review, and contracting; their economic and marketing policies; their selection of manuscript readers; their criteria for judging manuscripts; their interest in women's studies in language and literature; and any constraints they felt about publishing women's studies materials. On the other, the commission also wished to let the editors know about the identity and size of the potential market for women's studies publications, the value of women's studies as a field of inquiry and teaching, the nature and amount of research under way, and the work that remained to be done and to be published.

Encouraged by the publishers' receptiveness and eager to disperse the findings of the conference to women's studies scholars and teachers, Joan E. Hartman and Ellen Messer-Davidow, the editors of this two-volume work, arranged several workshops: one, Women in Print, in December 1976 at the MLA meeting in San Francisco; another in June 1979 at the National Women's Studies Association conference in Lawrence, Kansas; and a third in November 1979 at the American Educational Research Association conference in Cleveland, Ohio. Meanwhile, we were planning this publication to enlarge on matters discussed at the April 1976 conference and to reach a wider audience than we could through conferences. In soliciting contributions, we emphasized the provisional nature of *Women in Print*: the two volumes inquire into possible directions for research, make a preliminary survey of the available resources, and provide a tentative guide to our needs in research and publication.

The essays of *Women in Print I: Opportunities for Women's Studies Research in Language and Literature* fall into three categories: fundamental tasks of scholarship—bibliography, archival research, and linguistic analysis; women's literatures of special concern to feminists—lesbian, black, and working-class; and national literatures—German, Russian, Hispanic, French, and British. It might appear to the reader that one body of literature has been omitted, that of our own nation, but the literatures (in their justly plural form) of the United States supply much of the illustrative material for the first six essays, on the Anglo-American bibliographic tradition, archival research on Southern women writers, Anglo-American linguistic research, lesbian writers of the United States and lesbian expatriates in Paris, black American women writers, and working-class women's literature, particularly of this country. These essays attest to the rich diversity of a tradition that has been too rigidly confined to authors of one sex and one race, a few classes and regions, and certain genres and subjects. Like Hispanic literature, which is the product of some two dozen countries and populations, and French literature, which is provincial and francophone as well as Parisian, our literature has been written by authors of both sexes and all races, classes, and regions; they are dwellers at home and abroad, users of various dialects, chroniclers of different cultural histories, and crafters of diverse forms.

Having decided to examine literature and its study in these various categories, both conventional and new, we attempted to ensure continuity among the essays by asking the authors (1) to designate works, authors, periods, and topics that afford opportunities for research and publication; (2) to indicate the kinds of publications needed for research and teaching by format and content; and (3) to consider questions of canonicity, that is, why certain works are included in the literary canon while others are excluded and how the body of received works can be enlarged. In short, our aim was twofold: to reclaim and to revise. While the proponents of other critical approaches—such as reader-response criticism, poststructuralism, Marxist criticism, and the sociology of literature—are also questioning canonicity, we specifically wished to expose the operations of a gender system in literary endeavors. To narrow the scope of the ambitious charge we gave our contributors, we added that the essays need be only tentative and illustrative, not exhaustive. Within the space allowed, some authors chose to limit themselves to a period, some to a region or literary culture, and some to a theme.

The essays of *Women in Print I* exhibit recurrent concerns—notably, the absence of women's works from the canons of literature and "authoritative" scholarship, the pervasive attitudes that relegate women writers and scholars to a separate and secondary sphere, and the techniques that keep literature and criticism primarily the domain of white middle-class heterosexual males. Most conspicuously excluded not only from the literary canon but also from traditional inquiry, publication, and teaching are lesbian and black women writers. In "Out of the Archives and into the Academy: Opportunities for Research and Publication in Lesbian Literature," Karen M. Keener declares that the writing, reading, publication, and study of lesbian literature have been severely constrained by the fear and hatred of lesbianism in society. This literature is subjected both to the censorship that its authors and scholars impose on themselves because they fear retribution and to the censorship of publishers, who are unwilling to undergo the anticipated consequences of publishing this literature—small sales, moral and critical condemnation, and possible obscenity charges. And it is also subjected to an academic censorship (too slippery to prove but too insistent to mistake) imposed through pressure on the faculty who treat lesbian literature: their contracts are not renewed, their literary interests are discouraged, their research is actively directed, and their peace is often disrupted. As Erlene Stetson points out in "Black Women in and out of Print," the relation of black women to publishing arises from causes both historical and present. Subjugated, excluded, and deprived during and after slavery, black women are now powerless to direct their lives in a white male-run economy, which the publishing and literary establishments replicate morally and financially. White male editors, publishers, scholars, and reviewers are unable to move beyond ignorance, fear, or disgust in reading what black women write about—lives, experiences, and histories that do not support the white patriarchal myths of America. With negligible participation in publishing as decision makers and with few resources (including white-skin privilege) to create their own media, black women have had little chance to put their words into print. Their literary disenfranchisement has not stopped them from writing, but it has resulted in a scarcity of publications—primary sources, teaching materials, critical studies, and outlets for research and writing.

The separate and secondary sphere to which women writers and scholars have been consigned is implied and on occasion named. According to Susan L. Cocalis, Kay Goodman, and Sara Lennox, the authors of "Women in German Language and Literature," the term *Frauenliteratur* (or *Frauendichtung*), which is applied to both works and writers, signifies the subjective literary forms (short lyric poems, letters, and autobiographies) and the sentimental and domestic themes used by women writers. German literary historians of the nineteenth century, postulating that women could not master the "serious" genres (the historical novel, the drama, the epic poem, the novella), elaborated a gender-based system of classification and evaluation. The histories and anthologies of that period, as well as of subsequent ones, either fail to include female authors or, when not adhering to an alphabetical arrangement, list them together under a gender heading, regardless of their different styles, genres, periods, and topics. In "Opportunities for Scholarship in Eighteenth-Century British Literature," Katharine M. Rogers describes a treatment of women writers that must arise from the same mentality that designated a *Frauenliteratur*: the femaleness of authors is almost never overlooked by critics and scholars, and it almost always evokes denigration. Women who wrote in many genres came to be known only for those that fit the "feminine" pattern (sentimental novels, Gothic romances, or local-color fiction), for their connections with literary men of the period, or for their extraliterary reputations. While Rogers declares that female authors "must be evaluated as men are—in the context of their period and the mainstream of literature—not isolated in a literary ghetto with its own separate standards," she also desires a greater understanding of the education, relationships, status, constraints, and attitudes that colored the lives of the eighteenth-century English women writers, considered both collectively and individually.

While the differences between women and men are often maintained in literature as in life to the detriment of women, the essays on Russian and French literatures show that femininity (that is, the characteristics the culture ascribes to women) can be a positive distinction. Certainly both literatures do have misogynistic traditions of cruelly or comically portraying all that is female; but in "Women's Studies in Russian Literature: Opportunities for Research and Publication" Barbara Heldt points out that Russian literature also has a tradition of the strong, intense central female character: most commonly a young woman who establishes her independence or acts out the ideas of society, this protagonist, as the center of identity and intensity, is often depicted by her male author not as the Other but as the "Self, a better or worse self, perhaps, but always one more fully or intensely realized." These characters, with their heightened awareness, moral capacity, and courage, may be created to represent the fully human condition. Christiane P. Makward and Sylvie Weil's essay, "Directions in French Women's Studies," contains an account of the "writing-in-the-feminine" movement that began in France in the mid-1970s with the first radical critiques of male-centered philosophical discourse and with a poll "on the question of 'the sex of writing' " in a prestigious French literary journal. The French feminists involved in this movement asserted not the similarities between the sexes but "the difference of the feminine and postulated a nonmasculine relation of women to language." At first these matters were discussed in critical and theoretical writings, but they soon became the principles, as well as the subjects, of creative writing that has attempted innovations in specifically female language, form, imagery, and rhythm.

Like many of their colleagues, Heldt, Makward, and Weil mention the wealth of women's writings that remain deposited in the national archives and libraries. The books and manuscripts that gather dust in institutional collections have at least been preserved, and some have been published. That they do not circulate is only one manifestation of the neglect that categorically seems to befall women's writings somewhere along the way toward preserving, publishing, reprinting, reading and teaching, interpreting, and evaluating them. The greatest beneficiaries of all these public and scholarly attentions are the canonized works of literature, criticism, and scholarship. In this volume, several essays examine the criteria that support literary reputation and canonization and that screen categories of works from consideration. In "Working-Class Women's Literature: An Introduction to Study," Paul Lauter argues that a definition of working-class literature, and subsequently the criteria for evaluating it, must be founded on a description of its distinctive forms and features. The concepts and criteria that have been derived primarily from a high-culture, written literature inadequately illuminate and assess, for instance, oral works, works of mass culture or popular culture, and works created incrementally and collaboratively by a group in social settings in which artist and audience are not separate entities. Critics often judge working-class literature deficient because they use irrelevant criteria. Deborah S. Rosenfelt's essay, "The Politics of Bibliography: Women's Studies and the Literary Canon," shows in detail how criteria may act as "filters" to screen works by and about women from the literary canon and from scholarly study. For instance, such criteria as "universal" and "regional," which traditional critics have used to distinguish works as "greater" or "lesser" on the basis of presumably inherent literary qualities, actually tend to separate and devalue women's writings. Producing blunt, categorical judgments rather than sensitive evaluations, they reflect the social, political, and intellectual assumptions of those who wish to preserve not only the canon and its study but also their own privileged roles in criticism. Such assumptions infuse bibliographic selection, scholarly interests and interpretations, critical evaluations, and canonization, and they become almost irrevocable because bibliography, evaluation, and the canon precondition and reaffirm one another.

While Rosenfelt looks at some of the dynamics that produced the literary canon, Elizabeth A. Meese looks toward some strategies that will enlarge it. In "Archival Materials: The Problem of Literary Reputation," she contends that the "discovery, publication, and analysis of women's archival materials are a necessary beginning to the reassessment of women's place in the literary canon and of the canon itself." Scanning the contributions of Southern writers that are beginning to emerge from institutional archives, organizational files, and attics, she shows that female literary work has often differed from the kinds of work celebrated in the canon—authorship, especially of imaginative literature; achievement in the "major" genres; and the endowment of works with a universal import. The unearthing of these materials will establish the nature, diversity, and depth of women's literary contributions; reveal additional works and writers that deserve attention; and aid in the writing of biographical and critical studies that will in turn support new assessments of women's accomplishments and of existing canonical assumptions.

The essays of *Women in Print I* not only challenge the stereotypical treatment of women and their works but also stress the importance of treating women's literatures with a sensitivity to the differences that are determined by time and nation, by cultural plurality within a given community, by authorial definition, and by particular scholarly tasks. In "Opportunities for Women's Studies in the Hispanic Field," Jean Franco explains that Hispanic scholars deal with the literatures of nineteen Spanish-speaking countries of the Americas, as well as those of Spain and of the Spanish-speaking minority of the United States. In each of these countries and in some individual communities, the women's movement is in different stages, and the social, political, economic, and cultural conditions vary. The scholar has first to identify these conditions and then to determine how they not only influence women's lives but often appear in their art. The cultural plurality that characterizes the field of Hispanic women's literature and, even more complexly, the study of the literature produced by all communities of women can be seen again and again in the study of language. H. Lee Gershuny, whose essay "Language and Feminist Research" surveys diverse areas of linguistic study, cites experiments with groups in which such considerations as the sexual composition of the group and the type of task assigned can shape the language used by participants. One of her main points is that masculinist linguistic research is insensitive to cultural plurality. Traditional linguists, she reports, instead of working from a notion of language performance (that is, the actual uses of language in particular situations), employ a concept of "competence" to explore the intuitive knowledge of sounds, meanings, and syntax possessed by the speakers of a language. Because the concept of competence is based on the model of white middle-class males operating in a homogeneous speech community, traditional linguists must disregard differences or classify them as deviant.

The essays in this volume advocate female voices, female values, and female pluralism. They ask that literature by and about women be viewed as rich and varied and that it be studied for itself, without narrow assumptions and inappropriate criteria. Tillie Olsen once observed in a conversation that the criterion she applies to literature, criticism, and scholarship is, Does it enrich or impoverish literature? (Univ. of Cincinnati, 26 Oct. 1978). Others, whose criteria are more restrictive, ask, "Is it a great work? Is he a major author? Is it a serious genre?" and these criteria, ranking both works and writers, do not enhance the study of literature. To value, as Deborah Rosenfelt points out, is not to elevate the few and discard the rest. On the contrary, valuing leads us to expand our understanding and appreciation of the diversity of literary works and the breadth of their study.

The essays of *Women in Print I* present an array of resources, ideas, and directions for women's studies research and publication in language and literature. They reveal their authors in the midst of that generous activity of enlarging and enriching our views of language, literature, and ourselves.

Joan E. Hartman and Ellen Messer-Davidow
College of Staten Island, City University of New York
University of Cincinnati

The Politics of Bibliography
Women's Studies and the Literary Canon

Deborah S. Rosenfelt

The introduction to this volume describes the remarkable growth of women's studies in language and literature over the past decade. The proliferation of women-and-literature classes has generated, and has been generated by, a corresponding proliferation of research, scholarship, and critical theory. Unfortunately, there is a frustrating discrepancy between this abundance and its documentation in convenient bibliographic resources and aids to research. In the last few years, though, some important new research tools have emerged to facilitate work in this area, and more are in progress; the Appendix to this essay surveys some of these aids to research. My main purpose, however, is not to provide another bibliography but, rather, to explore the theoretical and practical problems involved in using existing bibliographic resources, revising those that are inadequate, and creating new ones. These problems are of fundamental importance to feminist scholars and teachers in defining and performing the bibliographic tasks that will give shape and substance to women's studies in language and literature and in carrying out the larger task of revising the literary canon.[1]

The term "bibliography" covers a multitude of forms, from book-length checklists of all an author's publications to publishers' catalogs of their latest offerings; from multivolume biobibliographies of many authors in various periods to selective topical bibliographies published in obscure journals; from catalogs of unpublished archival materials to periodicals for monitoring critical studies; from exhaustive listings of the contents of national libraries to course reading lists. Whatever the particular bibliographic form, the basic function is obvious: to inform us of materials that we might otherwise not know about. Cumulatively, though, bibliographies and aids to research perform another function: they map the contours of a discipline. In literature, they tell us what to read—by whom and about whom. The listing of a literary or a critical work in those places where scholars look for guidance—annual MLA bibliographies, specialized topical bibliographies, research guides, and publication histories—is analogous to the reporting of a current event in the media: if the event gets coverage, it is news; if it gets none, it is not. Further, human and literary events that receive repeated coverage acquire a certain categorical significance. Taxonomic decisions, then, quickly become political ones. By their inclusions and even more by their omissions, the bibliographies of our profession have done injustice to the contributions of women writers to our literary heritage.[2]

Two obvious distinctions between bibliographic categories will help to clarify this generalization and to locate more precisely the places in the bibliographic process where women writers begin to disappear. The first distinction is between bibliographies that document primary materials written by particular authors—essays, autobiography, letters, journals, diaries, imaginative literature—and those that list secondary studies about authors and their works—bibliography, biography, criticism, concordances, etc. In documenting primary materials, bibliographies make accessible the publication histories of given writers. In choosing the genres of writing to be included, particularly those to be used as taxons (bibliographic categories), primary bibliographers also make some judgments about what constitutes significant literature. In documenting secondary works, bibliographies guide us to the resources available for studying those writers and those literary works. By their very existence, they also tell us which writers and which works have been validated by critical consideration.

The second distinction is between those bibliographies that are comprehensive—the *British Museum Catalogue,* the *National Union Catalogue, Books in Print,* title registers, guides to archival holdings—and those that are selective, offering documentation for the "important" writers of a given era or nationality. For the purposes of this essay comprehensive bibliographies are of less concern than selective ones, because they include *all* the works in a given category: all the contents of a national library or archive, all the books published in a certain country in a certain year, all the articles published in a certain periodical within a certain time period. They require neither choice nor value judgment at the bibliographic level;[3] thus, they are not discriminatory, in either sense of the word. Comprehensive primary bibliographies like the *BMC*, the *NUC*, and even the relatively comprehensive *Cambridge Bibliography of English Literature* volumes do include the names of literally thousands of women writers.

Selective bibliographies, on the other hand, are discriminatory; that is, they involve choice—about whom to include and whom to exclude, what materials to scan, and even how to define "literature." The process of choosing involves, of course, applying clearly defined criteria to a given body of material. But this process inevitably calls into play bibliographers' less conscious assumptions about what constitutes significant literature, and it is at this point that bibliographies can become discriminatory in the other sense of the word. Also, to the extent that some bibliographers rely on the work of their predecessors, they can—without acknowledgment or awareness—transmit the discriminations of one generation to the next. The consequences are serious, for the selective bibliographies and guides to research, especially the more prestigious and popular, not only represent the canon of "great" works but help to define it. Precisely because they are selective, they bestow not only accessibility but legitimacy on both literary works and studies of them. The major reviews of research, the annual bibliographies in the scholarly journals, the research guides combining the publication histories of given authors with reviews of studies about those authors—it is these bibliographies to which teachers and students of literature turn, both for information and, implicitly, for advice. These are the works, the authors, the critical studies that *matter*. A book like Jackson Bryer's *Sixteen Modern American Authors: A Survey of Research and Criticism* (New York: Norton, 1974), in addition to guiding its reader to the "best" literary criticism, implicitly identifies as "major" the sixteen writers it includes. Only one woman writer, Willa Cather, appears among the sixteen. The proportion is fairly typical. Somehow, in the selection processes, more women writers are filtered out than their numbers and the significance of their contributions would justify.

Elaine Showalter, in a review essay for *Signs*, points to one obvious reason for the sparsity of women writers in bibliographies of critical studies:

> It is still astounding to read the annual PMLA bibliographies and discover the discrepancies between the critical energies lavished on male writers of very modest attainments and the underdevelopment of research on scores of women novelists, dramatists, and poets, whose books are unobtainable, whose lives have never been written, whose letters are uncollected, and whose works have been studied casually, if ever.[4]

Showalter, of course, is deploring not the content of the MLA bibliographies themselves but the trends in criticism they reflect. As Walter Achtert, director of research programs at MLA, remarked at the conference on women and publishing that gave rise to this volume, bibliography cannot really lead the profession; it can, on the whole, only follow. His statement is partially true: bibliographies of critical studies cannot make up works that do not exist and they are not the final cause of the discrepancy Showalter describes.

Rather, criticism and bibliography, operating as linked and mutually reinforcing historical processes, have inevitably perpetuated the cultural and aesthetic biases of society as a whole and the profession in particular. That is, if women writers suffer critical contempt or neglect, they will not find their way into the bibliographies and guides to research that help determine the works most of us read and teach and write about. Thus they will continue to suffer critical neglect. The primary task of feminist scholars in language and literature is to break this vicious circle, a task that requires a more precise understanding of its dynamics. An examination of some of our profession's bibliographical tools will illustrate concretely both the extent of women writers' underrepresentation and the attitudes and processes responsible for it.

Let me begin with an example from my own admittedly limited venture into bibliography. Five years ago, Florence Howe and I began work on a Goldentree bibliography[5] of women writers in England and the United States from the Middle Ages to the present. Although we had guessed at the magnitude of women's literature from our own teaching and research, we were nevertheless overwhelmed by the sheer number of writers we identified—a thousand women who merited inclusion as the authors not of unpublished manuscripts but of published works. Because Goldentree bibliographies, designed as reference tools for college students and teachers, are highly selective, we were able to choose only 150 writers. After eliminating juvenalia, children's books, and publications of individual stories, poems, pamphlets, and plays, we still had close to ten thousand entries, probably three fourths of them works written by the women themselves and the rest critical studies. To include as many primary entries as possible, we decided to omit critical studies for the women writers covered in the earlier volumes of the Goldentree series. That decision, unfortunately, saved little space. The thirteen literary bibliographies already published in the series (not counting the single volumes for Chaucer and Milton) contain ten times as many male writers as female writers (977 to 86, by a quick count), and over half the female writers appear in two volumes, Darwin Turner's *Afro-American Writers* (New York: Appleton, 1970) and Ian Watt's *The British Novel: Scott through Hardy* (Northbrook, Ill.: AHM, 1973).

We can be grateful for Turner's and Watt's acknowledgments of the rich achievements of black American women writers and Victorian women novelists. Unfortunately, Watt and Turner were the exceptions, the rare bibliographers whose political orientation or, in Turner's case, ethnic identification made them sensitive to the literary implications of class, race, and sex and to the need for bibliographic affirmative action to amend the status quo. The other bibliographies in the series exhibit in various ways an untroubled androcentric perspective—that is, a kind of tunnel vision focused almost entirely on the male (usually the white middle-class male) as cultural norm. Take, for example, the bibliography *American Literature: Poe through Garland* (New York: Appleton, 1971), a collection emphasizing, according to its compiler, Harry Hayden Clark, the writers' contributions to "the short story, literary theory and criticism, social or travel commentary, history, and letters" (p. v). Clark includes economist Henry George, naturalist John Muir, historian John Fiske, and Confederate poet Henry Timrod, but he leaves out (among many others) Margaret Fuller, Elizabeth Cady Stanton, Mary Hunter Austin, and Charlotte Perkins Gilman, all of whom made significant contributions to at least one of the genres named. Only three women writers appear: Emily Dickinson, Sara Orne Jewett, and Constance Fenimore Woolson.

A similar failure in perception (for what else can one call the apparent obliviousness to women writers of considerable stature?) appears in Blake Nevius' *The American Novel: Sinclair Lewis to the Present* (Northbrook, Ill.: AHM, 1970), a Goldentree bibliography that exemplifies with particular clarity the circular relation between critical attention and bibliographic recognition. This volume focuses on secondary works, and Nevius explains that certain regrettable omissions reflect not so much his judgment as "a dearth of extended or serious commentary on these novelists and, incidentally, the degree to which studies of the contemporary American novel have concentrated on a half dozen writers" (p. v). The disproportion in his compilation of forty men and eight women is not his fault, since it reflects the real imbalance Showalter noted between the critical energies devoted to male as opposed to female writers. Yet the absences Nevius particularly regrets are all of men (John Cheever, Herbert Gold, Paul Bowles, James Purdy). Anyone relatively knowledgeable about women's literature will regret a good many other omissions, including Djuna Barnes, Kay Boyle, Zora Neale Hurston, and Anaïs Nin.

This androcentric perspective is the underlying cause of the cycle of exclusion, the filtering out of women writers disproportionately to their numbers and the significance of their contributions. As many cultural critics have documented far more thoroughly, the academic and literary establishment that makes critical decisions is and always has been a patriarchal institution, sharing and often helping to perpetuate the vision of man as norm, woman as other. Sometimes the simple obliviousness of androcentrism gives way to the false chivalry or open hostility of sexism. Here is George Watson Cole, a scholar of some repute, writing for the Bibliographic Society of America in 1929 about the founding of the American Library Association:

> On September 15, 1853, there was held in New York the first American Conference of librarians. Fifty-three delegates were in attendance, all of them men. . . . Then in the rooms of the Pennsylvania Historical Association, on October 4, 1876 . . . the American Library Association was organized. The total attendance was 103, of whom there were 11 ladies, who, taking their lives in their hands, ventured into this den of bibliothecal lions and—wonderful to relate—escaped in safety. An Englishman . . . was also present.[6]

Cole's recognition that bibliographic circles are patriarchal is commendable, but his patronizing tone is as suggestive as his statistics on women's status in them. I encountered his statement during the same week that a bibliothecal lion visiting at the Huntington Library remarked to me confidently over lunch that if any American women writers had been lost and neglected, it was certainly because they deserved to be. At least the libraries are open to women now; but although no contemporary Virginia Woolf need curse their closed doors, society is still not free of the assumptions that made culture a male domain. The persistent attitude among many male and some female scholars that women as a class, if noticed at all, are not to be taken seriously means specifically that, though "great" women writers are often acknowledged as such, "minor" women writers are perceived as *more* minor than their male counterparts. Only the pervasiveness of this profound androcentrism can account fully for the imbalance between the critical attention devoted to male writers and that devoted to female writers.

This androcentric bias has manifested itself in a variety of bibliographic processes and critical assumptions that have functioned as filters in the screening out of women writers. Simple perpetuation of the same bibliographic entries from era to era is one such process. Clark, for example, probably inherited some of his inclusions as well as some of his omissions from another bibliographer, Jacob Blanck, head of a bibliographic project that reveals under scrutiny some of the more subtle mechanisms and attitudes responsible for the secondary status of women in bibliography. In the early 1940s, under the auspices of the Bibliographic Society of America, Blanck began work on a selective but relatively extensive bibliography describing first editions of belletristic works by American writers who died before 1930. In the preface to his *Bibliography of American Literature* (New Haven: Yale Univ. Press, 1955–69), Blanck explains its scope:

> This, then, is a selective bibliography. It is limited to the material which constitutes the structure of American literature of the past

> one hundred and fifty years. It is not an attempt to evaluate the American author or his work, for that is not the province of the bibliographer. . . . In a bibliography each meets on common ground. . . . We have attempted only to describe bibliographically the work of certain American authors who, in their own time at least, were known and read. Present popularity, or the lack of it, was not a factor in deciding whether the inclusion of an author was appropriate. If for a period . . . an author's works enjoyed something resembling recognition, then such productions were within our scope.
>
> The thought was to present a list of American works which, for any reason, were considered significant in American . . . literature. (I, xi)

This passage contains only one explicit criterion for inclusion: an author must have been at some period "known and read" and "considered significant." "To the bibliographer," Blanck writes, "a titanic classic is no more important than the poorest production of the less talented author" (I, xi). How, then, *did* the selection of some three hundred authors from thousands of candidates take place? The process had two stages. First, a supervisory committee of the Bibliographical Society of America (five scholars, all male) drew up a preliminary list. Then the committee sought consultation by publishing its list in the *Library Journal* (15 June 1944, pp. 549–50) and by circulating it among MLA scholars and specialists in American literature. The committee's original list included 46 women and 224 men. In the completed volumes of the bibliography, only one female writer was dropped from this published list, compared with seven men, but only one was added, compared with eleven men. None of the consultants' additions or deletions challenged in any serious way the results of the selection process that had taken place in preparing the list for general dissemination. Apparently, the consultants shared whatever values determined the original selections. In practice, these values constituted hidden criteria, since the staggering disproportion between male and female writers simply cannot be explained by Blanck's single criterion. The early and middle nineteenth century produced hundreds of women writers (including Hawthorne's maligned hordes of scribbling women) who enjoyed considerable popularity and reputation in their own day and who were considered significant by their contemporaries. Yet among Blanck's omissions are seven of the ten women writers whom Ann Douglas Wood selected as especially popular and interesting exemplars of the "sentimental" school.[7] Blanck tells us in his preface that Rebecca Harding Davis and Mrs. E. D. E. N. Southworth (one of Wood's ten choices) were excluded because "these nominations were not supported by a majority of the persons invited to express opinions . . ." (I, xii). In fact, the supervisory committee had eliminated these two women even before publishing its preliminary list in the *Library Journal.*

Obviously criteria other than recognition by one's contemporaries mattered here, criteria never articulated but certainly having something to do with judgments of literary merit, Blanck's disclaimer notwithstanding. No doubt a good many women omitted from this bibliography were victims of the "minor women writers are more minor than minor male writers" syndrome, but another critical filter, more precise and complex, also reduced their numbers, through a double bind familiar to feminist scholars. On the one hand, a body of prejudice held that domestic and sentimental concerns were the proper sphere of women writers, especially in the nineteenth century; on the other hand, a set of values, both social and aesthetic, tended, as the genteel tradition faded into the past, to patronize or dismiss precisely those concerns as beneath the dignity of a significant writer. This interpretation is substantiated by the fact that the one woman writer added to the list during the consulting process was Caroline Kirkland, who came back into fashion in the early twentieth century because her realistic fiction about the American frontier distinguished her clearly from the sentimentalists.[8] Thus the domestic and sentimental women novelists and poets who were so significant a part of the nineteenth-century literary scene virtually disappear from bibliographies, criticism, and literary history in the twentieth century. Until recently we have assumed that their works are shallow and mawkish and have not taken the trouble to reexamine their writing to see if any of it has literary and social value. The point here is not that sentimentalism is good or bad but, rather, that a number of popular female novelists were eliminated from an influential bibliography even though the criteria for their omission were never articulated. Without the rise of feminist criticism and scholarship, the role of these writers in literary history would probably have been obliterated.

Another group of women, one with a very different perspective, is equally invisible in this bibliography: the suffragists. True, most of the suffragists wrote not belles lettres but political essays; also true, one major male writer, William James, was eliminated in the final round because he wrote philosophic essays rather than imaginative literature or criticism. Yet his elimination seems anomalous, since the bibliography includes less notable males known only for their nonfiction prose, little if any of which was devoted to the arts. Among them are Silas Weir Mitchell, a prominent physician known even in his own time mostly for his medical theories (Mitchell's medical advice contributed to Charlotte Perkins Gilman's nervous breakdown); John Muir, the naturalist; and four once influential but now discredited historians, three of whom reappear, like Muir, in Clark's Goldentree volume—John Fiske, John Motley, Francis Parkman, and William Hickling Prescott.

Several of these embodied in vivid prose enduring myths about the American experience, including the ethnocentric vision of evil redskins and courageous pioneers, but surely their histories were no more significant than the *History of Women Suffrage*, by Elizabeth Cady Stanton and others, nor did any of them write autobiographies so vividly literate as Stanton's *Eighty Years and More*. Stanton, of course, is absent. The absence of Gilman and Austin here, unlike their omission from the Clark bibliography, is justified: they died after the cutoff date for inclusion. Yet both the Blanck and the Clark bibliographies suggest that nonfiction prose is more likely to qualify as "literature" when written by men than when written by women—particularly, perhaps, when the content is explicitly feminist. Thus both the domestic, sentimental women writers and the feminists have suffered the neglect of these exemplary literary bibliographers. The contributions of black writers like Phillis Wheatley, Frederick Douglass, and W. E. B. Du Bois suffer similar neglect in these bibliographies. Finally, we must point to the biases of class and race, as well as of sex, to explain a list that, like Blanck's, includes in the category of minor male writers so many upper-middle-class Easterners trained in Ivy League schools—a group similar, one may assume, to the body of scholars who selected them.

Still, Blanck does list a good many women writers who disappear from the more selective bibliographies that reflect the mid-century emphasis of our profession on a handful of literary "greats"—another of the critical filters that screen out women disproportionately. The introduction to an important anthology of American literature, Perry Miller's *Major Writers of America* (New York: Harcourt, 1962) articulates with particular clarity the scholarly attitudes responsible for stressing a pantheon of "greats" at the expense of the rest of our literary heritage:

> *Major Writers of America* is made possible at this point in time . . . because the study of American literature—inside and outside the university—is now systematic and mature. . . . Today, after seven or eight decades of skirmishing the battle for American literature is won. . . . The canon is at long last becoming established. . . . Yet it is incumbent upon us to make clear which are the few peaks and which the many low-lying hills. We must, if we can, suppress an undiscriminating pedantry by distinguishing just wherein the great are truly great. We must set apart those who belong to world literature rather than merely to local (or to what is worse, regional) patriotism. We must vindicate the study of American literature. . . . (p. xvii)

Although Miller is writing the introduction to an anthology, not a bibliography, the critical assumptions here also inform much of the bibliographic work of the past three decades and determine which writers receive the critical attention that gains their entry into the selective bibliographies. Miller assumes:

- that scholars are obligated to make value judgments setting apart the "peaks" from the "low-lying hills"—those who belong to "world literature" from those of local or regional interest—and that these value judgments have some kind of permanent validity
- that this process of naming the "greats" and discarding the rest is necessary to vindicate the study of American literature
- that the canon of American literature is becoming more or less firmly established

Miller's first assumption—that the critical establishment has an obligation to distinguish the truly great writers from the run of the mill, the works of world literature from those of merely regional significance—rests on the convergence of two literary traditions, one longstanding and the other more recent. The approach to literature through its "greats" has classical antecedents; in English literary history, the man of letters as arbiter of public taste, revealing the glories of some writers and consigning others to oblivion, has spoken in the authoritative and influential voices of Samuel Johnson, Matthew Arnold, and F. R. Leavis. Miller's "we" is the American equivalent of these English men of letters—a "we" who assume a fraternity of shared background, education, taste, and public responsibility, a "we" who can agree on literary "touchstones." Miller implies, in the opposition between "regional" and "world" literature, the old criterion of universality, the belief that the touchstones selected by that fraternity, transcending geographic boundaries through a special union of significant theme and once appropriate form, will appeal to rational human beings everywhere. The very homogeneity of the literary aristocracy both here and abroad leads these men of letters to equate their own taste with a universal aesthetic response and to ignore literatures by those outside their own traditions. For example, it would never have occurred to Miller, or to most of us today, to include in the definition of American literature the great orally transmitted poetry cycles of the first Americans—the Indians.

Thus, feminist criticism (and Marxist criticism before it) has questioned the use of "universality" as a critical concept. No one who has read Florence Howe on James Joyce, Ellen Cantarow on William Butler Yeats, or Kate Millett on Lawrence, Mailer, and Miller;[9] no one who has ever tried to persuade a male reader steeped in the romantic poets and in Hemingway, Faulkner, and Joyce to appreciate the virtues of Doris Lessing (who, not incidentally, is omitted from Paul L. Wiley's 1973 Goldentree bibliography, *The British Novel: Conrad to the Present* (Northbrook, Ill.: AHM, 1973); and certainly no one familiar with the recent critical work of lesbians and women of color will ever again be able to use the term "universality" with comfort. The point is that if the "we" who decide what is "great" and what is "universal" are the educated upper middle class, predominantly white and predominantly male, and if that "we" regard "regional patriotism" as a variety of aesthetic sin and do not regard certain literatures at all, then the topography of "great peaks" and "low-lying hills" will reflect the real expanse of literature only a little more accurately than the maps of medieval cartologists diagram the earth. Moreover, the very distinction in value between "regional" and "universal" is sex-biased: "regional" is more often applied pejoratively to women, and "universal" is usually reserved as an accolade for men. Thus many women writers who have infused their written work with imagery drawn from the regions that nurtured them have been dismissed as narrow local colorists, although, as feminist critics are fond of pointing out, few writers could be more regional than Emerson or Thoreau or Faulkner. This distinction is another of those critical filters that have screened out a disproportionate number of women.

Miller also inherited a more recent tradition that originally arose to challenge the classicists' messy concern with supratextual matters like morality, politics, and history. When Miller was writing, the New Criticism and related schools of intrinsic criticism had dominated literary scholarship and theory for more than a decade, clearly prescribing the essential qualities of "great" works: irony, paradox, symbolism, metaphor, ambiguity, and impersonality.[10] Because the New Criticism valued works that could be analyzed as autonomous, self-contained structures without reference to the artist or to the historical era, certain genres (like poetry and fiction) became more highly regarded than others (like autobiography or essay). In fact, the very definitions of literature shifted under the influence of the various intrinsic critical schools. Memoirs, diaries, personal essays, letters—forms in which women writers have excelled—were increasingly considered subliterary genres, except for those works that had been acknowledged as literature for so long that their status was secure: Franklin's *Autobiography,* but not that of Linda Brent, Elizabeth Cady Stanton, or Mary Hunter Austin; Emerson's or Thoreau's essays, but not those of Margaret Fuller. In addition, fiction, poetry, or drama that engaged in an impassioned examination of specific social issues was deemed suspect; it was propaganda, not art—unless, of course, its internal symbolic structure gave it a universality transcending the temporal concern. I do not mean to develop another attack on the social irresponsibility of the New Criticism, but I do want to point out that, in its ostensibly more "scientific" approach to literary analysis, it provided an aesthetic rationale for focusing on a relatively few works, writers, and genres at the expense of much of our literary heritage.

This dual critical heritage, then, posits a select few works of literary genius and a select body of critics with the taste and/or training to bring their merits before the public. Small wonder that Nevius, the Goldentree bibliographer, found a disproportionately large body of significant criticism on a "half-dozen writers" or that teachers and students who rely on his and similar bibliographies absorb and transmit unspoken assumptions about who *the* important writers are. Small wonder too that all but a handful of women writers (inevitably the same handful) have been omitted from literary histories, anthologies, critical theories, and most bibliographies. Yet this "great works" approach, in spite of its long preeminence in various guises, is only one possible avenue to literary scholarship. Elaine Showalter, using a term she borrows from John Gross, describes the effect of this "residual Great Traditionalism" on the study of women writers and demonstrates its limitations in *A Literature of Their Own: British Women Writers from Brontë to Lessing* ([Princeton: Princeton Univ. Press, 1977], p. 7). Her book offers a model for a literary criticism encompassing not only the "greats" but also many good and productive writers, significant in their own right, without whom the "greats" could never have written.

Miller's second assumption—that the process of naming the "greats" and discarding the rest is necessary to vindicate American literature—is even more strongly linked to its historical context. Even as late as 1962, American literature as a field of study had still not achieved total victory in its struggle for legitimacy; not so long ago American literature had been regarded in the academy as slight and faddish compared with the classics and with the "great tradition" of English literature. Miller's metaphors of battle suggest the intensity with which Americanists fought to win for their literature a respectable position beside these older literatures. In a way, then, Miller was trying to do for American literature precisely what scholars in women's and ethnic studies are now trying to do for women's and ethnic literatures—to expand the canon. The embattled Americanist, though, instinctively chose an exclusive rather than an inclusive strategy, a literary tokenism that would allow the most assimilable to rise but would not question the established literary order. The problem with this defensive posture, of course, is that it shuts out segments of American literature just as the prior chauvinism of the English literateurs shut out most of American literature. The more one realizes how closely Miller's argument is bound to the historical realities of his own era, the less reason there is for accepting it in our own.

The problems with Miller's third assumption, that the canon of American literature is or can be more or less firmly established, appear also in one of those influential, highly selective guides to research so valuable to every scholar in American literature, Lewis Leary's *American Literature: A Study and Research Guide* (New York: St. Martin's, 1976). In a chapter called "Major American Writers," Leary acknowledges, unlike Miller, that the term "major" is troublesome and relative, having meant different things in different eras. Yet he goes on to say that in our time there has been "a kind of consensus" in which forty-five great writers "have been recently named and examined in detailed bibliographical essays." He discusses the content of four collections that emphasize major writers. Only three of the writers are women: Ann Bradstreet, Emily Dickinson, and Willa Cather. Leary himself notes the omission of Edith Wharton and Gertrude Stein from Jackson Bryer's survey of research and criticism, cited above, but the list of notable female omissions should not, of course, stop there. Side by side, Miller's and Leary's comments show that a limited number of writers, almost all of whom are male and white, are validated again and again as "great" or "major," that it is their names that keep appearing in the bibliographies and guides to research, their lives that are studied and documented, and their works that provide, in an endless cycle of self-replication, the criteria and theory for deciding what *is* of literary value. In this way, the canon itself, to the extent that critics and scholars of successive eras have defined it, becomes one of the critical filters through which many women writers have been unable to pass. Leary's chapter on bibliographical guides makes one more link in the cycle of exclusion. Here he recommends, among a few other works, the six Goldentree bibliographies in American literature, praising them as "especially useful" (p. 65); in another chapter, he reiterates that these volumes give "excellent guidance" (p. 73). So they do, if one is not looking for guidance to works by or about female writers.

The assumption that the canon has been established, that critical opinion has identified *the* "major writers," and that these choices will remain essentially unchanged seems to embrace not only a reverence for tradition but an acceptance of the laws of a Darwinian aesthetic: that the best and fittest, or at least the most prolific and influential, will survive or, conversely, that the works that have survived and have had repeated critical validation are in fact the best and the fittest. This very assumption helps to exclude women and minority writers from legitimate consideration in criticism and the classroom and, as we have already seen, has limited their appearance in the selective bibliographies of our field.

Besides, if history has anything to teach us about the present, the assumption is highly questionable. The canon has undergone major revisions before, in the face of considerable resistance from conservative members of the academy. Carl Van Doren, writing an article called "Toward a New Canon" published in the *Nation,* 13 April 1932, commented that "the canon of American literature refuses to stay fixed." Noting that Bryant, Longfellow, Whittier, Holmes, Lowell, Irving, Howells, and Cooper had failed to hold their own against Emerson, Hawthorne, Thoreau, James, Twain, Melville, Dickinson, and some twentieth-century writers, Van Doren pointed out that the literary establishment resisted these changes because of its vested interest in the conservative classics, which had been comfortably published and taught for so long; because of a patriotism hostile to the newer writers' harsh criticisms of America; and because of "the natural inertia with which each age resists the age that follows it." In effecting a thoroughgoing revision of the canon, he remarked:

> Not much help can be expected from the American academy or from the universities. They will do no more than wait till the work has been done by actual workers. Then they will hold on to the revised canon with stubborn opposition to any further changes which some later age may have to insist on.[11]

We are in just such a later age now, and Van Doren's remark has the ring of prophecy. Jay B. Hubbell's book *Who Are the Major American Writers?*, from which Van Doren's remarks are quoted, documents again and again the relativity of the canon, which changes as each age questions the literary judgments and reputations of the age that has preceded it.

The canon, then, is not a given, unchangeable corpus of received works, nor are the standard canonical works the only meritorious ones. One of the important tasks feminist scholars interested in bibliography are now undertaking is to press for the inclusion of the many worthy women writers recovered and reevaluated during the past decade and for the inclusion of feminist critical studies of both male and female writers in the selective bibliographies that reflect and help shape the literary canon as a whole. Adding these names and works is one way in which bibliography can begin to lead the profession. For one of the legacies of women's studies in literature is that it has forced us to reconsider what we value in literature and why and, for that matter, what we call "literature" and why. Students of women's literature have challenged old and often unspoken assumptions about literary value and have begun to pose new criteria for assessing works in all the genres. One can only hope that in the future many more scholars and bibliographers will have a fundamental understanding of these issues, so that their work will adequately reflect the cultural diversity of our society and its literary modes.

The second contribution of feminist scholars concerned with bibliographic issues is of course the publication of separate or supplementary bibliographies devoted exclusively to materials on women's contributions. The Appendix to this paper considers some of the products of this endeavor more specifically. Much of this bibliographic work entails important original research: identifying women writers, clarifying their publication histories, making their works available for evaluation. Even bibliographies that simply detail the publication histories of relatively unknown women writers can offer valuable information to critics exploring a particular author's artistic development, reception at a given time, or influence and relation to other contemporary writers, works, and currents in culture and society.

Feminist scholars must also turn their attention to unraveling some of the problems of attribution inherited from their bibliographic predecessors. The *British Museum Catalogue*, for example, has twenty-five pages headed simply "A Lady." About a century ago Ralph Thomas, having tried to identify some of the women who used this pseudonym, published *Aggravating Ladies: Being a List of Works Published under the Pseudonym of "A Lady," with Preliminary Suggestions on the Art of Describing Books Bibliographically* (London: Quaritch, 1880). This pamphlet cited 151 works by nineteenth-century English writers who signed themselves "A Lady" and whose identities had "resisted all enquiry in the most aggravating manner" (p. 1). The unyielding anonymity of these women is not the fault of the frustrated Thomas or of the *BMC*, but it does suggest one connection among patriarchal ideology, bibliography, and the canon. Women writers for decades attracted critical notice that was often patronizingly or scathingly *ad feminam*. How much more modest, decorous, and safe, then, to publish as "a lady" than under one's own name. Yet, lumping together the works of an indeterminate number of authors under this heading has undoubtedly contributed to their neglect by the scholars of a later generation. Probably not all these anonymous literary efforts would be worth recovering, but the law of averages alone suggests that among them are some undocumented, undiscovered works of real value.

Some women writers, of course, chose to hide their gender behind male pseudonyms rather than have their works identified as the products of a female pen. Shakespeare was not a woman, but Vernon Lee, John Oliver Hobbes, Michael Field, and A. M. Barnard were—respectively, Violet Paget, Mrs. Craigie, an aunt-niece team of Katherine Bradley and Edith Cooper, and Louisa May Alcott. Undoubtedly there are other women writers whose identities have been masked under male names. Other women who wrote chose never to publish, not only because they feared notoriety but also because they considered their writings unpublishable or uninteresting. Sometimes, of course, they were right; but new research suggests the existence of rich stores of "hidden" women's literature, often in nontraditional genres (notes, journals, memoirs, letters, diaries), and new critical theories are being developed to accommodate such works.[12] Clearly, a great deal of original research remains to be done before bibliographies can adequately outline the dimensions of women's contributions to literature. Such research will provide the basis for a more holistic understanding of literary history.

Finally, feminist scholars must of course find ways to monitor more systematically and coherently the growing wealth of secondary studies on women writers, both by making existing resources more responsive to our needs and by creating new resources. The work already under way, in creating new bibliographies of secondary studies on women writers and in enlarging current bibliographies to include them, has encountered certain difficulties, both conceptual and practical.

For one thing, women's studies does not lend itself to the traditional taxonomic categories established for studies in language and literature. First of all, women's studies is interdisciplinary; its scholars have found their analyses the richer for crossing the boundaries between, say, history and literary criticism. For example, though Carroll Smith Rosenberg's pioneering article on female subculture, "The Female World of Love and Ritual: Relations between Women in Nineteenth-Century America" (*Signs,* 1 [1975], 1–29), is essential reading for anyone interested in women and literature in America, it would traditionally appear in a historic bibliography. Thus, one must check interdisciplinary and often incomplete bibliographic sources like *Women's Studies Abstracts* before one can feel relatively comfortable about having covered all the bases. *Signs: A Journal of Women in Culture and Society* publishes annual review essays on women's studies scholarship in a variety of fields, but while these essays provide some remedy to this problem, they are inevitably highly selective themselves, offering important analytic overviews of major scholarship rather than comprehensive listings of the year's work.

Second, a great deal of interesting work in women's studies has approached literary questions from a pedagogical perspective, often in sources more likely to reach the attention and the bibliographies of educators than of modern language professors. Because the "first generation" of women's studies scholars were hungry for publications in their new field, they knew about the Clearinghouse on Women's Studies of the Feminist Press and the syllabuses, bibliographies, and critical/pedagogical essays in its Female Studies series. But because that basic hunger has been appeased and because such resources are documented only erratically in the references modern language professors generally consult, these aids are less familiar to a newer generation. While the 1976 *MLA International Bibliography* did include Florence Howe's important article "Feminism and the Study of Literature" (*The Radical Teacher,* 3 [1976]), it did not include the essays in criticism, teaching and bibliography that appear regularly in the *Women's Studies Newsletter,* nor did the 1977 *Bibliography* include such publications as the NCTE's *Responses to Sexism: Classroom Practices in Teaching English, 1976–77* (1976), assembled by the Committee on the Role and Image of Women. This work contains, among other useful pieces, a concise article by Carolyn Allen on feminist literary criticism and Susan Waugh Allen's "Basic Resource Bibliography for the Teacher of Women in Literature."

Third, the filiations of women writers seldom correspond to the neat chronological and geographical categories that have so far governed the arrangement of most bibliographic sources in our profession. For example, a brilliant chapter in Ellen Moers's *Literary Women: The Great Writers* (Garden City, N.Y.: Doubleday, 1976) points out connections among Harriet Beecher Stowe, George Sand, George Eliot, Elizabeth Barrett Browning, and Emily Dickinson—writers of one century but three different countries, whose ties with one another constitute part of a literary tradition very different from the one we usually associate with the bibliographic category "Victorian."

If secondary studies of women writers often defy traditional boundaries of era, nationality, and language, so too do studies on such topics as Images of Women in Literature or Female Style. Anyone who has ever tried to use the annual MLA bibliographies can attest to their inconvenient documention of such studies. Suppose, for example, that you wish to find significant articles written in the past year on "female style." You do not want to limit the topic by genre, but you do decide to focus on works written in English about British and American women writers. You begin by checking General Literature and Related Topics, including Esthetics, Literary Criticism and Literary Theory, Literature, General and Comparative, Themes and Types, and Bibliographical, before moving on to English Literature I, General and Miscellaneous. Still ahead, after a couple of hours of eye-aching labor, remain the entries for each period in England and America—and probably the volume on linguistics.

Happily, bibliographers at MLA headquarters are now engaged in a thoroughgoing revision of taxonomic procedures for the annual bibliographies. They will almost certainly incorporate a subject index with categories for women both as writers and as images in literature, a measure that will greatly simplify the prolonged gleaning of relevant items from the thousands of irrelevant ones. The process could be further simplified, and the importance of women writers as a category acknowledged, by the inclusion of one heading for women's studies in language and literature for each appropriate location in the main texts of the bibliographies. American Literature has the analogous heading

Afro-American for both the general introductory section and for each century; extensive cross listing at the end of the introductory section refers researchers to other citations. The ethnic studies sections document ethnic Americans not as "images in" the written or spoken word but only as producers of it, an omission the subject indexes will correct. Feminist scholars would benefit from a similar classification for women, one acknowledging their presence as contributors to culture and as shapers of language, literature, and critical thought. Apparently, though, MLA bibliographers may do away with the separate classifications for ethnic studies, on the grounds that articles on individual writers should be given under the names of those writers and that limited cross listing and the subject index will meet remaining needs. I would argue that as long as ethnic minorities and women constitute social categories with experiences and traditions recognizably different from those of the dominant culture, they deserve bibliographic headings of their own. In any case, feminist scholars in literature should continue to provide friendly pressure and concrete suggestions to ensure a more convenient indexing of relevant studies and should also make sure to send bibliographers at the MLA and other scholarly centers copies of their own publications, especially those that have appeared in the interdisciplinary journals and lesser-known periodicals that have often provided outlets for feminist critical studies.

Today, feminist scholars are going about the necessary task of creating new resources devoted exclusively to women's studies in language and literature; in doing so they will have to give careful attention to problems of selection and arrangement. In an editorial in *Women and Literature* (4 [Spring 1976], 4), Janet M. Todd wrote:

> The discipline itself is in a fluid state, and so when the bibliographer excludes or includes an item, she does so by instinct rather than by method. Unlike Marxist and Structuralist criticism, women's studies in literature has as yet no clear theoretical base. As our study moves beyond the necessary description of female history and literature into their rigorous analysis, we should have the theoretical tools to make selection a more methodical task and bibliographies consequently more coherent.

Todd goes on to mention an additional problem faced by feminist bibliographers: the discrepancy between their financial and technical resources and those available to established bibliographies like those of the MLA. She argues both for more external funding for independent bibliographers in women's studies and for increased collaboration between these bibliographers and established resource centers. "With adequate annual and chronological bibliographies," she concludes, "we may define our discipline and provide its history. Without such a history we remain as alone in our separate studies as Wollstonecraft and her sisters considered themselves in theirs."

One final proviso in closing: in creating our own bibliographic resources, and thereby defining and refining our discipline, we need also to maintain the curious double consciousness that has always accompanied women's studies: while establishing a room of our own, we must make sure that we are also a presence in the house as a whole. Since bibliography helps to define the literary canon, feminist scholars cannot leave unchallenged the bibliographic aids to research that enshrine a few great works by a few great writers (predominantly male, white, and middle-class) and ignore the rest of literature. The old approach is already undergoing a necessary reevaluation, as the monolithic formalism of the intrinsic critical schools give way to critical pluralism and as a new and more sophisticated literary history becomes increasingly respectable. The bibliographies of our profession can begin to lead this movement by documenting the contributions of all the contributors—male and female, Anglo and ethnic—to our rich and diverse literary heritage.

Notes

1. Throughout this paper I am indebted to Ellen Messer-Davidow for help far exceeding mere editorial assistance. Not only her ideas but some of the language in her comments on various drafts have found their way into this version. Her exacting and detailed critiques make her virtually a coauthor.
2. I am focusing my analysis in this paper on the category of sex without trying to explore fully the complicated interactions of gender with race, class, and sexual preference. Obviously, women of color have suffered a dual invisibility in literary history (threefold if they are lesbians), an invisibility described with painful clarity by Barbara Smith in "Toward a Black Feminist Criticism" (*Conditions: Two,* 1 [Oct. 1977], 25–44). Much of what I say here applies to the literature of people of color, but the precise historical processes affecting the relation of that literature to the literary canon as a whole are not always the same as those affecting the works of (white) women. I encountered blatant racism in some of my research, but I felt that its impact on bibliography required a separate study. An important work in progress by Paul Lauter will contribute a great deal to our understanding of the historical processes that have shaped the literary canon; his probing questions about canonicity underlie much of this paper.
3. Comprehensive bibliographies do, of course, reflect and perpetuate discriminations that occur before the bibliographic stage. If most of the articles in a given periodical in a given period are on male writers, comprehensive bibliographies can only reflect that bias. More important is the point made by Ellen Messer-Davidow in an editorial comment:

   While comprehensive bibliographies may not themselves discriminate, they do reflect and transmit discriminations that were operative in the collecting and preserving of materials. An example: the letters, journals, and published works of . . . women writers . . . were often preserved because their correspondents were famous literary, scientific, and political figures, or because they were . . . members of aristocratic families. . . . Meanwhile correspondence between women writers is lost.
4. *Signs,* 1 (1975), 442.
5. Under the general editorship of O. B. Hardison, the series was published by Meredith Corporation until 1971; since then the publisher has been AHM Publishing Corporation, Northbrook, Ill.
6. "A Survey of the Bibliography of English Literature," *Papers of the Bibliographical Society of America,* 23, No. 2 (1929), 4.
7. "The Literature of Impoverishment: The Women Local Colorists in America, 1865–1914," *Women's Studies,* 1 (Nov. 1972), 3–45.
8. This view comes from Langley Carleton Keyes's article on Kirkland in *Notable American Women: A Dictionary,* II (Cambridge: Harvard Univ. Press, 1971), 337–39. The Keyes article itself reflects both the prejudice against sentimentalism and its association with women writers: "In an age when most Americans were imbued with the romantic outlook, and when nearly all novelists, certainly all lady novelists, were sentimentalists, her early work ran counter to the prevailing tide" (p. 339).

9. Florence Howe, "Feminism and Literature," in *Images of Women in Fiction,* ed. Susan Koppelman Cornillon (Bowling Green, Ohio: Bowling Green Univ. Popular Press, 1972), pp. 260–64; Ellen Cantarow, "Why Teach Literature? An Account of How I Came to Ask That Question," *The Politics of Literature: Dissenting Essays on the Teaching of English,* ed. Louis Kampf and Paul Lauter (New York: Vintage-Random House, 1973), pp. 76–77; Kate Millett, *Sexual Politics* (New York: Avon, 1969).
10. Among the many articles discussing the influence of the New Criticism, I am especially indebted to the following: the essays by Louis Kampf and Paul Lauter in *The Politics of Literature;* E. D. Hirsch, Jr., " 'Intrinsic' Criticism," *College English,* 36 (1974), 446–57; Edward Wasiolek, "Wanted: A New Contextualism," *Critical Inquiry,* 1 (1975), 623–39.
11. Carl Van Doren, quoted in Jay B. Hubbell, *Who Are the Major American Writers?* (Durham, N.C.: Duke Univ. Press, 1972), p. 272.
12. I am thinking in particular of the work generated by the three-year project of the Modern Language Association's Commission on the Status of Women in the Profession, Teaching Women's Literature from a Regional Perspective, funded by the Fund for the Improvement of Postsecondary Education. Participants in this project, teachers and students throughout the country, have been unearthing samples of "nontraditional" literature. An institute in summer 1979, funded by the National Endowment for the Humanities, focused on issues in critical theory raised by these new materials.

Appendix

A Selective Review of Bibliographic Resources on Women Writers in England and America

At the moment, there is no adequate comprehensive guide to primary and secondary materials for women's studies in language and literature. The Modern Language Association's Division of Women's Studies, however, has now begun to prepare such a guide and has issued a call for participants. That project deserves the widespread support of feminist scholars. In the meantime, an essential resource guide is the four-volume *Notable American Women, 1607–1950* (Cambridge: Harvard Univ. Press, 1971), which contains bibliographies, some excellent and some competent, of most recognized American women writers. In addition, the first two volumes of *American Women Writers: A Critical Reference Guide*, ed. Lina Mainiero (New York: Ungar, 1979, 1980) are now available. This guide will also be an essential resource, but it does have certain limitations. It omits a number of important contemporary women writers and critics whose works have contributed substantially to the evolution of feminist literature and criticism, and most of its annotations abide by the editor's injunction to contributing authors to "go easy on feminist criticism" except as "a minor part of your article (perhaps 20 per cent)." Some leading feminist critics refused to contribute at all under these conditions, and the guide is less pioneering and less reflective of the important critical developments of the last decade than one might wish.

Two general annotated bibliographies of primary works deserve mention, although they are labors of love rather than of rigorous scholarship. The more comprehensive of the two is *Women and Literature: An Annotated Bibliography of Women Writers*, 3rd ed. (Cambridge, Mass.: Women Literature Collective, 1976), a highly selective but intelligent list annotated from a feminist perspective. My own *Strong Women: An Annotated Bibliography of Literature for the High School Classroom* (Old Westbury, N.Y.: Feminist, 1976) is still more selective, focusing on works easily available in paperback, written by women about strong female protagonists. Two important topical bibliographies, containing both primary and secondary materials, are Ora Williams' *American Black Women in the Arts and Social Sciences*, 2nd ed. (Metuchen, N.J.: Scarecrow, 1977), which documents black women's contributions in a number of fields, and Gene Damon and Lee Stuart's *The Lesbian in Literature: A Bibliography*, 2nd ed. (Reno, Nev.: Ladder, 1975).

A number of critical books and anthologies contain helpful bibliographies or checklists on works by women writers; among these are Nina Baym's *Woman's Fiction: A Guide to Novels by and about Women in America, 1820–1870* (Ithaca, N.Y.: Cornell Univ. Press, 1978); Barbara Christian's *Black Women Novelists: The Development of a Tradition, 1892–1976* (Westport, Conn.: Greenwood, 1980); Mary Anne Ferguson's *Images of Women in Literature,* 3rd ed. (Boston: Houghton, 1981); Dexter Fisher's *The Third Woman: Minority Women Writers of the United States* (Boston: Houghton, 1980); Jeannette Foster's *Sex Variant Women in Literature* (1956), 2nd ed. (Baltimore: Diana, 1975); Sandra M. Gilbert and Susan Gubar's *Shakespeare's Sisters: Feminist Essays on Women Poets* (Bloomington: Indiana Univ. Press, 1979); Ellen Moers's *Literary Women: The Great Writers* (New York: Doubleday, 1976); Elaine Showalter's *A Literature of Their Own: British Women Novelists from Brontë to Lessing* (Princeton: Princeton Univ. Press, 1977), which includes a bibliography mentioning the first works by women writers of the period covered in her study; and Ann Stanford's *The Women Poets in English: An Anthology* (New York: McGraw-Hill, 1972), which concludes with brief but helpful biobibliographies of British and American poets. Scholars interested in women's contributions to periodical literature can consult the bibliographies in Alison Adburgham's *Women in Print: Writing Women and Women's Magazines from the Restoration to the Accession of Victoria* (London: Allen and Unwin, 1972); Cynthia Leslie White's *Women's Magazines, 1693–1968* (London: Joseph, 1970); and E. M. Palmegiano's *Women and British Periodicals, 1832–1867: A Bibliography* (New York: Garland, 1976).

Primary bibliographies focusing on writers of a specific era, genre, or tradition have appeared with increasing frequency in recent periodicals. Among them are the following: Joyce Fullard and Rhoda W. Schueller, "A Bibliography of Eighteenth Century Women Poets," *Mary Wollstonecraft Journal,* 2 (May 1974), 40–46; Norman Greco and Ronaele Novotny, "Bibliography of Women in the English Renaissance," *University of Michigan Papers in Women's Studies,* 1 (June 1974), 30–57; Eugene L. Huddleston, "Feminist Verse Satire in America: A Checklist, 1700–1800," *Bulletin of Bibliography,* 32 (July-Sept. 1973), 115–21, 132; Jayne Loader, "Women in the Left, 1906–1941: A Bibliography of Primary Resources," *University of Michigan Papers in Women's Studies,* 2 (Sept. 1975), 9–82; and Joan Reardon and Kristine A. Thorsen, *Poetry by American Women, 1900–1975: A Bibliography* (Metuchen, N.J.: Scarecrow, 1979), which lists close to 9,500 volumes of poetry published by some 5,500 women. Most of these are annotated, and several contain secondary as well as primary entries. For archival materials, a project conducted by the Women's History Sources Survey is likely to prove useful as well to scholars in literature: *Women's Histo-*

ry Sources: A Guide to Archives and Manuscript Collections in the United States, 2 vols., ed. Andrea Hinding and Clarke Chambers (New York: Bowker, 1980).

Bibliographies and aids to research for secondary studies have appeared with increasing frequency in recent years. For an overview of bibliographic works on women's studies in a number of fields, researchers should consult Patricia K. Ballou, "Bibliographies for Research on Women," a review essay in the Winter 1977 issue of *Signs.* Ballou cites a number of general bibliographies useful in our discipline; one she omits is Merle Froschl and Jane Williamson, ed., *Feminist Resources for Schools and Colleges: A Guide to Curricular Materials,* rev. ed. (Old Westbury, N.Y.: Feminist, 1977).

There are now four book-length bibliographies documenting critical studies on women writers who have written in English: Paula R. Backscheider and Felicity A. Nussbaum, *An Annotated Bibliography of Twentieth-Century Critical Studies of Women and Literature, 1660–1800* (New York: Garland, 1977); Carol Fairbanks Myers, *Women in Literature: Criticism of the Seventies* (Metuchen, N.J.: Scarecrow, 1976), which contains citations for images of women in literature as well as for women writers; Narda Lacey Schwartz, *Articles on Women Writers, 1960–1975* (Santa Barbara, Calif.: American Bibliographical Center–Clio Press, 1978), a list of articles published in English about some six hundred women writers from the United States, Great Britain, Ireland, Australia, Canada, New Zealand, and Africa; and Barbara A. White, *American Women Writers: An Annotated Bibliography of Criticism* (New York: Garland, 1977). An increasing number of women writers have been treated in individual reference guides and some, like Jane Austen, in more than one. I cannot mention all these guides here, but among the most useful are the bibliographies included in the volumes of the Twayne and the University of Minnesota series and the reference aids published by G. K. Hall on Harriet Beecher Stowe, Katherine Anne Porter and Carson McCullers, Sylvia Plath and Anne Sexton, George Eliot, Edith Wharton and Kate Chopin, Elizabeth Gaskell, Christina Rossetti, Flannery O'Connor and Caroline Gordon, and Eudora Welty.

Of periodical resources, two in particular are essential. *Women Studies Abstracts* has provided annotations for important literary studies as well as a list of reviews in each quarterly issue since 1972. Although the list is inevitably incomplete, women's studies scholars in every field owe a debt of gratitude to its editor, Sara Whaley, and her team of volunteers. Of even greater usefulness to the specialist in women's studies in language and literature are the increasingly comprehensive bibliographies in *Women and Literature.* These bibliographies—the painstaking work of the general editor, Janet Todd; the bibliographic editor, Florence Boos; and a number of volunteers—began with an abbreviated compilation in the Fall 1975 issue. These bibliographies emphasize feminist materials and journals not included in the standard bibliographies, and in 1976 they began to cover all pertinent literature written and published in English—in Africa, Canada, and Australia as well as in Great Britain and the United States. Now funded by a small grant from the National Endowment for the Humanities, the bibliographies deserve additional support. Ideally they will eventually take the form of a computerized data bank, so that feminist scholars will be able to retrieve coherent categories of information. Finally, scholars may locate some of the special periodical issues devoted to essays on women and literature by consulting Margrit Eichler, John Marecki, and Jennifer Newton, comps., *Women: A Bibliography of Special Periodical Issues, 1960–1975* (Toronto: Canadian Newsletter of Research on Women, 1977), which contains a section on "Anthropology, Arts, and Literature."

For scholars trying to keep up with trends in feminist criticism, several review articles will prove helpful. A landmark essay is Elaine Showalter's "Literary Criticism," *Signs,* 1 (1975), 435–60. Annette Kolodny's review essay of the same title in *Signs,* 2 (1976), 404–21, contains sections on biographies and collected letters and on critical studies of individual writers as well as a section on feminist critical theory. Cheri Register's bibliographical introduction to Josephine Donovan, ed., *Feminist Literary Criticism: Exploratory Essays* (Lexington: Univ. of Kentucky Press, 1977) is also helpful, although already out of date (a tribute to the strides feminist criticism has made in recent years). Sara Lincoln's *The Female Phoenix: A Review of Books by, for, and about Women* (Ann Arbor: Univ. of Michigan Press, 1977) includes sections titled "A Feminist Perspective on Literary Criticism," "Literary Works about the Feminine Experience," and "Biography and Autobiography." The most recent overview of feminist criticism is Sandra M. Gilbert's "Life Studies, or Speech after Long Silence: Feminist Critics Today," *College English,* 40 (1979), 849–63. Scholars interested particularly in the relations between language and sex can consult Mary Ritchie Key's *Male/Female Language: With a Comprehensive Bibliography* (Metuchen, N.J.: Scarecrow, 1977).

Still to be devised is a systematic documentation of work in progress, especially since the demise of *Women's Work and Women's Studies,* 1971–1973/74 (New York: Barnard College Women's Center, 1972–75) (1971–72 vols. available from KNOW, Inc.; the 1973/74 vol. available from the Feminist Press). The new National Women's Studies Association might assume this task, but in the interim, scholars in language and literature could make more consistent use of the annual listings in *Concerns,* the newsletter of the Women's Caucus for the Modern Languages.

Archival Materials
The Problem of Literary Reputation

Elizabeth A. Meese

Feminist critics, faced with a canon of "great works" to be studied, written about, and taught, have undertaken to examine canonicity: the reasons for elevating certain works to the exclusion of others and the means by which works are (or should be) included in or excluded from a literary canon. We begin by assuming that both extrinsic and intrinsic criticisms, like descriptions of historical periods, embody the biases of those who determine critical standards and norms; we also assume, conversely, that critical standards and norms reflect the characteristics of the writers and works that provide the criteria for prevailing notions of "great literature." Critics, of course, aim for an objective, consistent, and humanistic approach as they assess literature, reviewing past judgments and attempting to validate those made in the present. They assume that they are themselves fair and that they apply criteria with an even hand. But this assumption is not justified; critics have traditionally adopted a stance of cultural homogeneity and, through unintentional parochialism or willful discrimination, they have disregarded works by women, blacks and working-class people—works that often defy the tidy schematics of traditional literary theory and practice. Whatever the particular theories and practices critics adopt, the consequence is that works by women are generally classified as relatively mediocre and relegated to obscurity.

The discovery, publication, and analysis of women's archival materials are a necessary beginning to the reassessment of women's place in the literary canon and of the canon itself. Specifically, women's archival materials can aid in clarifying the assumptions that underlie canonization and devising new, more inclusive criteria; in discovering additional writers and works deserving of literary attention and repute; and in developing fuller contexts in which to understand women's lives and works.

Canonical status and literary reputation seem to involve three major assumptions. First, literary reputation is apparently reserved, particularly for authors of imaginative works. Second, achievement in the novel, poetry, and drama—the "major" genres—is thought of greater merit than achievement in short stories, letters, diaries, children's works, travel literature, and other nonfictional prose—the "minor" genres. Finally, the works canonized are characterized as universal rather than regional.

Literary history records individual authors' contributions to literary culture, whereas archival materials reveal other roles through which literary contribution was possible. For instance, Elizabeth Palmer Peabody, like many other mid-nineteenth-century women, participated in the Concord conversation circle, one of the few opportunities women had to exercise their philosophical and literary imaginations. Peabody's letters to Theodore Parker, the transcendentalist theologian, display a fine sensibility at work, finer than is revealed in the more familiar portions of her *Record of a School,* anthologized by Perry Miller in *The Transcendentalists*. Miller's headnote describes her as "an intellectual spinster," exemplifying the critical diminution of a woman who was a social reformer, an educator, and the publisher of *The Dial.*[1] The cursory treatment of Peabody's accomplishments typifies the work done on women of the transcendentalist circle, with the exception of recent feminist studies and reprintings of Margaret Fuller.[2]

Harriet Monroe's role in the development of twentieth-century literature suggests another significant form of women's literary work. As the editor of *Poetry,* one of the best magazines devoted to verse, Monroe corresponded extensively with the writers of this century and won wide admiration for her editorial astuteness. Her correspondence should be published, her critical essays reevaluated, and her assistance to other authors appraised. Several women made significant contributions as journalists, notably Lillian Smith, who edited *Pseudopodia,* which became *The South Today;* Mary Ann Shadd, the black editor of a mid-nineteenth-century newspaper, *Provincial Freeman;* and Piney Woods Forsyth, editor of the *Advocate,* a Mississippi women's rights periodical. These writers frequently used their authority to support women's rights and antislavery coverage, and they hired other women to help them.[3] Women did have access to editorial and publishing roles, albeit often only through the death of a husband or a father. Women who acted as literary patrons also deserve greater recognition; Annie Fields, for example, the wife of a Boston publisher, was untiring in her efforts on behalf of Sarah Orne Jewett and Willa Cather, among others.[4] To appraise women's contributions to literary culture, critics need a fuller understanding of literary roles other than authorship.

But even when women managed to get into print—overcoming, as Tillie Olsen notes, economic, social, and educational obstacles—they seldom acquired significant literary reputations.[5] Literary scholarship is weighted toward poems and novels and, to a lesser degree, plays; it attaches no prestige to short stories, letters, diaries, children's works, travel literature, and educational treatises except insofar as they support the reputations of writers in "prestige" genres.

With the possible exception of the short story, which I discuss separately, the differentiation between prestige and nonprestige genres grows out of a critical tradition that opposes art and life. Critics hold that language functions differently in literature from the way it does elsewhere and that characters and events—the raw material of life—must be transformed into art if they are to become fit objects for study. The obvious practical and personal usefulness of letters, diaries, travel literature, treatises, and children's works militates against their acceptance in an "art for art's sake" system of valuation. Since women were deprived of a full education until almost the twentieth century, they wrote in the genres they could master without formal instruction. Moreover, being excluded from the aesthetic networks and institutions, women were inclined to write more for other reasons than "art's sake," an incentive that requires a sense of relation to artistic tradition, positive self-concepts, and cultural legitimacy.

The undervaluing of the short story presents a particularly interesting case. What, for example, is known of Katherine Brush, Mary Johnston, Margaret Leech, Kathleen Norris, Maristan Chapman, Elsie M. Rushfeldt, Ruth Barr Sanborn, and Caroline Slade, all of whom won O. Henry Awards in 1929?[6] Given the relatively short time that has elapsed since then, why are so many of their names unfamiliar? One might surmise that these women lost their places in literary history because they failed to publish novels or volumes of poetry, the prestige genres, whereas their male contemporaries published stories along with more highly valued works. But that hypothesis is not borne out: even those women writers who published in the "prestige" genres vanished from literary history.

To give women writers their due, we must point out meritorious features of neglected forms. Vast amounts of archival material should be described by genre and then evaluated. We need, for example, to understand the relation between Julia Tutwiler's treatises on education and other didactic works of the nineteenth century. Before we can feel secure in our judgments, we need careful comparative studies concerning the development of literary reputation generally (e.g., Lowell versus Berryman, Cather versus Dreiser, Rhys versus Hemingway). And we also need comparative studies of the aesthetic choices made by less well known writers, both men and women.

The final major charge leveled against women writers in particular is that their works remain "regional" rather than "universal." It is no coincidence that, with the exception of current publications by feminist presses, most works by women writers in print today simply demonstrate traditional concepts of literary development and achievement. Although we may see more than local color in the works of writers like Sarah Orne Jewett and Mary Wilkins Freeman, we recognize that they are widely available because they are viewed as creditable examples of the regional type. They fulfill the great design of literary history so well that they cannot be ignored altogether. They instruct students in a hierarchy of literary development—a progression (of "improvement") from local color to realism to naturalism.

"Regional" writing is neither better nor worse than writing that is supposed to be "universal." The issue resides in definition. Eudora Welty focuses the discussion well in the following observation:

> "Regional," I think is a careless term, as well as a condescending one, because what it does is fail to differentiate between the localized raw material of life and its outcome as art. 'Regional' is an outsider's term; it has no meaning for the insider who is doing the writing, because as far as he knows he is simply writing about life.[7]

Critics have applied the term "regionalism" to avoid judging work by more general literary and aesthetic standards. Every fabric is woven from local detail, but not every locale is equally familiar. Similarly unfamiliar are the lives chronicled when the narrow definition of literature as the works of the patriarchy is expanded to include works expressing a greater variety of experience (which is more truly "universal"). In the face of racial, sexual, and ethnic diversity, the critic is often an outsider, struggling toward a sense of significance. The Cajun stories of Ada Jack Carver, on one level, depict the small, isolated world of the Louisiana bayous but, as exotic as that place is and as firmly rooted in its details as the stories are, they direct us to compelling human concerns of cross-generational relations and of the conflict between old and new ways.[8]

In addition to the assumptions that have influenced women writers' literary reputations, some other causes of neglect surface in the course of archival work. The circumstances attending the preservation and location of women's papers have had a damaging effect on research.

Women writers have a tendency to destroy their unpublished papers and works, often viewing this material as private and irrelevant. Djuna Barnes (best known for her novel *Nightwood*) and Eudora Welty have both said that they intend to destroy personal documents. Ada Jack Carver had all her papers destroyed at her death, leaving only the stories in print and the letters and clippings saved by Cammie Henry of Melrose Plantation. Only one person has written a dissertation on Carver; he spent years collecting the essential biographical information, but he flounders in his critical analysis, obviously suffering from the lack of supporting personal data as well as from the absence of viable critical models for the analysis of women's writing.[9]

Researchers searching for papers may begin with conventional guides, like *American Literary Manuscripts,* that list repositories of the papers of such well-known literary figures as Willa Cather, Grace King, and Marianne Moore. The *Women's History Sources Survey* is much more useful in its scope and currency; field-workers have surveyed all the public repositories in the country, cataloging collections of women's material. Apart from consulting these indexes, researchers would be wise to begin at home. Public libraries, historical societies, attics, and basements are frequently better sources of women's manuscripts than are the rare book rooms and archives of large research libraries (the women's collections at Smith and Radcliffe are notable exceptions). Researchers in Alabama have located excellent collections by unlikely means: small-town libraries telephoned private citizens, a recycling center unearthed the record book from a black women's organization of the 1920s, and a garage sale yielded two boxes of a deceased professor's letters and manuscripts on women's education. The best strategy is to work through local contacts and to consider everything possible.

When housed in institutions, women's manuscripts are frequently found in collections cataloged under male family names. Often a woman's documents are preserved because her husband or father was important; unless researchers exercise care, women's work may be "lost" within collections listed only by male family names. Even though a woman's letters may be preserved, they are often seen only as an extension of her husband's work, as with Varina Howell Davis, "First Lady of the Confederacy" and wife of Jefferson Davis. (She was a prolific correspondent, and her letters display political astuteness, sensitivity, and intelligence.)

It is wise to consider the institutional politics underlying the development of archival collections. Archivists are primarily interested in collecting documents of obvious historical and literary value. This attitude results in collections that, in organization and content, mirror traditional academic attitudes toward significant figures and important events. Correspondence is cataloged one-sidedly—for instance, at Tulane University, we find the letters of Julia Peterkin, South Carolina Pulitzer Prize winner, to Lyle Saxon cataloged under his name, since local interests dictate his greater importance. On the whole, however, for archival research on noncanonical figures, it is difficult to make rules; aside from the few generalizations and cautions detailed above, each effort requires its own detective work, following clues and connections.

To reverse this state of affairs, a scheme for the publication of archival material is essential. Some of the women's manuscripts discovered through research meet prevailing literary standards for publication; these are the works with which we are inevitably most comfortable. But if the work of feminist reevaluation is to go forward, we need to promote the publication of other materials—bibliographies, biographies, archival manuscripts, biocriticism, and oral testimony. To illustrate the kinds of work that should be done, I will use my experience with Southern women's literature as a reference point for constructing what I hope will be some broadly useful guidelines for publishing priorities.

Severe problems exist for scholars working on obscure writers whose primary works are difficult to locate. Research on most women writers could be facilitated by the publication of bibliographical data, organized by author and subdivided according to region, topic, genre, and period. Several projects currently in progress promise valuable results. *Women's Records: A Preliminary Guide,* published by the Georgia Department of Archives and History, is a welcome addition to the research tools available for scholars interested in Southern women. Dolores K. Gros-Louis at Indiana University has compiled records of women's manuscripts and privately printed autobiographies, first-person memoirs, recollections and reminiscences. The bibliography contains descriptions of the materials and locations of manuscript holdings. In a project called First Person Female, Carolyn Rhodes at Old Dominion is compiling biographical sketches of American women writers. It is important that the *Women's History Sources Survey* receive sufficient support from scholars to permit the existing information on archival holdings to be updated and expanded to accommodate new and overlooked acquisitions. Activities of this kind represent useful directions for research, especially when manuscript locations are included with basic bibliographical and biographical data.

The dispersal of manuscripts and scarce publications in repositories throughout a state or many states is a problem for researchers working on most writers, but it poses greater difficulties with women's material, since these papers tend also to be cataloged deviously. Alabama researchers, for example, have discovered archival materials by Howard

Weeden, a twentieth-century woman painter and poet, scattered from Huntsville to Mobile. Similarly, Varina Howell Davis' letters are housed in a number of collections, among them the University of Alabama collection, the State of Alabama Department of Archives and History, the Southern Historical Collection at the University of North Carolina, Chapel Hill, and the New York Public Library. A computerized locator service for the manuscript holdings of public and private repositories would simplify archival work for everyone. Materials could be described and coded by location, with the database accessible from terminals throughout the country.

A magnificent, singular book-length manuscript (not one of the hundreds of fine out-of-print texts) is an extremely rare find. But I have discovered three—the diary of Sarah Gayle and the poetry and Japanese journals of Mary Fenollosa.[10] Publishing activity need not be restricted to book-length gems, however; anthologies of women's stories might be organized around a theme (e.g., Carver's stories on aging, Caroline Slade's on country women), a region, an economic class, an ethnic group, or a genre. Collections of letters reflecting a range of subjects concerning everyday life, female friends, familial relationships, and historical events could provide us with an entirely new perspective on the lives of most people. Women's letters written during the Civil War, when the men were away and the women assumed responsible roles, attack the fundamental stereotypes of the "Southern Belle." Southern family letters, like those still in the possession of the Kennedy family (Centreville, Alabama), suggest women's perspectives on war. It would be interesting to compare their views with those of Northern women or of women during the two world wars. Also, a compilation of women's treaties on education would be interesting and valuable; black and white women have addressed this subject for over a century. The relevant papers of a better-known educational theorist like Julia Tutwiler might form the basis for a collection that would include letters and diaries left by the many women who founded and taught in schools throughout the South.

Another kind of useful collection is exemplified by the Feminist Press's Zora Neale Hurston reader, *I Love Myself When I Am Laughing,* edited by Alice Walker (1979), which reprints selections from Hurston's out-of-print works. Publication of the reader followed revived interest in Hurston, primarily in her novel *Their Eyes Were Watching God,* but similar single-figure readers might well renew interest in such authors as Julia Peterkin, Elizabeth Madox Roberts, Ellen Glasgow, Margaret Walker, and Lillian Smith, to suggest only a few. Such readers could also contribute to the development of research by printing selected manuscript materials and thus making them accessible to a substantial audience. Roberts' widely dispersed correspondence and notebooks, for example, contain extensive and valuable commentary on the development of her works. Such materials, which are generally available in print for canonized male writers, have certainly encouraged research and criticism.

Sound biocriticism, such as we find in the better volumes of the Twayne Series, would militate against the general avoidance of writers—often female, black and regional—whose works seem impenetrable. Furthermore, publication of books like Thomas Landes' *Julia Peterkin* (Boston: G. K. Hall, 1976) encourages us to teach these writers, and by teaching them, we contribute significantly to the development of literary reputation. Frederick Ungar's controversial international encyclopedias of biocritical entries on women writers and the standard *Notable American Women, 1607–1950* (Cambridge: Harvard Univ. Press, 1971) provide brief surveys that call attention to figures deserving more extended consideration. Good preliminary biocritical works are needed for writers like Frances Harper, Nella Larsen, Toni Cade Bambara, and Wilma Dykeman. With writers whose body of works is extensive, such as Mary Noailles Murfree's or Harriette Arnow's, full scholarly-critical studies are in order.

We also need to publish women's oral testimony—oral history, personal narrative, and folklore. Such materials, if they have been collected, are most often found in smaller archives throughout the country, but frequently the scholar needs to collect the materials prior to publication. Like any written document, oral testimony may be valued intrinsically, for the beauty and artistry of the narrator's presentation, or extrinsically, for what it reveals about the diverse texture of women's everyday lives. One of the best ways to reconstitute the cultural heritage of women is to collect and analyze oral narrative. Spoken lives and re-created events, as recent collections of oral testimony demonstrate, often resemble literature in their design, verbal artistry, characterization, and power to affect the listener.[11] Even when oral works have little intrinsic value, they contain the kind of source materials from which many conventional literary works have been constructed; they provide insight into the worlds of our writers and their characters.

Over the past few years, the Modern Language Association's Commission on the Status of Women in the Profession has focused attention on the wealth of women's archival resources. Supported by grants from the Fund for the Improvement of Postsecondary Education, the Commission sponsored three years of research and teaching on women's regional literature. The project, directed by Leonore Hoffmann, engaged hundreds of scholar-teachers and student researchers throughout the country in the study of local archival resources. This activity culminated in a 1979 National Endowment for the Humanities

Summer Institute on Women's Non-Traditional Literature. For five weeks, twenty-five teachers explored the theoretical and pedagogical problems involved in the study of noncanonical material, preparatory to teaching courses in their own institutions and furthering research activities. These efforts have resulted in an extended network of feminist scholars committed to the discovery, development, and use of archival collections of material by women. On the strength of this fine beginning, the Modern Language Association Commission might well consider the procedures adopted by the National Historical Publications Commission Advisory Committee on Women's Papers. In 1974, the Committee drew up a list of over ninety women and women's organizations whose papers warranted publication or editing. It used as a standard the women's contributions to social history but excluded the works of creative writers and artists unless, like Harriet Beecher Stowe and Louisa May Alcott, their activities were significant in other ways. In addition to published guides like *American Literary Manuscripts,* the *Women's History Sources Survey* and the findings of these trained researchers might provide the basis for determining some sources for archival materials as well as some priorities for publication.

Promoting the recognition of women writers requires a particular vigilance on our part. We must ensure the availability of the literature that we believe people should read and that we wish to teach and discuss—a commitment that is currently being demonstrated by feminist presses throughout the country. We must work against the speed with which new books—many of them by and about women—go out of print or never appear in paperback editions. We need to make certain that someone keeps writers like Zora Neale Hurston, Elizabeth Madox Roberts, Nella Larsen, and Edith Summers Kelley in print, and we must also confront the more difficult task of bringing out easily available editions of lesser-known writers like Julia LeGrand, the Southern diarist, and Mary MacLane, the author of the autobiographical *I, Mary MacLane.* The judgments surrounding the publication and evaluation of writers like these are not made without difficulty. We can only learn to trust the strength of our academic and personal preparation to carry us through the uncharted territory ahead.

Notes

1. Perry Miller, ed. *The Transcendentalists* (Cambridge: Harvard Univ. Press, 1967), p. 141.
2. Most notable are Bell Gale Chevigny, *The Woman and the Myth: Margaret Fuller's Life and Writings* (Old Westbury, N.Y.: Feminist, 1976), and Paula Blanchard, *Margaret Fuller: From Transcendentalism to Revolution* (New York: Seymour Lawrence-Delta, 1978).
3. For further discussion, see Gerda Lerner, *The Majority Finds Its Past: Placing Women in History* (New York: Oxford Univ. Press, 1979), pp. 101–02.
4. Some of the letters to and from Annie Fields are available in a number of the works she wrote or edited: *Letters of Sarah Orne Jewett* (Boston: Houghton, 1911); *Authors and Friends* (Boston: Houghton, 1896); and *Memoirs of a Hostess* (Boston: Atlantic Monthly, 1922). These works demonstrate clearly how women fostered support networks for other creative women.
5. *Silences* (New York: Delacorte, 1978), pp. 22–46.
6. *O. Henry Memorial Award: Prize Stories of 1929,* ed. Blanche Colton Williams (Garden City, N.Y.: Doubleday, 1929).
7. Quoted by Gayle White, "Eudora Welty: 'The central thing is a sense of belonging,' " *Atlanta Constitution Magazine,* 15 May 1977, pp. 6 ff.
8. See the primary sources "The Raspberry Dress," *Century Magazine* (December, 1926), pp. 189–98, "The Old One" *Harper's* (October, 1926), pp. 545–54, and the biocritical sketch by Alice A. Parker, *American Women Writers From Colonial Times to the Present,* ed. Lina Mainiero (New York: Ungar, 1979), I, 306–08.
9. Oliver Jackson Ford III, "Ada Jack Carver: A Critical Biography," Diss. Univ. of Connecticut 1975. The Cammie Henry scrapbook of Carver clippings and manuscripts is at the Univ. of Northwestern Louisiana (Natchitoches, La.).
10. The work of Mary McNeil Fenollosa, wife of the Oriental scholar Ernest Fenollosa, has been considered only briefly in an article by Caldwell Delaney, "Mary McNeil Fenollosa, an Alabama Woman of Letters," *Alabama Review,* 16, No. 3 (July 1963), 163–73. Her papers are housed in the collection of the Museum of Mobile; her most successful works were three novels—*Truth Dexter* (1897), *The Breath of the Gods* (1904), *Red Horse Hill* (1907–08)—and a volume of verse, *Out of the Nest* (1899).
11. See, e.g., selections from Jane Katz, *I Am The Fire of Time* (New York: Dutton, 1975); *Mountain Wolf Woman, Sister of Crashing Thunder: The Autobiography of a Winnebago Indian,* ed. Nancy Lurie (Ann Arbor: Univ. of Michigan Press, 1961); Kathy Kahn, *Hillbilly Women* (New York: Avon, 1974); Beverly Hungry Wolf, *The Ways of My Grandmothers* (New York: Morrow, 1980).

Language and Feminist Research

H. Lee Gershuny

Feminist research in language operates within the theoretical framework of linguistic determinism and linguistic relativity known as the Sapir-Whorf Hypothesis (SWH). Stated simply, the major premises of the SWH are (1) that sensory data are *classified into categories* implicit in the language system and (2) that *the structure* of the language affects the way in which the world is perceived and conceptualized.

In suggesting that the limits of our language determine the limits of our world, the SWH has enormous implications for feminist research in every discipline, since these disciplines have been traditionally structured from masculinist points of view. As a result, language has both reflected and reinforced the cultural norms that consistently subordinate female-associated symbols. Stereotyped concepts of femininity and masculinity permeate the categories and models of many symbol systems with which humanity organizes its various worlds—literature, language, theology, psychology, sociology, and so on. For example, early American male writers repeatedly compared the qualities of the new world to those of female sexuality. Their metaphors express their conflict between raping and dominating the land and being nourished by "her" fertile beauty. An ambivalence born of an erotic desire for the virginal or seductive woman and a filial need for the protective mother's breast characterized men's language and their behavior regarding both "land-as-woman" and "woman-as-woman."[1] Their descriptions of the land modeled the white-male perception of woman so that land and woman each assumed the traits of the other. Characterizing the land as woman was affected not only by the lexicon (vocabulary) and semantics (meaning) of the language used but also by the androcentric cultural norms that suggested ways of classifying sensory data and establishing relations among classes. Since language patterns and cultural norms constantly influence and interact with each other, feminist research in language is interested in the ways in which concepts of femininity and masculinity affect both the features of a particular language and the taxonomies and models of a particular discipline. In actively applying the premises of the SWH, feminists hope to change the male-supremacist cultural world by changing language usage. They are not only ferreting out androcentricism in language and culture but also devising nonsexist language usage, defining themselves, and revaluing female qualities.

Sensory Data Are Classified into Categories. Sensory data have frequently been divided into opposed classes: animate/inanimate, day/night, subject/object, positive/negative, thinking/feeling, industrial/agrarian, good/evil, and male/female. These dichotomies are often defined according to stereotyped traits of masculinity (strong, assertive, independent, abstract, logical, etc.) and femininity (weak, passive, dependent, emotional, intuitive, etc.) that are ranked and valued. Classifying and arranging the world through language invariably suggest values. The more important values will be associated with masculine labels—"God created *man* in *His* image" (emphasis added)—and when male and female terms are paired, the former usually appears first, as in "Mr. and Mrs." The dominant class subsumes the subordinate and becomes the norm, as in English where the masculine terms—*man, mankind,* and *he*—absorb the feminine.

Language Structures Our World. Classifying the phenomenal and cultural worlds often structures them into superior-inferior hierarchies and positive-negative polarities. By definition, masculine traits are superior and establish the norm in most, if not all, studies of human behavior. In classifying the English language as "positively and expressly masculine," for example, Otto Jesperson concomitantly ranked masculine qualities as superior to feminine: "it is the language of a grown-up man and has very little childish or feminine about it." Similarly, in a study on stereotyping, clinical psychologists were more likely to attribute traits that characterize healthy adults to a man than to a woman, thereby suggesting that healthy women may not be perceived as mature adults.[2] Assumptions about the "nature" of females and males are hidden not only in the definition of a healthy adult but also in most clinicians' interpretations of the model. As feminist psychologists have pointed out, the definition of a healthy adult does not necessarily exclude women, even though it lists traits characteristic of the male stereotype. In addition to the culturally hidden biases in models and definitions, the personal biases of the researcher, practitioner, or clinician may affect research topics, methods, interpretations, and applications. A masculinist or feminist perspective, for example, suggests that sex bias reflects both the symbol system of the culture and the sexual identity of the encoder or decoder. (Generally, however, feminism has been excluded and denigrated by the established male biases.)

In documenting how linguistic features structure and perpetuate a pervasive androcentric bias, feminist scholars challenge the myth of scientific and linguistic objectivity. In the process, they demythologize male supremacy by demonstrating that it is an artifact of culture that underlies our values, power structure, and perceptions of self, other, and environment. The symbols of male supremacy construct the world in terms of sexual difference and dominance. As an integral part of our language and thought, they perpetuate and justify male power. Since a classifying system, by its nature, is bound to reflect and shape cultural biases, all people who use language—whether linguists who analyze and describe it or scholars who use it to classify and reorganize their systems of inquiry—are prey to the values and biases implicit in the language system.

Thus, feminist research in language (1) brings to consciousness the deep androcentric structures embedded in language theory and practice; (2) describes the features of female and male language from a feminist perspective; and (3) creates, as a result, new metaphors, methods, models, and meanings to change the limits of the masculinist world. These research goals are integral to the three interrelated research areas that I discuss:

1. *Linguistics*—theoretical considerations of the meaning and structure of language
2. *The language of social institutions*—language about women and men in the major fields of discourse and institutions of socialization
3. *Sociolinguistics and interpersonal communication*—language used by women and men in various social settings

Linguistics

In investigating the features of any language, feminist researchers have been primarily concerned with the ways in which gender has been marked by a given speech community at a given time (*synchronic* linguistics) and changed through linguistic usage and evolution (*diachronic* linguistics).[3] Such studies ask two major questions: (1) To what extent are linguistic theory and history based on androcentric premises and models? (2) What structural and semantic features differentiate gender in a given language and speech community? Although some feminists have studied language according to traditional linguistic categories—the phonological (intonation, pronunciation), morphological (word structure), syntactic (word order), and semantic (meaning)[4]—I have organized this overview in terms of linguistic issues raised by feminists. This approach seems appropriate here not only because of the androcentric bias in traditional linguistics but also because of feminists' distinctive emphasis and orientation within these categories.

Androcentricism in Linguistic Inquiry

Feminists conceive of language as human behavior interacting with many social and psychological variables that function beyond the closed system of Chomsky's formal linguistics. We are interested in developing theories based on linguistic "performance"—the actual use of language in concrete situations—and in redefining "competence"—the intuitive knowledge about sounds, meanings, and syntax that the speakers of a language possess. Chomsky's definition of the "competent" or ideal speaker proves inadequate since it is based on the model of a white middle-class male operating in a homogeneous speech community that exists only in the androcentric orientation of most scholars and not in any real speech community. Language, after all, does not operate in a vacuum, even in internal dialogue, but relates to the person using it and to the cultural values and sociopolitical rules governing the situation. Separating linguistic studies of theoretical "competence" from those of practical "performance" contrives a division between form and function and between linguistic theory and language behavior.

Based on androcentric models, even seemingly neutral linguistic data are bound to reflect not only the bias of the linguist in selecting illustrative data from *his* speech community but the subtly pervasive sexual biases embedded in the language as a result of larger sociopolitical inequalities. Although a dictionary, for example, is regarded as authoritative and neutral in defining and illustrating word meaning, feminist research has uncovered both the lexicographers' androcentric biases in devising illustrative sentences that stereotype and denigrate the feminine gender, and the larger cultural bias evident in the meaning, structure, and usage of the American-English lexicon: (1) terms with visible masculine markers, like *mailman* and *manpower*, outnumber the feminine by three to one; (2) negative connotation is more frequently a feature of feminine words than of masculine ones; (3) a greater number of negative words are associated with the feminine; (4) the feminine term is syntactically subordinated in that it generally appears second or last in word order—*guys and dolls, boys and girls, men and women;* and (5) word choice and meaning are based on stereotyped gender connotations; females *shriek, giggle, titter, purr,* and *cackle,* whereas males *roar, bellow, growl,* and *guffaw*. The masculine is established as the human norm—the average person is always masculine, as in "the man in the street" and "the average man"—and masculine terms are used three times more often than feminine terms in dictionary definitions and illustrative sentences.[5] Linguistic theorists, in selecting illustrative material, tend to be as affected by the traditional androcentric biases in methodology and data collection as are the lexicographers. In a paper on discourse analysis and the connective *otherwise,* the first in a series of eleven examples was: "Professor Arid must stop assaulting coeds. Otherwise he'll be arrested."[6] Chomsky, the father of the competence-performance dichotomy, used *he or she* once—"if a person matured into an amoeboid or mental midget, then he or she . . ."—and the generic *he* for all other pronominal references in his lecture "Rules and Representations."[7]

In diachronic linguistics also, feminists have reported androcentric interpretations of linguistic change. Wolfe, for example, points out that male scholars frequently ignore female-associated myths and metaphors in tracing word etymologies from cognates in comparative linguistics studies. They assume that early Indo-European cultures were as patriarchally oriented as our culture is today.[8]

Feminist research, then, suggests that androcentric bias in data collection and analysis characterizes not only linguistic and cultural inquiry but also any other systematization of data that trivializes linguistic sexism and denies the existence of the female orientation.

Gender Marking

Gender marking refers to the semantic (meaning) and structural features that differentiate gender in a given language. In arguing that sex-role stereotypes are embedded in gender marking, feminist linguists have challenged the traditional androcentric view that gender, in English, is based mainly on the classification of nominals according to their reference to biological sex, that is, "natural gender." With extensive illustrations of linguistic performance, feminists continue to demonstrate that gender referents (nominals that denote male and female gender) and gender markers (linguistic features that denote gender) carry the connotation of the sex stereotypes and, as a result, limit our social reality.[9]

The Semantics of Gender Marking. A word that has [+female] semantic space (i.e., meaning), like *nurse,* is usually negative in connotation and not as high in prestige as the [+male] counterpart, here *doctor.* There is no [+male] counterpart for *shrew,* but for the pejorative exclusively [+female] *spinster,* English provides the positive, exclusively [+male] *bachelor*. When [+female] in association, many words take on a narrow, more negative meaning than when referring to [+male]. The word *professional*, for example, suggests whore when used with a [+female] referent, but when used with a [+male] referent, the term has a more general meaning, suggesting competence and commitment to one's career or occupation.

If changes in the connotations of female-associated words from neutral or positive to pejorative are a prime indicator of changes in woman's condition, then research in diachronic linguistics suggests that woman's state has gradually deteriorated while man's has improved. Schulz notes:

> Again and again in the history of the language, one finds that a perfectly innocent term designating a girl or woman may begin with totally neutral or even positive connotations, but that it gradually acquires negative implications, at first perhaps only slightly disparaging, but after a period of time becoming abusive and ending as a sexual slur.

Schulz cites:

> *Lord*, for example, is still reserved as a title for deities and certain Englishmen, but any woman may call herself a *lady*. Only a few are entitled to be called *Baronet* and only a few wish to be called *Dame*, since as a general term, *dame* is opprobrious. Although *governor* degenerated briefly in nineteenth century Cockney slang, the term still refers to men who "exercise a sovereign authority in a colony, territory, or state." A *governess*, on the other hand, is chiefly a "nursemaid," operating in a realm much diminished from that of Queen Elizabeth I, who was acknowledged to be "the supreme majesty and governess of all persons" (OED). We might conceivably, and without affront, call the Queen's Equerry a *courtier*, but would we dare refer to her lady-in-waiting as a *courtesan*? *Sir* and *Master* seem to have come down through time as titles of courtesy without taint. However, *Madam*, *Miss*, and *Mistress* have all derogated, becoming euphemisms respectively for "a mistress of a brothel," "a prostitute," and "a woman with whom a man habitually fornicates."[10]

Stanley lists 220 terms for sexually promiscuous women in a constantly expanding lexicon, with only 22 for promiscuous men.[11]

Unmarked nominals, however, are presumed to have [+male] semantic space until feminine markers are added, as in poet/poet*ess*, major/major*ette*, steward/steward*ess*, and judge/*lady* judge. As indicated earlier, lexical pairs exist in English to mark gender semantically, as in *tailor* [+male] and *seamstress* [+female]. The implication is clear—not only do unmarked [+male] terms establish the masculine as the norm and the feminine as the deviant, but the addition of the feminine marker counteracts the positive connotation of the unmarked nominal.

The Grammar and Semantics of Generics. Gender marking in English becomes an even more contentious linguistic issue when we examine English generics that theoretically mean [+male], [+male and +female], or [+human, unknown sex]. But English generic terms are frequently masculine-marked, both morphologically (as in *man, mankind* and *he*) and semantically (as in occupational terms like *doctor, professor, manager,* and *boss,* until a feminine marker is added). In addition, feminists have cited contexts where words that might apply to either—*child, rider, people, students*—are actually [+male] in reference. Masculine-marked generics sound ridiculous when used to refer to the female population, as in the sentences "Man like other mammals breast-feeds his young" and "When we get abortion-law repeal, everyone will be able to decide for himself whether or not to have an abortion" (Nilsen et al., pp. 50–73, 145). Feminists argue that, although each sentence accords grammatically with the competence structural model, it does not work semantically because English speakers do not regard masculine-marked "generics" as terms with [+female] semantic space. Research has supported this contention by demonstrating that children and young adults of both sexes seldom select or include a female image when decoding generics like *man.*[12] Feminists also point out that *woman, she,* and other feminine-marked "generics" have been perfectly acceptable when used to refer to all-female populations but not in referring to groups of unknown or mixed sex. Even though the population of women is slightly larger than that of men, *womankind* is not used as a "true" generic and this point is cited as further evidence of the double standard embedded in English. In effect, English grammar and semantics have tended to minimize, subordinate, ignore, absorb, or subsume the contribution and existence of women, sometimes even erasing from language, history, and thought all evidence of the female experience.

Future Directions

In organizing the abundant data feminists are gathering to document linguistic sexism, we will need a viable theory of linguistic performance with grammatical rules that explain asymmetrical meaning and usage in gender-marked contexts—for example, where adjectives are used to describe females but not males or where titles of marital status (*Mrs.* and *Miss*) are used for females but not for males, who are referred to by professional titles (*Dr.* and *Prof.*) or last names. If possible, semantically marked [+female] adjectives could be classified according to such themes as sexuality, intelligence, and physical characteristics and compared with [+male] adjectives in the same classification. Is there a tendency, for example, to describe females as *bright* and males as *intelligent*? On a word-choice test, what adjectives and verbs would female and male participants choose for feminine- and masculine-marked subjects? Can the meanings of such lexical pairs (adjectives and verbs) be compared on the semantic differential where subjects measure the semantic space of selected words according to polarized scales selected by the researcher (strong/weak, active/passive, masculine/feminine, etc.)? Such investigations could test the feminist contention that the semantic space of English is structured according to sex-role stereotypes.

In reducing linguistic sexism, feminists have added such terms as *consciousness raising, Ms.* and *sexism* to the lexicon and changed usage to nonsexist alternatives like *chair* or *chairperson* and *fire fighter*. But feminists need to investigate the extent to which such changes appear in linguistic performance and whether nonsexist language usage correlates with nonsexist meaning and attitudes. Further research using the semantic differential, for example, would tell researchers whether the connotations of female-associated and nonsexist words are changing. Is one kind of nonsexist marker more positive in connotation than another? Have words like *spokesperson* and *anchorperson* become euphemisms for female referents? Or has the meaning of generics and established nonsexist alternatives actually changed, so that the former do include females and the latter do include males?

In short, the basic question feminists have asked in the past remains pertinent: To what extent do linguistic features and theoretical systems reflect sex bias?

The Language of Social Institutions

Feminist descriptions of the verbal and nonverbal language of major institutions of socialization (e.g., education, mass media, work, law, religion, courtship, and marriage) chiefly concern what the culture is saying *about* females and males. Since language and culture shape each other, using sexist language limits the cultural world to sexist beliefs. Sexist language maintains a double standard and code—one for and about females and the other for and about males. If the language of textbooks, religious codes, and law defines women as inferior to men, then our beliefs and behavior will reflect those values. Feminist investigations consistently confirm the pervasiveness of not only the linguistic sexism just described but also the polarization and conflict of the sexes in culture.

Language about Females and Males

Numerous content analyses of words and images that differentiate and convey sex roles have been published by informal women's groups, government commissions, and scholars from virtually every discipline.[13] Their results have appeared in journals operated by women and in those established by men. Bosmajian, for example, found that the language of legislatures and courts has traditionally defined, labeled, and stereotyped women as (1) mothers and wives, (2) infants and incompetents, (3) vamps and profligates, and/or (4) nonpersons and nonentities. Such paternalistic beliefs limit women's political and economic rights and also attempt to keep them from hearing or speaking improper language. State laws, for example, have allowed only men to use obscene or lascivious language and then, only outside the hearing range of women (Nilsen et al., pp. 77–92). In business texts, the female secretary is frequently reminded in word and image that she has less intelligence than her male boss and virtually no independent judgment. She is advised to lower the high register of her voice and to correct the bad speaking habits that she, as a woman, is believed to have. Apart from demeaning women, social institutions establish double standards of linguistic performance that require conformity to sex-role stereotypes (Nilsen et al., p. 154).

The data collected in content analyses of the language of various social institutions reflect the following patterns:

1. *Stereotyping.* Roles of females and males are stereotyped and mythologized in words and images. Males are cast as leaders, businessmen, and professionals; women, as wives, mothers and prostitutes.

2. *Negativity.* The female stereotype is negative and inferior by definition. Women are described in terms of their physical appearance whereas men are described in terms of their careers and accomplishments. Behavior described in a man as *assertive* is described in a woman as *pushy, bitchy,* or *castrating.* Female traits in a male are almost always described in negative terms—*effeminate, dependent, emotional,* and so forth.

3. *Low-status roles.* The jobs associated with women carry little power and prestige. Secretarial positions for example, are archetypically feminine; executive positions, requiring more intelligence, are archetypically masculine.

4. *Subordination.* Females are defined in relation to males instead of their own terms and are stereotypically viewed as subordinate to males and dependent on them. They usually appear after men in a listing or discussion. Robin Lakoff was described as "George Lakoff's wife and *also* a Professor of Linguistics at Berkeley" in "Notes on the Contributors" (*Semantic Syntax,* 1974, emphasis added).

5. *Invisibility.* The feminine gender is omitted from "generic" words and not represented in references to historical and cultural contributions. Even in discussions of female achievements, women may disappear syntactically in passive constructions: "quilts were made; quilting was done."[14]

6. *Trivializing.* Women's accomplishments, conversations, and is-

sues are dismissed and/or trivialized as hysterical overreactions or plain gossip. "When the neurotic woman gets cured, she becomes a woman. When the neurotic man gets cured, he becomes an artist."[15]

Future Directions

The more we feminists reveal how verbal and nonverbal language sustains and perpetuates male dominance in every phase of life, the more we challenge the assumptions of biological determinism inherent in the sex stereotypes. The repeated protests of those authorities who trivialize the issues of linguistic sexism and nonsexist usage serve to dramatize the importance of language as a source of social control.

Although cultural sexism has been amply documented, continual research is needed to determine the extent to which language, attitudes, and behavior have changed and the degree to which language usage reflects actual changes in the condition of women. Is the image of women changing in consort with a changing reality? For example, in analyzing the dialogue of female and male characters in the literature of female and male writers in the *Ladies' Home Journal,* 1900–20, Berryman found that, while the image of woman changed from that of wife and mother to that of unmarried career woman, female speech patterns remained the same. Berryman suggests that even today, although women's behavior may convey a positive image, their demeaning speech patterns may negate their efforts.[16] Some of the most important questions in sociolinguistics today deal with the features and implications of women's language and linguistic style.

Sociolinguistics and Interpersonal Communication

Is there a women's language? If so, what are its features and under what conditions is sex-differentiated usage observed? Although these questions have always interested observers of linguistic behavior in a variety of cultures,[17] they have recently gained more attention from feminist linguists and sociolinguists who seek (1) to describe the features of sex-differentiated verbal and nonverbal language usage; (2) to explain why the differences take certain forms and appear in certain contexts; and (3) to uncover androcentric biases in research.

Generally, sociolinguists acknowledge that sex differences in language cannot be explained by the same theories that account for ethnic, racial, class, and geographical dialects, since women and men communicate freely within these groups (Trudgill, pp. 84–102). After reviewing interdisciplinary language studies, Thorne and Henley suggested that sex-differentiated language was generated from

> . . . the social elaboration of gender, the structure of male dominance, and the division of labor by sex (the interests, activities, and

position of women and men in society, including the socialization of children, and forms of social bonding). (p. 14)

Similarly, Lakoff asserts that woman's subordination and powerlessness are reflected not only in the ways women are spoken of and are expected to speak but in the ways in which they actually speak.[18]

Researchers have varied the social context, the problem-solving tasks, and the composition (female-male, female-female, and male-male) of small communication groups to examine how a complex interaction of variables impinges on language usage. While linguistics, sociolinguistics, interpersonal communications, and social psychology overlap in these studies, the common concern here is the extent to which biological sex differences interact with psychological, sociological, and political gender differences to create sex-linked linguistic features.

Features of Sex-Differentiated Language

Before I briefly outline some of the sex differences that have been postulated, prescribed, and empirically observed in extensive reviews of the literature (see Key, and Thorne and Henley), I must point out that, since linguistic (verbal and nonverbal) behavior functions as an integral part of the social context, this section, of necessity, merely describes tendencies in female and male language users, not the operating rules of model languages.

Sex differences have been observed (1) in traditional linguistic parameters of written and spoken English—phonology (pronunciation, intonation, pitch), and style—and (2) in verbal and nonverbal features of interpersonal communication. Most studies have assumed that, though females and males have access to the same grammatical and lexical features, women would more frequently use patterns that betray uncertainty and reflect submission to male dominance. Content has been analyzed to determine whether topic and lexical choices of females and males cluster around sex-stereotyped categories. Other researchers have suggested that if it is true that females and males learn "genderlects"—that is, sex-linked language—then subjects should be able to distinguish between the speech of women and that of men and even to generate the criteria for such discriminations.

Phonology—Pronunciation. Studies finding significant differences between female and male pronunciations—for example, in the male use of *-in* and the female use of *-ing* in verb endings (as in *fishin'* and *fishing*)—as well as related research[19] suggest that working-class women are more likely than working-class men to use phonetic forms that resemble the prestige style of the white middle-class male. Trudgill's explanation for this type of sex-linked phonetic variation is that women, because of their subordinate social position, are more status-conscious than men are. Consigned by their biological sex and physical qualities to a low social status, they are forced to rely on linguistic cues and other symbols to signal a higher rank (Trudgill, pp. 84–102).

Phonology—Pitch. Women's speech is variously stereotyped as high-pitched, loud, simpering, shrill, whiney, giggly, breathy, and thin—qualities opposite to, and less desirable than, those of men's speech.[20] The larynxes of preadolescent boys and girls are the same size, relative to height and weight, but adult judges have been able to identify the sexes of children, aged four to fourteen from their voices.[21] The implication is that cultural expectations and sex-role identification play a more significant role than does anatomical development in sex-differentiated voice features.

Phonology—Intonation. Researchers have found that women tend to conform to role expectations by intoning assertions as questions, by speaking more emotionally and expressively than men do, and by using more "polite" and cheerful patterns than men do.[22]

Syntax. Researchers have identified syntactic patterns that they believe women tend to use more frequently than men:

1. Intensifiers: *so, such, quite, rather, vastly,*
2. Modal construction: *can, could, shall, should, will, would, may, might*—words that suggest doubt about events that did or will take place,
3. Tag questions: a shortened yes/no question added to a declarative statement, as in "Women's speech is different, isn't it?"
4. Modified imperative constructions: (a) interrogative structures in lieu of commands, as in "Do you mind turning down the volume?" (b) modals and polite forms, as in "You could return the book tomorrow if you'd like"; (c) longer sentences to avoid brusqueness, as in "Would it be all right with you if I gave you a credit tomorrow instead of today?" (see Lakoff; Key, pp. 75–77).

In addition, women tend, more often than men, to break off their sentences without finishing them (Jesperson, *Language,* pp. 237–53). Researchers suggest that the uncertainty, tentativeness, and submissiveness evident in women's speech patterns show that language behavior conforms to sex-role expectations.

These patterns have been investigated (1) by asking subjects to identify the sex of the writer or speaker from both linguistic data collected by the researcher and data appearing in popular culture; and (2) by analyzing and quantifying lexical and syntactic features in fictitious female-male dialogues.[23] Since such studies were based on contexts (magazines, cartoons, and fiction) that may have already stereotyped women's speech, these findings merely suggest rather than confirm that women are more likely than men to use tag questions, lengthy messages, unfinished sentences, and intensifiers.

Lexicon. Lakoff suggests that sex-linked vocabulary is consonant with occupational and sex roles. She notes, for example, that women involved with the subtleties of home decorating and fashion are likely to make color distinctions that a man would consider "trivial and irrelevant to the real world." In addition, she observes that men are more likely than women to use strong expletives like *shit, damn,* and *hell* while women are more given to weak expressions like *oh dear* and *goodness sakes;* and she identifies lexical terms that are largely confined to female use: *adorable, charming, sweet, lovely,* and *divine.* Berryman's analysis of male-female dialogue in the *Ladies' Home Journal* confirms as characteristic of women many lexical features that Lakoff (pp. 3–73) and Kramer ("Women's Speech," pp. 43–56) defined as female. Women characters used more exclamations, intensifiers, and qualifiers (adjectives and adverbs that reduce the intensity of a statement—*sort of, kind of, somewhat*) (Berryman, pp. 3–13). Similarly, Gleser and her colleagues found that females used more words implying opinion, emotion, or desire; made more references to self; and used more modal forms, expressing possibility rather than certainty. Males, on the other hand, used significantly more words implying space, time, quantity, and destructive action. Swacker's study of the speech patterns of seventeen males and seventeen females also cited lexical variations in their use of numerals. Females not only used fewer numerals in their descriptive passages but also qualified half their numerals with indicators of approximation: "about six books."[24] In characterizing the overall content and style of sex-differentiated speech, research has usually confirmed sex-role expectations.

Semantics. Nilsen's research with elementary school children suggests that the reference and meaning of masculine-marked English generics may be more confusing to girls than to boys. Similarly, Schneider and Hacker's study of pictures submitted by introductory sociology students for "generic" *man* (e.g., *social man, political man, economic man*) and terms without the *man* label (e.g., *social behavior, political behavior*) indicates both that women are seldom pictured as part of "generic" *man* and that the meaning of generics differs for female and male decoders (Nilsen, "Grammatical Gender, pp. 106–108, and Schneider and Hacker, pp. 12–18). Eble, too, notes that the connotations of words differ along sex lines. The meaning changes in relation to the speaker's sex: "You caught me with my pants down" is a "metaphorical admission of embarrassment on the part of a man, but is almost always interpreted literally and physically if a woman says it."[25]

Style. The existence of a discernible women's language implies the existence of a women's linguistic style, that is, a consistent pattern of sex-differentiated language use in speaking and writing. Linguistic parameters (phonology, semantics, lexicon, and syntax), the mode of communication (oral or written), and, of course, the social context would need to be considered in determining the features of a women's style. Although "stylistics" has historically been an important element of literary analysis and criticism, interactive styles—women's speaking styles—have been the concern in sociolinguistic studies.

Feminist critics have discussed at length how the "content" of women's writing differs from that of men since women experience a different world, feelings, and concerns and thus bring to writing a different sensibility. To find an artistic voice that is authentically her own, a woman author must violate the conventions of "feminine" passivity and subordination. The conflict between feminine socialization and artistic creation—an assertive and independent act—raises questions about the existence and nature of women's style of writing and its correlation with folklinguistics (beliefs about female and male language based on the stereotypes).

Most feminist studies of "women's style" in writing have focused on individual writers, proceeding from their particular features to the more general tendencies in women's written language. These studies attempt to show that women's writing may (1) reflect their social condition, (2) express conflict between sex-role expectation and artistic sensibility, or (3) devise new forms and metaphors in wrenching language from patriarchal meanings and contexts.[26]

Sex-Linked Features of Interpersonal Communication

Although the distinctive characteristics of male and female communication patterns may not be defined as rigidly in American English as they are in cultures with less sex-role flexibility, we can nevertheless identify a prescriptive code of linguistic behavior for female-male interactions. Determining the rules of interactive "grammars," however, is far more complex than analyzing the content of written language. Researchers must not only classify the linguistic features elicited but interpret the data in the light of the structure of the situation, the personality and social class of each participant, and the effect of one variable on another. Thorne and Henley identified seven factors in communicative events that are relevant to studies in sex-differentiation in language: (1) the *locations* (night clubs, classrooms, offices, "natural" or contrived settings), (2) the various *participants* (senders, receivers, addressors, and addressees; the sex of those speaking, spoken to, and spoken about—considerations regarded separately and/or in combination), (3) the *channels* (written, spoken, nonverbal), (4) the *codes* (linguistic, paralinguistic, kinesic, interactional), (5) the *forms of messages* and their *genres* (wordplay, jokes, verbal dueling, narratives), (6) the *attitudes* and *content* that a message may convey on the topics being discussed, and (7) the *events* themselves, taken as a whole (Thorne and Henley, pp. 12–13). Studies of sex differences in group communication generally concentrate on verbal and nonverbal interactive patterns and on the overall interactive style—task, performance, conformity, bargaining, coalition formation, and leadership.

Verbal Interaction Patterns. According to Baird's review of the literature, most studies of face-to-face female-male interactions contradict the popular belief that women talk more than men. In fact, women tended to speak less than men and to acquiesce to male interruptions and dominance. Men spoke not only more often than women, but at greater length and interrupted women more frequently than women interrupted them. In general, men tended to use verbal and nonverbal cues to direct the topics of conversation toward occupational and male-oriented interests.[27]

Valdés-Fallis recently tested the belief that women have a greater "natural" sensitivity to men's verbal and nonverbal cues than other men do. She examined the code-switching patterns (the tendency to switch from one language pattern to another) of Mexican-American bilingual females first in face-to-face interactions with males and then in response to taped male speech. In the live interactions, female speakers tended to follow the language switching and the kind of switching pattern initiated by the male, but in the taped-speech situation, when tacit male approval was eliminated, their sensitivity to the switching styles on the stimulus tapes did not differ from men's. Valdés-Fallis' experiments challenge another folklinguistic belief, that women are "naturally" sensitive to verbal and nonverbal language cues; her findings suggest that such "sensitivity" is more a function of perceived power relationships (i.e., women's perceived powerlessness in a given social situation) than of a "natural" tendency to submit to the mythical "strength" of male speech.[28]

Nonverbal Interaction Patterns. To date, Henley has conducted the most extensive feminist review of the literature on sex-differentiated nonverbal communication. The parameters of nonverbal language that Henley identifies (gestures, demeanor, posture, personal space, timing, touching, eye contact, and facial expression) are analogous to verbal parameters (syntax, lexicon, semantics, and phonology) in communicating, maintaining, and ritualizing the symbol systems and social structures of male dominance.[29]

The same form of behavior (for example, smiling, shaking hands, or touching) may be used to express differences in status and solidarity between equals (close and distant) and nonequals (superior and subordinate). In citing evidence for sex-differentiated smiling, Henley noted that women and men smile not only in different ways but for different purposes. A woman is more likely to show her teeth or use a coy "lip-in" smile as a gesture of subordination to the person she is meeting. In an informal study of smile elicitation, Henley's students found that females not only returned smiles more often than males did but returned them more to males than to other females. Males were more inhibited about returning smiles to males than to females. Mothers were observed to smile when talking to their children whether or not they were saying something positive, whereas fathers smiled mainly when saying something friendly or approving (Henley, p. 177).

Women's frequent smiling reflects their socialized acceptance of male domination and of the programmed admonition to remain pleasant and pretty for men no matter what. The expressions of anger and indifference that are more characteristic of men's facial expressions suggest their strength and power to oppose, attack, withhold information, and "be cool"—unmoved and unemotional. Whatever the nonverbal cue, Henley found that the "same behaviors exhibited by superior to subordinate are those exhibited by men to women; and women exhibit to men the behaviors typical of subordinate to superior" (Henley, p. 180). She concludes that sex-differentiated language is less a matter of inherent differences between men and women than it is of pervasive differences in power.

Interactive Styles. Jenkins and Kramer, in their review of communication in women's consciousness-raising (CR) groups, suggest that the competitiveness characteristic of androcentric models of group interaction is antithetical to the goals of leaderless women's CR groups. Both the kind of interaction—shared narratives—and the groups' purpose—the revaluation of women and women's concerns—are integral parts of the new feminist consciousness. Sharing and unmasking (self-disclosure) replace masculine behavior—remaining secretive and competing to win. As a result, women may not be using the same communication strategies as men. Nevertheless, society expects them to conform to the male model of leadership and to use male problem-solving methods.

Although research in group communication generally suggests that sex-role expectations are reflected in sex-differentiated behavior, we must ask whether we are measuring sex differences or male standards. Jenkins and Kramer emphasize the importance of revaluing women's strengths—for instance, women's affiliative, emotionally supportive, interactive styles of behavior, such as narrating to illustrate a concept rather than to manipulate the audience. In CR groups, more occurs than the simple raising of sociopolitical consciousness: an authentic women's language is expressed in the structure and process of feminist interactions.[30]

To examine a context where a woman's control of her world rests on her verbal abilities, Johnson analyzed the interactional style of a Texas madam. Both the madam (Miss Hilda) and her "girls" were aware that the prostitute's art is more mental and verbal than sexual. The girls and their male clients recognized Miss Hilda's superior verbal ability, saying that she "could walk out on the floor right now, take any man to the bedroom, and talk him out of even the deed to his house."[31] The researcher found that Hilda consistently used more jokes, toasts, rhymes, and proverbs than anyone else, while reinforcing a strong pride in her womanhood. Her jokes did not demean women, whores, or old or weak men. Johnson believed that Hilda's strong presentation of herself as a woman enhanced her role as social controller (p. 224).

Androcentric Biases in Sociolinguistic and Communication Research

Whatever the approach or set of variables, a researcher should realize that male sociopolitical dominance acts as a hidden assumption in any empirical study of language difference. Sex bias must be considered in every step of the research design: statement of the problem, methodology, data collection and analysis, interpretation, and generalization of the results. In reviewing the literature or gathering data on communication behavior, we should question whether measures of difference can actually be value-free. When sex differences in communication behavior occur at specified times under specified conditions, can we consider them characteristic? When these differences reflect gender-role expectations, we need to examine the factors underlying these expectations, such as stereotyped definitions and male standards of behavior. Sause, for example, in his content analysis of the language of kindergarten children, acknowledged that as interviewer he may have inhibited his female subjects, who were more accustomed to interacting with women, and that as experimenter he may have chosen materials that were sex-biased toward the boys.[32] Henley has reported that in studies of nonverbal communication definitions, selection of material, research design, and interpretation of data frequently assume that male behavior is the norm and that female behavior is deviant. Stereotyped sex differences in nonverbal behavior may be found because the sterotypes have been built into the research design. One study, for example, used different semantic scales on the semantic differential to rate the posture of female and male figures. The researchers used sex stereotypes not only as the basis for the semantic scales but also as the justification for using different measures for female and male figures (Henley, p. 141).

Future Directions

Feminist research points beyond patriarchal paradigms to new theoretical frameworks and methods that (1) include a feminist perspective, that is, the female experience and perception of "reality," (2) revalue women's language and style, and (3) redefine problems and problem-solving processes. Progress in this direction will require further study of women's language in women's contexts.

All features of sex-differentiated language usage, both verbal (oral and written) and nonverbal, need additional empirical research in a variety of contexts. Comparative studies investigating possible changes in sex-differentiated usage during periods of change in women's consciousness, for example, could be studied more easily in written language and could tell us something about the interrelations of language, sex, and society. Other studies are needed to compare the sex-differentiated usages of different social classes in the same culture and to compare usages between cultures (e.g., American English and British English). Finding that women's language reflects the same patterns cross-culturally and differs significantly from men's language would strengthen our argument that language maintains the social order.

Because women have been writing for centuries—unpublished letters, journals, and diaries as well as published fiction, poetry, drama, and nonfiction—comparative analyses of past and present women's styles seem to be promising avenues of investigation, as do synchronic comparisons of female and male language in a given period. Since Kolodny published *The Lay of the Land,* a study of early American male writing, she has been gathering data for *The Lay of the Land, Part II,* a synchronic study of female writing.[33] In addition to overall writing style, the ways in which female and male writers treat male and female dialogue in fiction and drama present rich areas to investigate, especially as reflections of changing sex images and values.

Even if females and males use a similar lexicon, do they agree on the connotation? Does meaning vary with the sex of coder and decoder? The area of sex-differentiated semantics is virtually untapped. For example, would the decoder's sex determine the gender evoked by nonsexist words like *flight attendant* or *spokesperson*? Would females and males rate the connotative meanings of nonsexist terms and [+female] and [+male] pejorative terms differently on a semantic differential? Investigations of these questions might tell us whether sex-differentiated language use implies sex-differentiated semantics. If it does, then females and males may use the same words to refer to different "realities."

We also need studies of verbal and nonverbal language in "natural" settings, where groups communicate for their own purposes rather than the experimenter's. These studies might address questions like these: (1) How do women's and men's groups differ in the expression of power? (2) Does the expression of power change for each sex in mixed-sex groups? (3) How does each sex treat violations of group norms in mixed and homogeneous groups? Such research should avoid the pitfalls of androcentricism: blaming the victim, justifying the status quo, and focusing on stereotyped differences between the sexes as opposed to differences in the situation. It is not always clear, for example, whether a language pattern (e.g., tag questions) is used by females and males for the same purpose. If an interpretation is based on stereotypes, then the researcher may be ignoring important situational factors and may miss the broader significance of the sex difference in language use.

We might examine the ways in which authority is conveyed and maintained in verbal interaction, such as interruptions, pauses, and silences used to express domination or submission, and the differences between women's and men's groups in the kind and quantity of supportive and assertive language used. Kramer recommends a "social psychology approach which considers such mediating variables as a person's social identity, social relationships, cognitive organization of the situation and expectations of the speakers" ("False Truisms"). In considering the definition and expression of dominance such an orientation would be likely to pay more attention to individuals than to the separate but related social structure that traps women in masculine standards.

In short, in their analyses of linguistic data and interactive styles, feminists are focusing on theoretical frameworks and methodologies. As a result, their interpretations of data suggest that differences between females and males in using linguistic and interactive rules are a function more of situational differences than of sex differences. The features of "women's language" may actually be the expressions of the powerless and may be sex-linked only when power is ritualized through sex-role double standards and sexual politics. Nevertheless, we need a coherent interdisciplinary theory that will explain and predict particulars of sex-differentiated language use.

Toward Liberating Language

In response to linguistic sexism, professional organizations (e.g., the National Council of Teachers of English and the American Psychological Association) and publishing houses (e.g., McGraw-Hill and Scott Foresman) have issued nonsexist guidelines for writers and editors. Of course, some establishment writers continue to trivialize or ridicule changes in gender markers by insisting that *he or she*, *anchorperson*, *chairperson*, and so forth are awkward and inefficient terms that degenerate English usage.

But feminists, "declining" to use patriarchal generics, have devised new pronoun declensions. Orovan suggested *co* for common gender, but this word had limited usefulness in alternative–life-style communities.[34] Marge Piercy, in her novel *Woman on the Edge of Time,* coined the pronoun *per* to refer to the androgynous beings of the future and made other morphological and semantic changes to reflect the new consciousness. Champions of pronoun change have not gathered wide support, but feminists continue to invent pronouns, portmanteau words, neologisms, and puns—*Ms.*, *herstory, Manglish, gynergy, phallustine, testeria, mythogynies,* and *cosmosis*—and to rename themselves—*women* to *wimmin,* Cooperman to Cooperperson, and Elana Nachman to Elana Dykewoman.[35] A new consciousness implies a new language that calls attention to inequities of patriarchal paradigms and that in turn creates a new perception and awareness. Although coinages have appeared in literary, critical, and philosophical works, little has been done to compile the *lingua femina* that feminist writers are developing. Much more needs to be asked. For example, do feminists use language differently from other women? In their theories of "competence," linguists have seldom considered speakers' linguistic alterations, and psycholinguists have virtually ignored the development of female and male speech play.

But feminist wordplay is more than witty neologisms. In gaining access to and control of oral and written media, women come out of the closet. They are now free to say publicly what their diaries whispered privately. Although many women may use familiar words, they have wrenched these words from patriarchal associations and charged them with new meanings. Old metaphors have been revived in feminist contexts and examined from feminist perspectives, as with *androgyny* and *dyarchy,* and pejorative [+female] terms are being returned to their sources, rejuvenated, and ameliorated.[36] Note what Daly has done to *spinster, crone, lesbian,* and *revolting hag* in *Gyn/Ecology* (Boston: Beacon, 1978). As a philosopher and poet, Daly gives new meanings to old words by creating juxtapositions that shatter patriarchal assumptions and liberate language and consciousness from sexist semantics. "The sisterhood of man," for instance, lends generic weight to *sisterhood* while emasculating the pseudogeneric *man* (*Beyond God the Father,* p. 9).

The linguistic inventiveness of feminists suggests that the direction of feminist research in every field of discourse requires a reinterpretation of the term *method. Method* must be extracted from its usual semantic field of androcentric biases and redefined by feminist research:

> The method of liberation, then, involves a castrating of language and images that reflect and perpetuate the structures of a sexist world. It castrates precisely in the sense of cutting away the phallocentric value system imposed by patriarchy, in its subtle as well as in its more manifest expressions. (Daly, *Beyond God the Father,* p. 9)

Thus, feminist research in language needs to move toward seven basic goals: (1) revealing androcentric bias in thinking, structure, and semantics; (2) raising woman's consciousness and improving her condition both conceptually and practically; (3) revealing the interplay of women's consciousness and language; (4) investigating differences and commonalities of women's and men's languages across cultures and within pluralistic societies; (5) redefining *method* structurally and semantically; (6) describing feminist language in inventive contexts with new meanings; (7) developing theoretical/aesthetic frameworks that integrate both abstract/empirical data and intuitive/deductive thinking and that will ultimately transcend gender politics.

Notes

1. Annette Kolodny, *The Lay of the Land: Metaphor as Experience and History in American Life and Letters* (Chapel Hill: Univ. of North Carolina Press, 1976), pp. 66–89.
2. I. K. Broverman, D. M. Broverman, F. E. Clarkson, P. S. Rosenkrantz, and S. R. Vogel, "Sex-Role Stereotypes and Clinical Judgments of Mental Health," *Journal of Consulting Psychology,* 34 (1970), 1–7. Otto Jesperson is quoted from his *Growth and Structure of the English Language* (New York: Free, 1968), p. 2.
3. In this discussion, I describe features of English exclusively, although French, Spanish, German, Dutch, Norwegian, and Japanese have also been investigated.
4. Mary Ritchie Key, *Male/Female Language* (Metuchen, N.J.: Scarecrow, 1975), pp. 68–84.
5. See H. Lee Gershuny, "Sexist Semantics in the Dictionary," *ETC.: A Review of General Semantics,* 31 (1974), 159–69, and Alleen Pace Nilsen, "The Correlation between Gender and Other Semantic Features in American English," Linguistic Society of America, San Diego, Calif., 28 Dec. 1973.
6. Cheris Kramer, "False Truisms: Androcentrism and Language Study," MLA Convention, New York, 27 Dec. 1978.
7. Noam Chomsky, Stanford Univ., Stanford, Calif., Jan. 1979; cited by Sharon R. Veach, "Generic Apologia," *Women and Language News,* 4, No. 2 (1979), 8.
8. Susan J. Wolfe (Robbins), "Patriarchal Paradigms for Language Change," MLA Convention, New York, 28 Dec. 1978.
9. Alleen Pace Nilsen, Haig Bosmajian, H. Lee Gershuny, and Julia P. Stanley, *Sexism and Language* (Urbana, Ill.: NCTE, 1977), pp. 43–74.
10. Muriel R. Schulz, "The Semantic Derogation of Woman," in *Language and Sex: Difference and Dominance,* ed. Barrie Thorne and Nancy Henley (Rowley, Mass.: Newbury, 1975), pp. 65–66 (hereafter referred to as Thorne and Henley).
11. Julia P. Stanley, "Paradigmatic Woman: The Prostitute," in *Papers on Language Variation,* ed. David Shores (Birmingham: Univ. of Alabama Press, 1977), pp. 303–21.
12. See Joseph W. Schneider and Sally L. Hacker, "Sex Role Imagery and the Use of the Generic 'Man' in Introductory Texts," *American Sociologist,* 8, No. 8 (1973) 12–18, and Alleen Pace Nilsen, "Grammatical Gender and Its Relationship to the Equal Treatment of Males and Females in Children's Books," Diss. Univ. of Iowa 1973, pp. 106–07.
13. Content analysis classifies verbal or other symbolic material into categories so that the rate, frequency, and distribution of the content can be measured. It is meant to provide an objective, systematic, and quantitative description of communication content. In the light of the SWH, we can see how the definition of categories may reflect the bias of the researcher. Published analyses include *Dick and Jane as Victims: Sex Stereotyping in*

Children's Readers, (Princeton, N.J.: Women on Words and Images, 1972); U.S. Commission Report on Civil Rights, *Window Dressing on the Set: An Update* (Washington, D.C.: GPO, 1978); Nilsen et al.; Vivian Gornick and Barbara K. Moran, eds., *Woman in Sexist Society* (New York: NAL, 1972); Rosemary Radford Ruether, ed., *Religion and Sexism* (New York: Simon 1974); and Barbara Grizzuti Harrison, *Unlearning the Lie: Sexism in School* (New York: Liveright, 1973).

14. Patricia Mainardi, "Quilts: The Great American Art," *Radical America,* 7, No. 1 (1973), 64–68.
15. Otto Rank; quoted in Anaïs Nin, *Diary* (New York: Harcourt, 1974), I, 291.
16. Cynthia L. Berryman, *The Language of Women as a Reflection of the Image of Women in a Mass-Circulation Magazine: An Analysis of* Ladies' Home Journal *Fiction, 1900–1920* (ERIC ED 125 025), pp. 12–13.
17. See Otto Jesperson, "The Woman," *Language: Its Nature, Development and Origin* (New York: Norton, 1964), pp. 237–53, and Peter Trudgill, "Language and Sex," in his *Sociolinguistics: An Introduction* (Baltimore: Penguin, 1974), pp. 84–102.
18. Robin Lakoff, *Language and Woman's Place* (New York: Harper, 1975), pp. 3–50.
19. John L. Fischer, "Social Influences on the Choice of a Linguistic Variant," in *Language in Culture and Society,* ed. Dell Hymes (New York: Harper, 1964), pp. 483–88, and William Labov, *Sociolinguistic Patterns* (Philadelphia: Univ. of Pennsylvania Press, 1972), pp. 243, 301–04.
20. Cheris Kramer, "Women's Speech: Separate but Unequal?" in Thorne and Henley, pp. 43–56.
21. Jacqueline Sachs, Philip Lieberman, and Donna Erickson, "Anatomical and Cultural Determinants of Male and Female Speech," in *Language Attitudes: Current Trends and Prospects,* ed. Roger W. Shuy and Ralph W. Fasold (Washington, D.C.: Georgetown Univ. Press, 1973), pp. 74–84.
22. Lakoff, pp. 8–19; Key, pp. 15–31; and Ruth M. Brend, "Male-Female Intonation Patterns in American English," in Thorne and Henley, pp. 84–87.
23. Cheris Kramer, "Folklinguistics," *Psychology Today,* 8 (1974), 82–85; Cheris Kramer, "Stereotypes of Women's Speech: The Word from Cartoons," *Journal of Popular Culture,* 8 (1974), 627–29; Marie A. Garcia-Zamor, "Child Awareness of Sex Role Distinctions in Language Use," Linguistic Society of America, San Diego, Calif., 28 Dec. 1973; and Berryman, pp. 1–13.
24. Goldine C. Gleser, Louis A. Gottschalk, and John Watkins, "The Relationship of Sex and Intelligence to Choice of Words: A Normative Study of Verbal Behavior," *Journal of Clinical Psycholgy,* 15 (1959), 182–91, and Marjorie Swacker, "The Sex of the Speaker as a Sociolinguistic Variable," in Thorne and Henley, pp. 76–83.
25. Connie C. Eble, "How the Speech of Some is More Equal Than Others," Southeastern Conference on Linguistics, Charlotte, N.C., 17 Oct. 1972.
26. Julia P. Stanley and Susan W. Robbins, "Toward a Feminist Aesthetic," Conference on Language and Style, New York, 16 April 1977.
27. John E. Baird, Jr., "Sex Differences in Group Communication: A Review of Relevant Research," *Quarterly Journal of Speech,* 62 (1976), 181.

28. Guadalupe Valdés-Fallis, "Code-switching among Bilingual Mexican-American Women: Towards an Understanding of Sex-Related Language Alterations," *International Journal of the Sociology of Language,* 17 (1978), 65–72, and "Speech Accommodation in the Language of Mexican-American Bilinguals: Are Women Really More Sensitive?" MLA Convention, New York, 29 Dec. 1978.
29. Nancy Henley, *Body Politics: Power, Sex, and Nonverbal Communication* (Englewood Cliffs, N.J.: Prentice-Hall, 1977).
30. Lee Jenkins and Cheris Kramer, "Small Group Process: Learning from Women," *Women's Studies International Quarterly,* 1 (1978), 82.
31. Robbie Davis Johnson, "Folklore and Women: A Social Interactional Analysis of the Folklore of a Texas Madam," *Journal of American Folklore,* 86 (1973), 212.
32. Edwin F. Sause, "Computer Content Analysis of Sex Differences in the Language of Children," *Journal of Psycholinguistic Research,* 5, No. 3 (1976), 324.
33. Annette Kolodny, "To Render Home a Paradise: Women on the New World Landscapes," in *Women's Language and Style,* ed. Douglas Butturff and Edmund L. Epstein (Akron, Ohio: Univ. of Akron, 1978), pp. 36–46.
34. Casey Miller and Kate Swift, *Words and Women: New Language in New Times* (Garden City, N.Y.: Anchor-Doubleday, 1977), p. 116.
35. Varda One, "Manglish," unpublished paper; Emily Culpepper, "Female History/Myth Making," *Second Wave,* 4, No. 1 (1975); Ann Sheldon, Letter, *Village Voice,* 17 Dec. 1970; Juli Loesch, "Testeria and Penisolence—A Scourge to Humankind," *Aphra: The Feminist Literary Magazine,* 4, No. 1 (1972–73), 43–45; Katy Barasc, Letter, *Matrices,* n. d.; Mary Daly, *Beyond God the Father* (Boston: Beacon, 1973), p. 172; Julia P. Stanley, ed., *Matrices,* n.d.; and Stanley and Robbins, p. 16.
36. In "The Androgyny Papers," *Women's Studies: An Interdisciplinary Journal,* 2, No. 2 (1974), 139–271, Cynthia Secor examines *androgyny* from a contemporary feminist perspective. Mary Daly, in *Beyond God the Father* discusses both *dyarchy* and *androgyny.* As metaphors of female-male integration and equality, these terms become alternatives to the language of hierarchy, dualism, and fragmentation.

Out of the Archives and into the Academy

Opportunities for Research and Publication in Lesbian Literature

Karen M. Keener

The publication of lesbian-feminist works and the visibility of an evolving lesbian culture are among the most promising developments in and outside academe in the 1970s. But homophobic taboos, still very strong in society and academe, continue to foster neglect. Prejudicial views constrain lesbian literature more than any other body of literary works, restricting its writing, publication, distribution, reading, and study. Anyone interested in research and publication in lesbian literature should approach this field armed with a realistic assessment of its difficulties.

Certainly, recent social and economic changes have encouraged some lesbian writers to reveal themselves in their work and lives and have allowed a strong lesbian voice to heighten the reputations of a few writers—Rita Mae Brown's, for example—but the lessons of the past still exert their force. The story of Radclyffe Hall exemplifies the fate of a respected writer who chose to write openly on lesbian themes. After the publication of *The Well of Loneliness* (1928; rpt. New York: Pocket, 1950) and its obscenity trial, Hall was removed from the listing of notable writers in Fred B. Millett's *Contemporary British Literature: A Critical Survey and Two Hundred Thirty-Two Author Biographies* (1935; rpt. New York: Harcourt, 1969), was no longer acknowledged in the literary community at large, and was even shunned by some of her former lesbian friends because she had called attention to them. The threat of similar penalties made self-revelation inconceivable for well-established writers, like Willa Cather, and forced others, like May Sarton, to defer speaking openly about their relationships with women until their literary reputations were established.

The apparent abundance of lesbian literature in feminist and alternative bookstores today is somewhat misleading, for it must be viewed in the context of the earlier shortage: very few works were published in the past seventy-five years and almost none before this century. In fact, with the exception of a few paperback novels and some privately printed books, relatively little overtly lesbian material was published before 1970. In the past ten years, newly founded feminist presses have produced a variety of lesbian newspapers, journals, pamphlets, and books, thus giving writers an incentive to write openly. With an eye to sales, commercial films have taken up a few lesbian works: Bantam, for instance, purchased the rights to Rita Mae Brown's *Rubyfruit Jungle* (New York, 1977), once the Daughters, Inc., edition (Plainfield, Vt., 1973) had proved successful. Commercial publishers, however, cannot be depended on to keep such works in print. By 1978, *The Well of Loneliness* was out of print in paperback, and *Patience and Sarah* (Greenwich, Conn.: Fawcett, 1973) was out of print in both paperback and hardcover. Academic presses and journals have published few works of lesbian-feminist scholarship. Jeannette Foster's vitally important *Sex Variant Women in Literature* was turned down by academic presses in the 1950s and again in the 1970s. Foster had the book printed at her own expense in 1956 (New York: Vantage), and Diana Press (Baltimore, Md.) reprinted it in 1975.

In addition to self-censorship by writers and selective censorship by publishers, an insidious form of institutional censorship constrains academic women from reading and writing about lesbian literature. The hatred and fear of lesbianism carry over to lesbian literature and its study: the existence of this literature is denied or deemed unimportant, and those who study it are assumed to be lesbians—and therefore undesirable as members of an academic staff. Women interested in the subject are faced with these attitudes at every point in their academic careers. In pursuing degrees, they are actively discouraged by professors and thesis advisers from studying lesbian literature. As scholars doing research in this area, they are said to be too narrowly and inconsequentially focused. An article on lesbian literature listed on a résumé has often kept an applicant from being considered for a teaching job. Finally, the charge or even the suspicion of lesbianism has led to dismissal (usually for other stated reasons) and to forced resignation.[1] Given these conditions governing research, hiring, and firing, it is understandable that virtually no academic women have chosen, until very recently, to study lesbian literature openly.

Toward a Definition of Lesbian Literature

The phobia about lesbianism that has impeded the open writing, abundant publishing, and dedicated study of lesbian literature has also made definition itself a major critical problem. In the first place, the narrowly sexual definition of the word "lesbian" excludes women of earlier centuries whose romantic—but usually nonsexual—friendships were in other respects very much like relationships between twentieth-century lesbians. My definition of lesbian literature will include writers and works that are not obviously lesbian as well as those that are not lesbian in the strictly sexual meaning of the word. (Although biographical and social materials can help immensely in the task of definition, the scholar who uses them is likely to find her interpretations of this material and even her recourse to it challenged.) Second, while it has long been the practice to categorize works by period, genre, and topic, few scholars are disposed to accept the validity of grouping works by their sexual content or affectional perspective. Finally, in defining lesbian literature one faces the obvious difficulty of constructing a category that can include such disparate writers as Sappho, Emily Dickinson, Radclyffe Hall, Willa Cather, Rita Mae Brown, and Adrienne Rich.

While the few works that overtly portray sexual relationships between women and speak to lesbian concerns are the obvious candidates for this category of literature, a more inclusive definition helps us to understand the unique vision that woman-identified writers have brought to bear on life and expressed in their works.[2] Like all writers, women writers whose affectional preferences are for women think, feel, and view the world in ways that transcend explicit sexuality. To define our literature in fully human rather than narrowly sexual terms will require describing a lesbian epistemology—an aesthetic sense and a world view that inform the works of lesbian writers.

In the absence of such an epistemological description—which must come from, not before, thorough study—my working definition of lesbian literature includes a wide variety of writers and works. Central among these are the lesbian writers whose works deal with overt lesbian themes: well-known writers like Sappho, Gertrude Stein, Amy Lowell, Radclyffe Hall, Rita Mae Brown, and Adrienne Rich; and less-known writers like Sarah Aldrich, Pat Parker, Judy Grahn, Elana (Nachman) Dykewoman, Bertha Harris, Olga Broumas, and Monique Wittig. Other writers subsumed in my definition are those who have had significant woman-identified relationships and whose works may portray coded lesbian relationships: Willa Cather, Edna St. Vincent Millay, Virginia Woolf, Vita Sackville-West, Colette, Emily Dickinson, Sarah Orne Jewett, and Lillian Hellman. Finally, I include any works of literature that explicitly or implicitly portray female-female relationships marked by love, caring, and nurturance.

I distinguish four groups of lesbian writers according to the distinctive biocritical research problems associated with each. The first group, the writers of any period who are almost entirely unknown, requires extensive primary research aimed at recovering their works and gathering information about their lives. Their works, whether unpublished or published, are almost completely forgotten. Once texts and biographical materials have been located through archival research and other means and made available for study, we must undertake the same tasks of interpreting and evaluating that we do for writers in the other groups. A second group includes writers whose works are known and studied but whose primary affectional relationships with women have seldom been recognized. A third, very exceptional group consists of the lesbian women who lived and wrote in Paris more or less openly, from about 1900 to 1940. The fourth group comprises lesbians writing openly today.

Interpreting Covert Lesbian Writers

The difficulty of recovering information about past lesbian writers is compounded at all points by concealment and obliteration. Few lesbians lived openly as lesbians until the mid-twentieth century, and woman-identified writers have left little explicit biographical information about their relationships with women. Further, many writers have coded the lesbian references in their work by using inexplicit language to describe relationships between women, both fictional and nonfictional, and by avoiding clear gender references in poetry. Some women with lifelong same-sex bonds, such as Katherine Bradley and Edith Cooper (who wrote together under the pen name Michael Field) and Sarah Ponsonby and Eleanor Butler (known as the Ladies of Llangollen), referred to each other in terms usually reserved for sexual endearment but insisted that their affection was platonic. *Orlando* (New York: Harcourt, 1973) never alludes directly to the close though brief relationship between Virginia Woolf and Vita Sackville-West that inspired its exploration of Vita's dual sexual nature. Because the pronoun "you" is not gender-marked in English, many love poems written by women are presumed to address men although there may be obvious evidence to the contrary. Some women poets have even changed gender-marked pronouns in their love poems from feminine to masculine before publication: Emily Dickinson is a notable example.

Biographical and textual materials have been destroyed by the writers themselves or, more frequently, by others. Sappho's story provides the best-known example of systematic obliteration: she was defamed by later Greeks, and only a few fragments of her poetry survived destruction by Christians. Letters and diaries have been burned by writers just before their deaths or by relatives, executors, and lovers immediately after. Amy Lowell asked Ada Dwyer to burn their love letters, and Dwyer did burn them a few days after Lowell's death, later regretting the act. Some of the personal diaries and letters of even such an openly lesbian woman as Natalie Clifford Barney were destroyed by her literary executor. Vita Sackville-West's diary concerning her relationship with Violet Trefusis, published with additional biographical sections in Nigel Nicolson's *Portrait of a Marriage* (New York: Bantam, 1974), is an important exception to these search-and-destroy missions. In other cases, material still exists but is withheld from researchers by family or other interested parties or by the conditions of wills. Examples include some Willa Cather letters and some Marks-Woolley papers.

By revision and excision, editors, translators, and publishers have attempted to remove lesbian allusions from literary works. Some sixteenth-century love sonnets by Louise Labé seem, in French, to address a woman, but in English translations they clearly address a male lover. William Michael Rossetti chose to omit the Sappho poems from his edition of Christina Rossetti's works, as he reported in his introduction to the volume. Edna St. Vincent Millay has been widely acknowledged as a Bohemian and an advocate of free love, yet her relationships with women (as in the poem "Interim") have been pointedly ignored. Dickinson's poems and letters have been selectively anthologized and reprinted to disguise her strong attachments to women.

Biographical and critical treatments of women writers need thorough review and revision as we begin to perceive the patriarchal and homophobic biases handed down to us in the guise of scholarly objectivity. Existing biographical treatments often contain humorous and sometimes ludicrous attempts to conceal, avoid, or rationalize the obvious. For example, W. G. Rogers' *When This You See, Remember Me: Gertrude Stein in Person* (rpt. Brooklyn, N.Y.: Greenwood House, 1971), a personal reminiscence of Stein and Toklas first published in 1948, scrupulously avoids acknowledging the conjugality of their relationship while unintentionally revealing it in many anecdotes. Other biographers have bent the facts to emphasize Emily Dickinson's unrequited love for a clergyman (or for one of the other male candidates) and Sarah Orne Jewett's friendships with men, completely ignoring the emotional influence and aesthetic effects that relationships with women had on these writers. In fact, almost every article and book giving attention to a woman writer's life describes her associations with men as if they were the center of the writer's—and the woman's—universe.

Many writers have censored their own work to conceal information about their personal lives. While we can only imagine what such censorship has cost in works left unwritten, the effects of concealment prompt major critical questions about existing texts. Willa Cather's need for concealment may well have damaged her work. Might the faults of narration in her novels have resulted from the use of a camouflaged narrator? Could she have improved *A Lost Lady* (New York: Knopf, 1923) and others of her novels by casting the narrators as women? Other writers have concealed information about their private lives by encoding lesbian experiences through innovative or distorted language, structure, and plot, achieving varying aesthetic effects. Do the pronoun confusions make some of Dickinson's poems more effective or simply more puzzling? Do some of Stein's startling experimentations with language and literary structure result in part from her need to conceal? Early in her career, Stein wrote an autobiographical story, in a fairly traditional narrative form, about a lesbian relationship among three women (*Q.E.D.*, written in 1903). It remained unpublished until after her death (available in *Fernhurst, Q.E.D. and Other Early Writings* [New York: Liveright, 1973]); yet during her lifetime she published a more experimental—and clearly heterosexual—version of the same story as "Melanctha."

The need to conceal and avoid lesbian subject matter has been especially limiting to American women writers who are also members of racial minorities. These writers continue to face a multiple bind: racism, sexism, and homophobia in the society at large; sexism and homophobia in their communities of birth; and racism in the mostly white lesbian community. Barbara Smith describes the effects of these limitations on the critical reception of black women's writing in "Toward a Black Feminist Criticism" (*Conditions: Two,* 1, No. 2 [1977]) and emphasizes the need for an awareness of lesbian-feminist themes in approaching black women's works. She then employs this perspective in discussing a lesbian motif in Toni Morrison's *Sula* (New York: Knopf, 1973). Other feminist scholars are beginning to apply lesbian-feminist awareness in reexamining the works and lives of black women writers of the past. Gloria T. Hull, through careful reading of published and unpublished work, has found undeniable lesbian themes in the poetry of Angelina Weld Grimké (" 'Under the Days': The Buried Life and Poetry of Angelina Weld Grimké," *Conditions: Five,* 2, No. 1 [1979]). Like other lesbian poets before her, Grimké changed some of the pronouns in her poems from feminine to masculine before her work reached publication.

The encoding of certain information and experiences by lesbian writers creates special problems in literary interpretation. How do we decode with a reasonable degree of certainty that the interpretation contributes to our understanding of writer and text? I suggest we proceed, with writers for whom there is any evidence to warrant this approach, from the following hypothetical questions: What *if* this writer has encoded sexual or affectional preference in her work? What *if* the writer's primary aesthetic and emotional influences derive from her relationships with women? Might her attempts to camouflage or conceal these preferences and influences help explain critical and interpretive problems with her work? Such questions are clearly relevant to the proper interpretation of the texts, particularly for earlier writers who faced strong pressure to conceal their affectional preferences.

The Paris Lesbians

A good deal of biographical material and literary work survives from a number of lesbians, many of them expatriate Americans, who lived and worked in Paris from approximately 1900 to 1940. These women, who can be called a group in only the loosest sense, include Gertrude Stein, Alice B. Toklas, Natalie Clifford Barney, Renée Vivien, Romaine Brooks, Djuna Barnes, Radclyffe Hall, Colette, and Margaret Anderson. They are exceptional for being the first-known women since Sappho's time to live and write openly as lesbians, though some, of course, were less open than others.

Literary works and biographies of several of these women are available in print today, and scholars are currently at work on biographical materials and private papers. Two interesting biographies of Barney were published in 1978 (George Wicks, *The Amazon of Letters: The Life and Loves of Natalie Barney* [New York: Popular Library], and Jean Chalòn, *Portrait of a Seductress*, trans. Carol Barko [New York: Crown]), but neither thoroughly surveys her remaining personal papers located in Paris. One inadequate and unsympathetic biography of Radclyffe Hall has been published by her literary executor, Lovat Dickson (*Radclyffe Hall at the Well of Loneliness* [New York: Scribner, 1975]). Many of her papers, as well as those of Stein, remain unexamined. Anderson's memoirs have been published, but she has not been the subject of biographical or critical study. James Mellow, in *The Charmed Circle* (New York: Avon, 1974), explored the relationships in Stein's circle of friends, but no large-scale study has focused on the relationships among lesbians in Paris during this time. Such a study should explore their biographies and their aesthetic concerns as well as their literary influences, their interpersonal support, and the literary effects of expatriation.

An examination of the Paris group and the friendships among its women may provide answers to several questions about lesbian literature and culture. How, for instance, does a support system affect what a lesbian allows herself to write? Does a lesbian writer need to separate herself geographically and emotionally from the restrictions of family and early-life associations, as in the extreme of expatriation, in order to write more openly? Are the causes and consequences of separation or expatriation for lesbian writers different from those for nonlesbian writers? Further, at what point in the life of a group does a distinct culture begin to take shape, and what influence does a group's culture have on the literature its members produce? In other words, how do literary, personal, and social factors interact in a lesbian culture? Does literary work shape the cultural and personal identities of lesbians, and how do changed cultural and personal self-concepts shape new directions in lesbian literature?

Reflection on the Paris group raises some other, more specific questions for research. One question addresses the sources lesbians choose to use in their writing. While many lesbian works have images and themes in common, Sappho, her poetry, and the ideals embodied by her colony on Lesbos provided particularly rich sources for the Paris lesbians. Her love of beauty in language, music, nature, and women so inspired Natalie Clifford Barney and Renée Vivien that they modeled themselves after her and even traveled to Lesbos in an attempt to refound her colony. Another question addresses critical reception. A brief glance at the critical attention given to Stein and Barnes prompts speculation on why some writers' works and reputations survive while those of others have been ignored. Until the 1970s, everyone had heard of Gertrude Stein but few had read her; her works were not in print, and those who looked into them thought them "interesting" but difficult to understand. Undoubtedly her reputation has survived because her circle of friends included many well-known male American writers, because she was not an overt feminist, and because her work was too obviously significant to be ignored, whether read or not. Why, though, has Djuna Barnes remained unrecognized and her poetic masterpiece *Nightwood* (New York: New Directions, 1961) virtually ignored, in spite of its introduction by T. S. Eliot in the first American edition (1937)? Research in these areas could open up important new directions in interpretation of these and other texts.

Contemporary Lesbian Writing

Until recently, the work of lesbian writers has been marked by a deep self-consciousness when we have attempted to pursue our craft outside the closet. Our works have reflected the tension we feel between our urge to develop a positive self-image and the socially induced tendency to be self-denigrating. We are now struggling to divorce ourselves from the patriarchal culture, to redefine ourselves in our own terms, and to speak in our own voices. To achieve these goals, we are both experimenting with new forms, styles, and subject matters and borrowing from traditional ones.

Even a cursory survey of contemporary lesbian fiction reveals an abundant variety of traditional, experimental, and antitraditional forms and structures. Rita Mae Brown chose the picaresque form for *Rubyfruit Jungle* and a romance form for her most recent novel, *Six of One* (New York: Harper, 1978). Alma Routsong (using the pseudonym Isabel Miller) wrote *Patience and Sarah* (published privately as *A Place for Us* in 1969) as a historical novel in the romantic tradition but employed the successful device of alternating the distinct narrative voices of the two main characters. June Arnold's *The Cook and the Carpenter* (Plainfield, Vt.: Daughters, Inc., 1973; published under the pseudonym The Carpenter) recreates life in a woman's collective but uses invented third-person-singular pronouns such as "na" and "nan" to conceal the sex of the characters, thereby challenging readers to rethink their assumptions about sex roles. Some writers—undoubtedly influenced by the work of Stein, Barnes, and Lowell—are creating new linguistic and literary structures to express the cultural perspectives of women. Joanna Russ, who writes primarily science fiction, presents in *The Female Man* (New York: Bantam, 1975) four women from different cultural and time settings who portray four facets of the same female character. Monique Wittig employs nonlinear prose and modular structure in reworking patriarchal myths to make them conform to female experience. In *Les Guérillères* (trans. David Le Vay [New York: Bard-Avon, 1973]) and *The Lesbian Body* (trans. David Le Vay [New York: Bard-Avon, 1976]), both written originally in French, Wittig transmutes syntax to express women's vision.

The nonfictional prose of contemporary lesbian writers also shows a new awareness of lesbian language, culture, and identity. Works like Mary Daly's *Gyn/Ecology* (Boston: Beacon, 1978) and Susan Griffin's *Women and Nature: The Roaring inside Her* (New York: Harper, 1978) are infused with highly poetic, ritualistic language. Kate Millett's *Flying* (New York: Knopf, 1974) and *Sita* (New York: Ballantine, 1978) use autobiographical, confessional, and fictional techniques to explore painful personal experiences.

The inclination toward experimental forms and reshaped language is even more evident among the contemporary poets. Poems often exhibit loose, long, flowing lines; they are "rhetorical" (meant to be read aloud), incantatory, ritualistic, and passionate. While distinctly lacking in academic irony and allusions (of the New Critical type), they are frequently political. Their concrete, personal style gives heavy emphasis to certain "female" images: seas, shells, water, blood, moon, fish, and goddesses. Major lesbian poets include Rich, Griffin, Grahn, Broumas, Larkin, and Lorde. Little magazines, which have published a large amount of fine "minor" poetry, are a rich source for research; feminist journals are equally important sources, particularly because they are publishing the poetry of black, Chicana, Native American, and Oriental American lesbian writers with increasing frequency. Perhaps the best single source of contemporary lesbian poetry, *Lesbian Poetry: An Anthology* (ed. Elly Bulkin and Joan Larkin [Watertown, Mass.: Persephone, 1981]), includes the works of sixty-four twentieth-century lesbian poets and contains a bibliography of additional resources.

Lesbian and other feminist scholars have gained insights into the masculinist roots and biases of our language. Linguistic studies have demonstrated that women's use of language, both oral and written, differs from men's. The linguistic and literary structures we have inherited are demonstrably patriarchal in design and are suited to the institutional needs of patriarchal societies. Our ability to form ideas is circumscribed by the number of concepts our culture names and by the semantic demands and limited structures of the English sentence. We are further restricted by demands for rhetorical logic, by linear time frames, and by the polarized distinctions created by categorizing objects, ideas, people, and even types of literature. The new perspectives on language and its use that women writers have developed demonstrate that to expect women to use only inherited literary forms and language patterns is like asking them to express themselves only in a foreign language.

Literature and publishing have clearly helped us to establish local, national, and international lesbian connections and to move from self-conscious isolation toward more positive concepts of our culture. A review of lesbian publishing and culture since 1950 would include the Daughters of Bilitis and its founders, Del Martin and Phyllis Lyon; Barbara Grier and the *Ladder;* and the many newsletters, newspapers, magazines, and poetry collections born of the late 1960s (most of the serial publications have since been discontinued). We should also consider songwriters and their music, beginning with the album *Lavender Jane Loves Women* (New York: Women's Wax Works, 1974) and continuing through the current recordings on Olivia and other labels, and the showcases of women's musical talent—the National Women's Music Festival in Champaign, Illinois (discontinued after 1980), the Michigan Women's Music Festival, and the many other music festivals springing up since these two began in the mid-1970s. Lesbian and feminist theater collectives have formed in a number of cities, performing works written either by individual resident playwrights or by the members as a group. Because the study of lesbian art can enrich lesbian library activity and scholarship, we should also consider the work of lesbian painters, printmakers, photographers, and dancers. What, we may ask, are the concerns of lesbian artists, how do these concerns touch the lives of lesbians in general, and how does lesbian art relate to our literature?

Resources for Research

We know little about most women writers before the eighteenth century and even less about lesbian writers of any period. Two extremely important works provide an excellent starting point for anyone interested in researching the lesbian in Western literature, especially before the present century. Jeannette Foster's *Sex Variant Women in Literature* compiles information about lesbian writers and characters from biblical times through the mid-twentieth century. Completed in 1955, this pioneering study surveys French, German, and English literature for references to lesbian characters and provides biographical information about authors with affectional attachments to women. Equally important for its wealth of information is Lillian Faderman's *Surpassing the Love of Men: Romantic Friendship and Love between Women from the Renaissance to the Present* (New York: Morrow, 1981). Using both published and unpublished sources, Faderman explores women's romantic friendship patterns and society's shifting attitudes toward them through several hundred years of Western European and American history.

Several other, less ambitious works contain information on a variety of more recent lesbian writers and works. Dolores Klaich's *Woman + Woman: Contemporary Attitudes toward Lesbianism* (New York: Simon, 1974) includes a historical overview of lesbians in literature. Jane Rule's *Lesbian Images* (New York: Pocket, 1976) provides biographical information and criticism for twelve twentieth-century women writers, as well as surveys of lesbian fiction and nonfiction. Information on little-known lesbian literature since 1950 is now available in the Arno Press reprint of the *Ladder* (the longest continuously published lesbian periodical to date, which stopped publication in 1972) and in a paperback collection of reviews by Barbara Grier (originally published under the pseudonym Gene Damon), *Lesbiana: Book Reviews from the* Ladder, *1966-1972* (Reno, Nev.: Naiad, 1976).

Many scholars, some of them feminist, have the impression that black women have produced few lesbian works and that other minority women have produced none. The following sources will correct this error. *Black Lesbians: An Annotated Bibliography* (compiled J. R. Roberts and Barbara Smith [Tallahassee, Fla.: Naiad, 1981]) lists a variety of articles and literary works. *Conditions: Five,* specially titled *The Black Women's Issue,* contains several lesbian poems and essays. Of particular interest is the essay by Ann Allen Shockley entitled "The Black Lesbian in American Literature: An Overview" (pp. 133–42).

Azalea: A Magazine by Third World Lesbians has been published on a regular basis since 1977 (Azalea, P.O. Box 200, Cooper Sta., New York, N.Y. 10276). Black, Chicana, and Oriental American poets are represented in *Lesbian Poetry: An Anthology,* and an anthology of Latin American lesbian writing—to include articles, short stories, poems, and songs—is scheduled for publication in 1982. Also scheduled for 1982 is *Nice Jewish Girls: A Lesbian Anthology* (ed. Evelyn Beck [Watertown, Mass.: Persephone]).

The few critical articles written from a lesbian-feminist perspective and published in widely indexed journals are difficult to find because of the lack of cross-referencing and of a specific bibliographical listing. Bibliographic practices must change to make such articles more accessible. While some articles appear in feminist and women's studies journals—*Signs, Chrysalis, Quest, Hecate, Heresies*—most criticism and theory are published in lesbian-feminist periodicals—*Amazon Quarterly* (which has ceased publication), *Conditions, Sinister Wisdom, Feminary, Motherroot Journal,* and others. These publications, rarely taken by libraries and seldom indexed by women's studies bibliographies, are accessible primarily to subscribers and others who happen to know about them. A survey of *Women's Studies Abstracts* for the year from Summer 1977 through Spring 1978 revealed twenty-five entries indexed under the heading "Lesbians," but not one of these entries concerned lesbian literature or literary scholarship. Although *Women's Studies Abstracts* does not list the journals it covers, the dearth of entries for this category indicates that it does not survey most lesbian journals. Developments in contemporary lesbian writing and publishing have been outlined in special issues of two periodicals, both edited by Beth Hodges: *Margins* (Aug. 1975) and *Sinister Wisdom,* 1, No. 2 (1976), a special issue called *Lesbian Writing and Publishing.*

There are other valuable sources of information, contacts, ideas, and leads for anyone wishing to pursue the study of lesbian literature. From 1973 through 1978, an annual Lesbian Writers' Conference was held in Chicago on the University of Chicago campus. Academic and professional conventions have become increasingly important sources. Since 1973, the Modern Language Association convention program has included a variety of women's, lesbian, and gay sessions, which have been sponsored by individuals as well as by the Gay Caucus for the Modern Languages, the Discussion Group on Gay Studies in Language and Literature, the Women's Caucus for the Modern Languages, the Division of Women's Studies in Language and Literature, and the Commission on the Status of Women in the Profession. (Beginning in 1982 a Division on Gay Studies in Language and Literature, approved by the MLA Executive Council in 1981, replaced the Discussion Group.) Occasionally, the Midwest Modern Language Association has included convention sessions related to lesbians and literature and sponsored by the Women's Caucus and the Women in Literature and Women's Studies sections. The National Council of Teachers of English, which has a Gay Caucus and a Women's Committee, has included pertinent sessions at its annual conventions since 1976. The National Women's Studies Association, which has a Lesbian Caucus, has included lesbian-focused sessions at each annual convention since its first in 1979. Papers presented at many of these sessions may not be published for some time, if ever. Some will be rejected by journals, some are parts of larger works in progress, and some are informal presentations intended only for session participants. Also, many sessions focus on problems, questions, and discussion, and the panelists do not read or distribute papers. For these reasons, the sessions themselves are sources of current information unavailable anywhere else.

A very important source of information on current directions and interests in lesbian scholarship in all academic fields is "*Matrices: A Lesbian-Feminist Research Newsletter* (Julia Penelope [Stanley], General Editor, Dept. of English, Univ. of Nebraska, Lincoln 68508). *Gay Studies Newsletter* is published by the Gay Caucus allied to the MLA; *Concerns,* the newsletter of the Women's Caucus for the Modern Languages allied to the MLA, contains notices of interest to lesbian scholars. *Gai Saber,* a journal of interest to both lesbians and gay men, was published for several years by the Gay Academic Union but has been replaced by a newsletter. *BREFF* (Dept. of French and Italian, 618 Van Hise, Univ. of Wisconsin, Madison 53706) provides bibliographic information on books and articles concerning French feminists and lesbian writers, notices of conferences, and reports on work in progress.

Bibliographies listing lesbian material include *Women Loving Women: A Select and Annotated Bibliography of Women Loving Women in Literature* (ed. Marie Kuda [Chicago: Lavender, 1974]), *Women and Literature: An Annotated Bibliography of Women Writers* (3rd ed. [Cambridge, Mass.: Women and Literature Collective, 1976]; works with lesbian content are separately indexed); the bibliographic appendix in *Our Right to Love: A Lesbian Resource Book* (ed. Ginny Vida [Englewood Cliffs, N.J.: Prentice-Hall, 1978]); and *The Lesbian in Literature* (ed. Barbara Grier, 3rd ed. [Tallahassee, Fla.: Naiad 1981]; includes about 7,000 entries). Resources for research in lesbian history include *Gay American History* (ed. Jonathan Katz [New York: Crowell, 1976]); *Sinister Wisdom,* No. 5: *Researching Lesbian History; Gay Archivist: Newsletter of the Canadian Gay Archives* (Box 639, Sta. A, Toronto, Ont. M5W 1G2, Canada); *Lesbian/Gay History Researchers Network Newsletter* (1519 P St. NW, Washington, DC 20005); and the Lesbian Herstory Archives and its newsletter (Box 1258, New York, NY 10001). The Archives' unique collection includes not only print materials but tapes, pictures, and other artifacts. Finally, the office of the Women's Studies Librarian-at-Large (464 Memorial Library, 728 State St., Madison, WI 53706) has compiled several bibliographies that should interest feminist scholars in all the academic disciplines and that contain specific references to lesbian works, and the Lesbian-Feminist Study Clearinghouse (Women's Studies Program, 1012 Cathedral of Learning, Univ. of Pittsburgh, Pittsburgh, PA 15260) reprints articles, course syllabi, and other material relevant to lesbian-feminist scholars and teachers.

Lesbian Literature in the Classroom

Teaching lesbian literature in our classes, as well as discovering, interpreting, and evaluating it through our research, helps to rectify the neglect of lesbian works and the falsification of the writers' biographies. We can give our students an opportunity we did not have to understand this special aspect of women's experience, to view these writers as writers, and to sample work that, like other minority literature, has been categorically excluded from the curriculum. It is not only in the specialized courses that teaching these works is appropriate but in all courses that profess to have a broad focus or to present a diversity of works—introduction to literature, twentieth-century literature, nineteenth-century literature, surveys of national literatures, surveys of minority literatures, world literature, women's literature, and genre courses.

Selecting works for the classroom presents a logistical problem. Lesbian literature, unfortunately, has not yet cracked the covers of our textbooks. With the exception of a few texts specifically designed for women's literature courses, no textbooks and anthologies that I know of treat lesbian works, biography, and criticism openly. We need representation in the "standard" textbooks and anthologies, but we also need paperback works—bibliographies, biographies, fiction, poetry, drama, and nonfiction—by and about lesbian writers; these may be works that are currently available only in hardback, that have gone out of print, that have gone unpublished despite their creative or scholarly merit, or that are now being written. Paperback anthologies of lesbian writings are especially needed now to correct the false impressions made by the "standard" texts we must use until we have revised ones, to supplement the few available single-title lesbian works, and to allow students to purchase a variety of materials cheaply. The opportunities to revise and compile teaching materials of these kinds are wide open.

Because everyone, and especially a lesbian or a gay man, is bound to approach the teaching of lesbian literature with some apprehension, we need pedagogical studies to help answer questions about what to teach and how to teach it in the various literature courses. These studies could treat the issues involved in teaching lesbian literature and explain the practices. They could review the existing literature courses and the texts used at various academic levels and suggest ways of incorporating and presenting lesbian material. They could report on the new lesbian and gay literature courses, as well as on the new lesbian publications, teaching materials, and pedagogical resources.[3]

Along with arranging for revised textbooks, new anthologies, single-title works, and pedagogical studies, we need to enlarge our library collections to support the inclusion of lesbian literature in our courses. We should have the usual resources to which students and teachers turn in their study of a literature—bibliographies, biographies, critical works, periodicals, and a full complement of literary works. The task is large: texts and anthologies must be revised, new anthologies and single-title works must be published, and library collections must be expanded. But we should not wait until we have these materials—the inclusion of lesbian literature in our courses will enrich them now as well as provide an impetus to researchers, publishers, and textbook editors.

This survey of the opportunities for research in lesbian literature makes clear the vast amount of basic work yet to be begun. Past neglect, coupled with the negative effects of homophobia, presents us with a field containing many questions and few answers. The outlook, however, is positive. As indicated by the growing number of conference sessions, articles, and books on the subject, scholarship in lesbian literature is rapidly pushing back the frontiers of our ignorance. With great enthusiasm and with great hope for the future, I report that we have come too far to turn back now.[4]

Notes

1. Louis Crew and Karen Keener, "Homophobia in the Academy: A Report of the Committee on Gay/Lesbian Concerns" (*College English,* 43, No. 7 [1981]) documents the effects of educators' attitudes toward homosexuals.
2. I use the term "woman-identified" to describe women who maintain their primary relationships—those providing love, caring, and nurturance—with other women rather than with men, whether or not those relationships are sexual.
3. The National Gay Student Association keeps a file of syllabi for the specifically lesbian and gay literature courses that have been offered on college and university campuses across the country.
4. Special thanks are due to the women who contributed ideas, information, and editorial help to this article: Diane Griffin Crowder, Paula Bennett, Deborah Core, Judith McDaniel, and Julia Penelope.

Black Women in and out of Print

Erlene Stetson

> She's only the Sepia Nightingale. . . .The Queen of Blues. The Tragic Voice of the Twenties and Thirties. She started out in New Orleans. When she came to Harlem, the lines stretched for five blocks outside of Small's Paradise. The cover charge went to ten dollars, and *still* they stretched. She had rooms full of orchids. Cars a block long, proposals from European royalty. She only made a few records. And then she disappeared. . . . *Where is She?*[1]

The situation of black women in and out of print—mostly out—is evident to those of us who teach courses on black women writers, who do research and write criticism on black women's literature, and who are black activists. Like the Sepia Nightingale, too many black women writers have disappeared, and countless others have never been permitted to sing in public. Our relations with the publishing establishment differ from those of any other group. And the political knowledge we have gained in building a black feminist movement and in developing a black analysis of our lives enables us to understand these relations and suggests strategies for change.

The situation of black women in publishing reflects our generally embattled political position in the United States. As black women, we face both racial and sexual oppression, and we usually face severe economic oppression as well. Since we are powerless to control the most basic aspects of our lives in a white male-run economy, we have little participation in and impact on the institutions that enable writers to get their thoughts, visions, and creativity into print. If the routes to publication were not filled with obstacles, our way would still be blocked, for the publishing industry, academic as well as commercial, is run by white men with essentially two aims—making profits and preserving the status quo.

Much of what we have the opportunity to read, see, and hear is controlled by corporations that unabashedly pursue not truth or artistic quality but profit. Academic publishing is not exempt from the charge: university presses try to produce publications that will bring them, along with their editors and authors, both material rewards and enhanced status. White decision makers in publishing assume that books by black women are not "profitable." They say these books have "limited appeal," and their decisions not to publish, distribute, and otherwise promote such books ensure that the appeal remains limited. While publishers claim to respond to demand, they are in fact manipulating supply and demand to control the market economically and ideologically.

Very little that is written by women and black people, let alone black women, is amenable to the predominant white male ideology. The subject that black women write about most often—their lives—is frequently repugnant and threatening to white men. Descriptions of the massive oppression that we have experienced do not support white myths of American life. Our words for the most part diametrically oppose the notions white men want to be known, thought, and read, and our hopes and visions challenge the distribution of privilege according to race, sex, and class. In ignoring or actively rejecting visions of dissent, a press, like any other medium, reveals its political function as a purveyor of ideology, as an endeavor controlled by white men, and as a means for bolstering existing power relations.

When politics and profit do not supply motives for ignoring black women's writings, we can look to the white male aesthetic of the Anglo-American cultural tradition, which is not attuned to the spirit, form, and subject matter of black literature. Black history and black art are intertwined. For a long time, reading and writing were punishable crimes for black people in this country, and the full privileges of education are still denied blacks today. Every act of literacy, let alone every work of literature, can be regarded as both a personal triumph and a political event. But instead of creating impoverishment, repression generated a rich, spirited tradition of story, song, and folklore.[2] Black struggle and celebration, described in oral forms and in the earliest written forms, such as the slave narrative, continue to influence black literature. The continuity of subject and theme in black women's poetry, for example, comes as much from the authors' shared history and common experiences as from the influence of predecessors and contemporaries on each generation of writers. Presented with unfamiliar experiences, unconventional formal features, and uncompromising spirits, white male publishers mistake their own chauvinism for aesthetic judgment and reject the works of black women authors as lacking in literary merit. In the eighteenth and nineteenth centuries, much black poetry and prose was privately printed or published abroad, particularly by antislavery groups in England. Today the most politically incisive and artistically innovative works by black women are usually published by small or alternative presses, and many black women who now experience a measure of general popularity had published two or three volumes privately before their works were accepted by publishers. Publication by alternative means is still the rule rather than the exception.

It is frequently true that a black woman writer who is recognized and promoted by the publishing industry and literary establishment is a token, the exception they condescend to notice. The recent revival of Zora Neale Hurston exemplifies this demoralizing practice. Unable for most of her life to support herself as a writer, Hurston died penniless. Now that interest in her work has no monetary and emotional rewards for her, her reputation has soared. Moreover, she is portrayed as unique; no mention is made of the many black women writers forming the tradition from which she wrote. The public is kept in ignorance of black women writers—in the plural—and is allowed to think that black women are generally incapable of literary creation.

The discrimination against black women in publishing occurs not only in the inadequate printing and distributing of their works but also in decision making. Few black women hold influential positions in editing, promotion, and marketing. Virtually no black women review books for the publications whose favorable attention determines commercial, literary, or scholarly success. Apart from producing occupational and economic inequities, this situation contributes to the ignorant and neglectful treatment of black women's literary works. Their token representation on publishers' staffs might as well be total exclusion for all the effect it has: it renders black women writers powerless to gain access to the public, and it makes a mockery of the few works that are published. Greeted with little understanding by the white male editors who select manuscripts for publication, given inadequate or misleading promotion by white male marketing managers, and ignored or denigrated by white male reviewers, these works are doomed to fulfill the prophecy that black women's books don't sell.

A consideration of the situation of black women in publishing must mention their relation to feminist publishing, which, despite its marginal economic position, has done much in the last decade to publish works essential to women and to promote a self-defined women's culture. Although feminist presses and publications may be more responsive to publishing works by third-world women than are commercial presses and publications—let alone academic ones—the overall record of the feminists is discouraging, particularly in the light of their alleged commitment to all women. Only when the movement as a whole confronts the issue of racism in both its personal and political dimensions will white feminist presses become resources also for women of color.[3]

Finally, black women do not yet have their own presses. There is no network of newspapers, periodicals, and small independent publishers in the black feminist community—not only because our movement has a different history from that of the white feminists but also because we lack the leverage of class and white-skin privilege that white women have used to advantage in both establishment and alternative publishing. We desperately need to build our own black feminist publishing resources. When these exist, the situation of black women in publishing will change for the better.

The politics of publishing influence our reading, teaching, and study of black women writers. The key word in describing the results of black women's literary disenfranchisement is scarcity—scarcity of bibliographies, primary sources, texts, biocritical studies, and topical or contextual studies of the lives of black women (some topics might be black women in slavery, their economic status in the South and North, and their organizations and activities). Much remains to be done, both to reclaim the past and make it available and to gain control over our present and future.

Because of the absence of black women authors from the white literary canon and their invisibility in masculinist versions of history, there have been, until recently, few bibliographies devoted to their lives and work. Some general bibliographies, often quite old, yield material upon careful scrutiny, but incompleteness and inexactness abound, a situation not unexpected in view of the limited research that has been done.

The most useful bibliographies follow, listed by date of publication:

1. Monroe N. Work, *A Bibliography of the Negro in Africa and America* (New York: Wilson, 1928). Work was the director of the Division of Records and Research at Tuskegee Institute; his bibliography is still important for its comprehensive list relating to the pre–Civil War period. It is arranged by subject—labor, occupations, women, and so forth.

2. Dorothy B. Porter, "Early American Negro Writings: A Bibliographical Study," *Publications of the Bibliographical Society of America,* 39 (1945), 192–268. A checklist of writings from 1760 to 1835 with locations.

3. W. E. B. DuBois and Guy Johnson, eds., *Encyclopedia of the Negro: Preparatory Volume with Reference Lists and Reports* (New York: Phelps-Stokes Fund, 1945; rev. ed. 1946). The volume is preparatory but comprehensive as far as it goes.

4. Warren Brown, *Checklist of Negro Newspapers in the United States, 1927–1946* (Jefferson, Mo.: Lincoln Univ. Press, 1946). An indispensable checklist.

5. Erwin Welsch, *The Negro in the United States: A Research Guide* (Bloomington: Indiana Univ. Press, 1965). Useful as a basic introduction.

6. John P. Davis, ed., *The American Negro Reference Book* (Englewood Cliffs, N.J.: Prentice-Hall, 1966). Impressionistic but has some good chapters.

7. *The Negro in American Literature and a Bibliography by and about Negro Americans* (Oshkosh, Wis.: Wisconsin Council of Teachers of English, 1966). Consisting of over a hundred author entries, this source, though rather dated, is still the most useful for secondary school teachers. It needs the addition of a considerable number of black women that it has omitted.

8. Peter N. Bergman, *The Chronological History of the Negro in America* (New York: Harper, 1969). Events, laws, ideas, and brief biographies arranged by year from 1942 to 1968 as well as a bibliography of bibliographies. Useful in spite of errors in the text and the index.

9. Elizabeth W. Miller, *The Negro in America*, rev. ed. Mary Fisher (Cambridge: Harvard Univ. Press, 1970). Although this work has no sections specifically on black women, it includes women in its useful sections on the Negro and the professions and on the Negro and the labor movement. It covers the scholarly and journalistic fields and has a comprehensive scope.

10. Dorothy B. Porter, *The Negro in the United States: A Selected Bibliography* (Washington, D.C.: Library of Congress, 1970). This listing emphasizes recent monographs in the Library of Congress and is arranged alphabetically by author under broad subject headings.

11. Darwin T. Turner, *Afro-American Writers* (New York: Appleton, 1970). One of the Goldentree bibliographies, this listing, which contains over twenty-five writers, is now somewhat dated.

12. Russel C. Brignano, *Black Americans in Autobiography: An Annotated Bibliography of Autobiographical Books Written since the Civil War* (Durham, N.C.: Duke Univ. Press, 1975). This subject-oriented bibliography is practical and useful, but it needs to include still more black women.

13. Theressa Gunnels Rush, Carol Fairbanks Myers, and Esther Spring Arata, *Black American Writers Past and Present: A Biographical and Bibliographical Dictionary*, 2 vols. (Metuchen, N.J.: Scarecrow, 1975). Contains general bibliographies; lists of black and white

critics, historians, and editors; and biobibliographies of individual writers that indicate where writings are anthologized.

14. Wayne Miller et al., *A Comprehensive Bibliography for the Study of American Minorities*, 2 vols. (New York: New York Univ. Press, 1976). The section on black American literature in Volume I contains an essay on black American history and literature that largely neglects women. The thousands of entries are grouped by library holdings, guides to collections, encyclopedias and handbooks, periodicals, history, the civil rights movement, black nationalism, sociology, education, the urban situation, economics, health, religion, and several literary genres and topics.

15 and 16. Esther Spring Arata and Nicholas John Rotoli, *Black American Playwrights, 1800 to the Present: A Bibliography* (Metuchen, N.J.: Scarecrow, 1976), and Esther Spring Arata et al., *More Black American Playwrights: A Bibliography* (Metuchen, N.J.: Scarecrow, 1978). These volumes contain listings by author of the plays, film scripts, and teleplays performed, published, and anthologized; criticisms of the authors and of individual works; reviews of the plays; awards; and some general bibliography.

17. Albert Robbins, *American Literary Manuscripts* (Athens: Univ. of Georgia Press, 1977). Comprehensive in its coverage of black men but uneven and inconsistent in its coverage of black women.

18. Carol Fairbanks and Eugene A. Engeldinger, *Black American Fiction: A Bibliography* (Metuchen, N.J.: Scarecrow, 1978). Contains listings by author of short fiction, novels, biographies and criticism, reviews, and a general bibliography.

19. *Index to Black American Literary Anthologies* (Boston: Hall, 1979). Alphabetical listings of anthology editors, authors, and the titles of the anthologized pieces.

20. Edward Margolies and David Bakish, *Afro-American Fiction, 1853–1976: A Guide to Information Sources* (Detroit: Gale, 1979). Contains checklists, by author, of novels and short story collections published between 1853 and 1976 (no reprints); an annotated bibliography of secondary sources for fifteen novelists (including four women—Zora Neale Hurston, Ann Petry, Paule Marshall, and Toni Morrison); an annotated bibliography of bibliographies and general studies; and a chronological checklist.

21. Helen R. Houston, *The Afro-American Novel, 1965–1975* (Troy, N.Y.: Whitson, 1980). An annotated bibliography of fifty-six contemporary novels that includes the most recent criticism culled from important black periodicals: *Black World, CLA Journal, Freedomways,* and *Phylon*. A useful and descriptive bibliography of primary and secondary materials, this practical aid lists the works of each author and provides biographical statements.

Bibliographies specifically directed toward the lives and works of black women (there are not yet any bibliographies of individual black women) are a product of the 1970s. Some were first published in periodicals and many still are. A selection of those published as volumes follows:

22. Ora Williams, *American Black Women in the Arts and Social Sciences: A Bibliographic Survey* (Metuchen, N.J.: Scarecrow, 1973). Good as far as it goes, but much is overlooked or missing.

23. Lenwood G. Davis, *The Black Woman in American Society: A Selected Annotated Bibliography* (Boston: Hall, 1975). An excellent descriptive bibliography; the selective listing evaluates the importance of the works.

24. James Loewenberg and Ruth Bogin, *Black Women in Nineteenth-Century American Life* (University Park: Pennsylvania State Univ. Press, 1976). An excellent documentary history.

25. Phyllis R. Klotman and Wilmer H. Baatz, *The Black Family and the Black Woman* (Bloomington: Indiana Univ. Library, 1972; rev. ed., New York: Arno, 1978). An annotated list of the holdings of Indiana University; the revised edition contains some six hundred new entries and new subject headings. Helpful in its annotation, sometimes confusing in its subject headings and chronological listing.

26. Lenwood G. Davis and Janet L. Sims, *Black Artists in the United States: An Annotated Bibliography of Books, Articles, and Dissertations on Black Artists, 1779–1979* (Westport, Conn.: Greenwood, 1980). A bibliography of visual arts and black artists.

27. Janet L. Sims, *The Progress of Afro-American Women: A Selected Bibliography and Resource Guide* (Westport, Conn.: Greenwood, 1980). A listing of nineteenth- and twentieth-century materials (books, periodical essays, dissertations) pertaining to black women in the United States, arranged by subjects—arts, literature, magazines, family, education, economics, health and beauty, and so forth. The sections on sex discrimination, suffrage, and the feminist movement are helpful for black feminist research, as is the listing of special periodical issues on black women.

Among recently published biographical and bibliographical works is *American Women Writers*, ed. Lina Maniero (New York: Ungar, 1979–80). Although it lists more black women writers than do most purportedly comprehensive bibliographies, it is uneven in its coverage and unforgivable in its omissions. Black women well known for their achievements and historical importance—such as Mari Evans, Kristen Hunter, and June Jordan—have been casually omitted, while lesser-known white women—even Anita Bryant, whose "works" are picture-books and ghostwritten publications—are carefully included. This reference work forcibly reminds black women that the battles they thought they had won must be fought again and again.

A number of special collections and archives contain material important to researchers doing work on black women. I list here some of those that have published catalogs:

28. *A Classified Catalogue of the Negro Collection in the Collis P. Huntington Library* (Hampton, Va.: Hampton Institute, 1940). This collection contains important materials on slavery and reconstruction and includes letters, diaries, and memoirs not generally available, as well as archival and other material on women—among them, Jessie Redmon Fauset.

29. *The Arthur B. Springarn Collection of Negro Authors* (Washington, D.C.: Howard Univ. Press, 1948).

30. *The Catalogue of the Heartman Negro Collection* (Houston: Texas Southern Univ. Press, 1957).

31. *Dictionary Catalogue of the Schomburg Collection of Negro Literature and History, New York Public Library,* 9 vols. (Boston: Hall, 1962); 2-vol. supplement (1967).

32. *Catalogue of the Negro Collection at the Fisk University Library,* 6 vols. (Boston: Hall, 1974). This collection of more than thirty-five thousand volumes and pamphlets contains important materials on slavery and reconstruction and includes the Countee Cullen papers and materials on Pauline Hopkins, Jessie Redmon Fauset, Angeline Weld Grimké, Zora Neale Hurston, Georgia Douglas Johnson, and the Harlem Renaissance.

Other important Afro-American collections are to be found in the Chicago Afro-American Union Library, the Thomas F. Holgate Library at Fisk University (Nashville, Tenn.), the Amistead Research Center at Dillard University (New Orleans, La.), and the James Weldon Johnson Memorial Collection at Yale University (New Haven, Conn.). Important women's materials are in the Sophia P. Smith Collection at Smith College (Northampton, Mass.), the Arthur and Elizabeth Schlesinger Library at Radcliffe College (Cambridge, Mass.), and a largely uncataloged collection of black women's writings at the Bennett College Library (Greensboro, N.C.).

Much material on black women has not been preserved in libraries. Some may be found in organizational collections, such as those of the National Association of Colored Women (NACW) in Washington, D.C.; its minutes, notes, publications, and letters document the social-club activities of an educated and leisured group of black women at the turn of the century. And much undoubtedly remains to be discovered in closets and attics (see Gloria T. Hull's account of finding the papers of Alice Dunbar Nelson [cited on p. 102]). Generations of neglect have left to us the essential tasks of discovering, documenting, publishing, and interpreting the works of black women.

As anyone doing research on black women finds, the scarcity of relevant books increases the importance of periodicals, not only for articles and bibliographies but also for fiction, poetry, and other writing that has not been reprinted or anthologized. The *Index to Periodical Articles by and about Blacks* (formerly *by and about Negroes)* offers general help; it also indexes, of the periodicals listed below, the *College Language Association Journal,* the *Journal of Negro History,* and the *Negro History Bulletin.* The *CLA Journal* (Morehouse Coll., Atlanta, Ga.) provides its own yearly author-title indexes. *Obsidian* (Wayne State Univ., Detroit) provides a biannual cumulative index and is also indexed in the *American Humanities Index* and *Index of American Periodical Verse.* The *Journal of Negro History* (1916–), a quarterly that contains essays, reprints of historical materials, and book reviews, publishes a yearly author-title index. The *Negro History Bulletin* (1937–), a bimonthly that prints short articles and book reviews, is not itself indexed. *Black Heritage* (formerly *Negro Heritage,* 1961–), a bimonthly printed in Reston, Virginia, is indexed through 1968; more recent issues are indexed in the Aids File of the Schomburg Center for Research in Black Culture, New York Public Library. Still useful, though old, is the *Selective List of Government Publications about the American Negro* (Oxon Hill, Md.: Prince George's County Memorial Library, 1969; prepared by the Reference Dept., Oxon Hill Branch).

For writings that have never resurfaced and have been forgotten, there are innumerable black magazines to be explored. The *AME* (American Methodist Episcopal) *Church Review,* a nineteenth-century literary and religious quarterly published in Brooklyn, New York, seems to have been particularly receptive to black women. Yale University has fairly complete holdings of this journal, and the Schomburg Center has it completely microfilmed and partially indexed. Other magazines that warrant investigation are the *Colored American* (originally the *Weekly Advocate),* the *Anglo-African Magazine,* the *Southern Workman,* the *Challenge, New Challenge,* the *Crisis, Opportunity, Fire,* and *Survey Graphic.*

To benefit scholars, readers, and especially teachers, a substantial number of notable black women writers need to have their biographies written and their works reprinted, not only in hardbound volumes for libraries but in less expensive paperback format. I include in this group Lucy Terry (1730–1821), Phillis Wheatley (1753–84), Frances E. W. Harper (1825–1911), Charlotte L. Forten (Grimké) (1838–1914), Pauline Hopkins (1859–1930), Alice Dunbar Nelson (1875–1935), Angelina Weld Grimké (1880–1938), Anne Spencer (1882–1975), Jessie Redmon Fauset (1886–1961), Georgia Douglas Johnson (1886–1966), Nella Larsen (1893–1963), Eva Jessye (1897–), Margaret Walker (1915–), Gwendolyn Brooks (1917–), Alice Childress

(1920–), Ann Allen Shockley (1927–), Paule Marshall (1929–), Lorraine Hansberry (1930–63), Kristen Hunter (1931–), Toni Morrison (1931–), Sonia Sanchez (1934–), Alice Walker (1944–), Ellease Southerland (1946–), Ntozake Shange (1948–), and Gayl Jones (1949–).

In eighteenth-century American literature, two black women poets stand out. Lucy Terry, a freed slave and the first black American poet, wrote "The Bars Fight" (Aug. 1796), a poem narrating an Indian massacre in western Massachusetts. Bernard Katz and Jonathan Katz wrote *Black Woman: A Fictionalized Biography of Lucy Terry Prince* (New York: Pantheon, 1973), and the Katz-Prince Collection of their drafts, correspondence, notes, and related materials is on microfilm at the Schomburg Center. Their biography is slight, however, and this remarkable woman merits a scholarly study (she argued, unsuccessfully, for the admission of her son to Williams College and successfully presented her own case in court against an adversary who attempted to deprive her and her family of some land).

Phillis Wheatley, a slave in the house of a Boston shoemaker, was taught to read and write, and she began composing poetry when she was thirteen. In 1773, at the age of twenty, she was sent to England to restore her failing health; there she published a collection of poetry, *Poems on Various Subjects, Religious and Moral.* The book appears to have been a joint British-American venture, since the title page reads "Printed for A. Bell, Bookseller, Aldgate; and Sold by Messrs. Cox and Berry, King-Street, Boston, 1773," but there is no satisfactory account of this volume's publication history. Wheatley's poetry and letters have been reprinted and anthologized, and the list of scholarly, biographical, and appreciative writings on her is long. She was celebrated in her own time, particularly in England by antislavery writers, and was the only non-British woman to be included in Mary Scott's *Female Advocate* (London: J. Johnson, 1774), an important early feminist panegyric on literary women. Wheatley's poetry has been too easily placed in the eighteenth-century neoclassical tradition; there should be a reassessment of her as a black American woman and an exploration of the contradictions between her own experience and the poetic conventions she learned. In general, the poetry of early black women has been analyzed largely for considerations of race but not for those of sex and class.

The experience of slavery, spanning the eighteenth and nineteenth centuries, links these early poets with their successors and even, through history and memory, with writers of this century, although our knowledge is yet too fragmentary to document and assess these continuities. Many early writings on slavery, often in the form of poetry, were published in England under the sponsorship of the antislavery forces, who could count among them men with access to the press.

Some of these volumes, such as Maria Falconar and Harriet Falconar's *Poems on Slavery* (London: Egertons, 1788), are now rare and inaccessible and should be reprinted.

Slave narratives have long been an important part of the black literary tradition, but those by women have seldom been reprinted and are virtually unavailable in paperback. The ones listed here are particularly useful in teaching and research:

1. Nancy Prince, *A Narrative of the Life and Travels of Mrs. Nancy Prince* (Boston: privately printed, 1850; 2nd ed., 1853; 3rd ed., 1856).
2. Mattie Griffiths (Brown), *Autobiography of a Female Slave* (New York: Redfield, 1856; rpt. New York: Arno, c. 1975).
3. Harriet (Brent) Jacobs, *Incidents in the Life of A Slave Girl,* ed. Lydia Maria Child (Boston: privately printed, 1861; rpt. New York: Harcourt, 1973).
4. Elizabeth Keckley, *Behind the Scenes; or, Thirty Years a Slave and Four Years in the White House* (New York: Carlton, 1868; rpt. New York: Arno, 1968).
5. Bethany Veney, *The Narrative of Bethany Veney: A Slave Woman* (Worcester, Mass.: A. P. Bicknell, 1889; 2nd ed., 1890; rpt. Philadelphia: Bicknell, 1970).
6. Lucy A. Berry Delaney, *From the Darkness Cometh the Light: or, Struggles for Freedom* (St. Louis: J. T. Smith, 1891).
7. Amanda (Berry) Smith, *An Autobiography: The Story of the Lord's Dealings with Mrs. Amanda Smith, the Colored Evangelist . . .* (Chicago: Meyer and Brother, 1893; rpt. Chicago: Christian Witness, 1921).
8. Annie Burton, *Memories of Childhood's Slavery Days* (Boston: Ross, 1909).

Frances E. W. Harper, a prolific poet, also wrote what is believed to be the first novel published in this country by an Afro-American woman, *Iola Leroy; or, Shadows Uplifted* (Philadelphia: Garrigues Brothers, 1892; rpt. New York: Arno, 1969). The publication histories of this novel and of her many volumes of poetry not only document her literary career but also illustrate the opportunities for publication—and their lack—available to a black woman author before and after the Civil War. Harper's earliest volume of poetry was *Poems on Miscellaneous Subjects* (Boston: J. B. Yerrinton, 1854), which was subsequently published in Philadelphia. Other volumes are *Moses: A Story of the Nile* (Philadelphia: Merrihew, 1869); *Atlanta Offering: Poems* (Philadelphia: George S. Ferguson, 1895; rpt. New York: Arno, 1969)—and, I think, also reprinted as *Poems* [Philadelphia: George S. Ferguson, 1900]); *Idylls of the Bible* (Philadelphia: privately printed, 1901; rpt. New York: AMS, 1975); and *The Sparrow's Fall and Other Poems* (n. p., n. d.). *Sketches of Southern Life* (Philadelphia: Merrihew, 1873) has not been reprinted, nor has "The Two Offers," a story published in the *Anglo-African Magazine,* Sept. 1859, pp. 288–91, 311–13. We need a full-length study of Harper, who was a feminist, as well as studies of her poetry and fiction—studies, for example, of the flower imagery she uses to convey the faces, histories, and conditions of women (see such poems as "The Mission of the Flowers," "The Crocuses," and "Dandelions"), and of the portrayals of strong, often rebellious women that she wrote in an attempt to build a tradition of female heroism.

A less prolific contemporary of Harper, Charlotte L. Forten (Grimké), kept a journal of her times, 1854–64, which remained in manuscript for a century. *The Journal of Charlotte L. Forten,* edited by Ray Allen Billington (New York: Dryden, 1953; rpt. New York: Macmillan, 1961), should be reissued in paperback, and her best poem "The Angel's Visit," published originally in the anthology *The Rising Sun* (Boston: A. G. Brown, 1874), deserves to be included in new anthologies.

Two later writers of the nineteenth century have suffered from the same lack of attention as Harper and Forten. Pauline Hopkins' novel *Contending Forces* (Boston: Colored Cooperative, 1900) has been reprinted (Carbondale: Southern Illinois Univ. Press, 1978), but her *Winona: A Tale of Negro Life in the South and Southwest* and *Of One Blood; or, The Hidden Self* can be read only as originally printed, in monthly installments in the *Colored American Magazine* (1902–03). Alice Dunbar Nelson—writer, editor, journalist, teacher, and activist—has also been neglected. All her short stories, those that are scattered as well as those in *Violets and Other Tales* (Boston: Monthly Review, 1895) and *The Goodness of St. Rocque and Other Stories* (New York: Dodd, 1899), need reprinting, especially in paperback.

There are many lesser-known black women poets, novelists, short-story writers, and playwrights of the nineteenth century whose works are also candidates for reprinting and anthologizing. The irregularity of the citations will suggest our fragmentary knowledge of these women and the problems of locating their works:

1. Rosa and Maria, *Poems* (South Carolina: n. p., 1834).
2. Ann Plato, *Essays including Biographies and Miscellaneous Pieces in Prose and Poetry* (Hartford, Conn.: privately printed, 1841).
3. Clarissa M. Thompson, *Treading the Winepress* (Boston: n. p., 1885–86).
4. Henrietta Cordelia Ray, *Poems* (New York: n. p., 1887); *Commemoration Ode on Lincoln Written for the Occasion of the Unveiling of the Freedman's Monument in Memory of Abraham Lincoln, April 14, 1876* (New York: J. J. Little, 1893).
5. Katherine Davis Tillman, *Beryl Weston's Ambitions* (Philadelphia: n. p., 1888); *Aunt Betsy's Thanksgiving* (Philadelphia: AME Book Concern, n. d.).

6. Ada N. Harris, "Elsie," *AME Church Review,* 7 (1890).
7. Josephine D. Heard, *Morning Glories* (Philadelphia: n. p., 1890).
8. Amelia E. Johnson, *Clarence and Corinne; or, God's Way* (1890); *The Hazeley Family* (1894); and *Martina Meriden; or What Is My Motive?* (1901). All three works were published in Philadelphia by the American Baptist Publication Society.
9. Victoria Earle (Matthews), *Aunt Lindy* (New York: J. J. Little, 1893).
10. Eloise Bibb (Thompson), *Poems* (Boston: Monthly Review, 1895).
11. Mary Weston Fordham, *Magnolia Leaves* (Charleston, S.C.: Walker, Evans & Cogswell, 1897; 2nd ed., 1898).
12. Priscilla Jane Thompson, *Ethiope Lays* (Rossmoyne, Ohio: privately printed, 1900).

Out-of-print works of black women writers of this century have frequently been made available in hardbound reprints for libraries but intermittently, if at all, in paperback reprints for reading and teaching. It is a mark of the revived interest in Zora Neale Hurston that two of her works—her book on black folklore, *Mules and Men* (Philadelphia: Lippincott, 1935), and her novel *Their Eyes Were Watching God* (Philadelphia: Lippincott, 1937)—have been issued as university-press paperbacks (by Indiana Univ. Press and the Univ. of Illinois Press, respectively) and are thus likely to remain in print longer than they would have if they had been reprinted as mass-market or even trade paperbacks. In addition, a paperback collection of Hurston's short stories, *I Like Myself When I Am Laughing . . . and Then Again When I Am Looking Mean and Impressive,* has been edited by Alice Walker (Old Westbury, N.Y.: Feminist, 1979). Two additional novels, *Jonah's Gourd Vine* (Philadelphia: Lippincott, 1934) and *Seraph on the Sewanee* (New York: Scribners, 1948) should also be reprinted, as should her autobiography, *Dust Tracks on a Road* (Philadelphia: Lippincott, 1942).

Other writers of the first half of the century who would be better known if their works were more widely available are the novelists Jessie Redmon Fauset and Nella Larsen and the poet Georgia Douglas Johnson. Fauset published four novels—*There Is Confusion* (New York: Boni & Liveright, 1924), *Plum Bun* (London: E. Matthew & Marrot, 1928; New York: Stokes, 1929), *The Chinaberry Tree* (New York: Stokes, 1931), and *Comedy: American Style* (New York: Stokes, 1933)—in addition to poems, essays, and short stories. Larsen published two novels, *Quicksand* (New York: Knopf, 1928) and *Passing* (New York: Knopf, 1929). There are four volumes of Johnson's poems: *The Heart of a Woman* (Boston: Cornhill, 1918), *Bronze* (Boston: B. J. Brimmer, 1922), *An Autumn Love Cycle* (New York: Vinal, 1926), and *Share My World: A Book of Poems* (Washington: privately printed, 1962). These women are promising subjects for full-length biocritical studies, as are, for example, Sara Lee Brown Fleming (*Hope's Highway* [New York: Neale, 1918]), Mary Etta Spencer (*The Resentment* [Philadelphia: AME Book Concern, 1921]), Lillian E. Wood (*Let My People Go* [Philadelphia: AME Book Concern, 1922]), and Annie Greene Nelson (*After the Storm* [Columbia, S.C.: Hampton, 1942] and *The Dawn Appears* [Columbia, S.C.: Hampton, 1944]).

Some more recent black women writers whose works are in and out of print— but mostly out—are Dorothy West (*The Living Is Easy* [Boston: Houghton, 1948]), Sadie Mae Roseborough (*Wasted Travail* [New York: Vantage, 1951]), Dorothy Lee Dickens (*Black on the Rainbow* [New York: Pageant, 1952]), Kristen Hunter (*The Landlord* [New York: Scribners, 1966]), Carlene H. Polite (*The Flagellants* [New York: Farrar, 1967] and *Sister X and the Victims of Foul Play* [New York: Farrar, 1975]), and Sara E. Wright (*This Child's Gonna Live* [New York: Delacourt, 1969; rpt. Dell, 1971]). In addition there are Paule Marshall and Ann Petry. Marshall's two novels are *Brown Girl, Brownstones* (New York: Random, 1959; rpt. Old Westbury, N.Y.: Feminist, 1981) and *The Chosen Place, the Timeless People* (New York: Harcourt, 1969). Ann Petry's three novels are *The Street* (Boston: Houghton, 1946), *The Country Place* (Boston: Houghton, 1947), and *The Narrows* (Boston: Houghton, 1953); she has also published a collection of short stories, *Miss Muriel and Other Stories* (Boston: Houghton, 1971), and a historical novel, *Tituba of Salem Village* (New York: Crowell, 1964). All these authors warrant serious critical attention.

Autobiographies of black women present a promising field for research. A useful bibliography is Russel C. Brignano's *Black Americans in Autobiography* (Durham, N.C.: Duke Univ. Press, 1975). A glance at black women's autobiographies in print shows a substantial representation of entertainers: Marion Anderson, Pearl Bailey, Dorothy Dandridge, Katherine Dunham, Billie Holliday, Lena Horne, and Eartha Kitt. Less prominently represented are political figures—Ida B. Wells Barnett, Daisy Bates, Shirley Chisholm, Angela Davis, and Florynce Kennedy—and literary figures—Gwendolyn Brooks, Nikki Giovanni, and Lorraine Hansberry. One wonders what gets printed and why, what remains to be found, in manuscript, and also whether it is possible to find continuities between the narratives of female slaves and these later autobiographies.

Much needs to be done to make black women's literature a viable field of study and inquiry. We need bibliographies and archival catalogs; full-scale biographies and critical analyses of many writers, including some I have not mentioned; investigations of circles of black women writers and artists—for instance, the women of the Harlem Renaissance or women poets of the 1940s and 1950s, such as Margaret

Danner, Naomi Long Madgett, and Gloria C. Oden; thematic studies linking the works of various black women writers; the development of black feminist critical theory; and interdisciplinary research that connects literature, history, and the social sciences to illumine the lives and production, literary or otherwise, of black women. Exemplifying the biographical work that might be done on eighteenth and nineteenth century black women is Dorothy Sterling's *Black Foremothers* (Old Westbury, N.Y.: Feminist, 1979), a sensitive treatment of Ellen Craft, Ida B. Wells, and Mary Church Terrell written with historical insight from a feminist perspective. Carolyn Wedin Sylvander's *Jessie Redmon Fauset, Black American Writer* (Troy, N.Y.: Whitson, 1981) offers provocative insights, musings, and meditations on the life of Fauset. The new material Sylvander unearths reminds us all too well of the need to check even the most commonplace data on black women writers, since so much misinformation, even mythology, gets repeated from source to source. Going beyond Sylvander's probing analysis and thoughtful discussions of Fauset's essays and short fiction, Barbara T. Christian's *Black Women Novelists: The Development of a Tradition, 1892–1976* (Westport, Conn.: Greenwood, 1980) is a perceptive study of Fauset and other black women writers. Christian's landmark work is the finest example of black feminist criticism to date. Her consideration of the mulatto stereotype is the best study on the subject.

A feminist perspective—a woman-identified perspective—is essential to writing about black lesbian women. As authors, as literary characters, and as subjects of study, they have suffered total neglect if not brutal repression. Their versions of the black female experience are the least known, even though images of woman-identified black women would help to heal the battered psyches common to all black women in a black-woman–hating society. Homophobia and fear of reprisal have understandably kept many black lesbian writers from coming out in print, but some talented ones are emerging who need a place for their words. Audre Lorde, Pat Parker, and Ann Allen Shockley are three black women writers who have done courageous and pioneering work by writing positively about the black lesbian experience.[5]

It is important that as black feminists, we do much of the interpretation and criticism of black women's literature ourselves. This is not to say that others should not work on or write about black women; they should—but preference given to outsiders' views of black women is like preference given to men's views of women: the outsider's opinions are valued purportedly for their objectivity and quality but are actually preferred for their racist and sexist biases. Other people's versions of our lives and oppression should not be more authoritative than our own. Two essays that begin to establish a black feminist criticism are Gloria T. Hull's "Re-writing Afro-American Literature: A Case for

Black Women Writers" (*Radical Teacher,* 6 [1977]) and Barbara Smith's "Toward a Black Feminist Criticism" (*Conditions: Two,* 1 [1977]). At the same time, white feminist critics should incorporate literature by black women in their canon of women's writings and the black imagination in their account of the female imagination. Some examples of "benign neglect" that come to mind are Nina Baym's *Women's Fiction: A Guide to Novels by and about Women in America, 1820–1870,* Ellen Moers's *Literary Women,* and Patricia Meyer Spack's *The Female Imagination.* Mary Helen Washington, in "New Lives and New Letters: Black Women Writers at the End of the Seventies" (*College English,* 43 [1981], 1–16), documents other omissions and also discusses the dangers of tokenism in the new (white) feminist rewriting of literary history; she is currently compiling an anthology of literary criticism by black women.

A variety of materials can be made available more quickly and economically by publishing anthologies than by reprinting single titles. Currently, only a handful of anthologies about black women are in print, and more are clearly needed, particularly specialized ones. Toni Cade Bambara has put together a pioneering anthology, *The Black Woman* (New York: NAL, 1970), that contains poetry, fiction, and prose. Among its theoretical essays, "A Historical and Critical Essay for Black Women in the Cities," by Pat Robinson and Group, remains important. A more recent and ambitious anthology is *Sturdy Black Bridges: Visions of Black Women in Literature,* ed. Roseann P. Bell, Bettye J. Parker, and Beverly Guy-Sheftall (Garden City, N.Y.: Anchor-Doubleday, 1979), which also contains a mixture of poetry, fiction, and prose—historical, critical, and theoretical essays and conversations with black women authors. It is an ambitious attempt to document black women's literary history, though some black feminists regard the book as homophobic and male-identified. Published by the Feminist Press in 1982 is *But Some of Us Are Brave: Black Women's Studies,* edited by Gloria T. Hull, Pat Bell Scott, and Barbara Smith. A collection of articles, some new and some reprinted, oriented toward research and pedagogy, the anthology includes Gloria T. Hull's "Researching Alice Dunbar Nelson: A Personal and Literary Perspective," Alice Walker's "One Child of One's Own: A Meaningful Digression within the Works," Michelle Wallace's "A Black Feminist's Search for Sisterhood," Mary Helen Washington's "Teaching Black-Eyed Susans," Jean Fagan Yellin's "Afro-American Women, 1800–1910: A Selected Bibliography," and Erlene Stetson's "Studying Slavery: Some Literary and Pedagogical Considerations."

Good anthologies with a historical focus are badly needed. *Black Women in White America* (ed. Gerda Lerner [New York: Pantheon, 1972]) is long on chronology and short on interpretation and imagination. *The Afro-American Woman: Struggles and Images* (ed. Sharon

Harley and Rosalyn Terborg-Penn [Port Washington, N.Y.: Kennikat, 1978]) is a slight, impressionistic volume, but Dorothy Porter's introduction contains a valuable list of collections and repositories with holdings on black women.

There are two excellent anthologies of fiction, both edited by Mary Helen Washington: *Black-Eyed Susans: Classic Stories by and about Black Women* (Garden City, N.Y.: Anchor-Doubleday, 1975) and *Midnight Birds: Stories of Contemporary Black Women Writers* (Garden City, N.Y.: Anchor-Doubleday, 1980). Erlene Stetson's *Black Sister: Poetry by American Black Women, 1746–1980* (Bloomington: Indiana Univ. Press, 1981) contains a range of poems by fifty-eight representative black women poets from the eighteenth century to the twentieth. Mari Evans' anthology *Black Women Poets, 1950–Present* (Garden City, N.Y.: Doubleday) is scheduled for publication in 1982. An ambitious recent anthology is *The Third Woman: Minority Women Writers of the United States,* (ed. Dexter Fisher [Boston: Houghton, 1980]); this collection brings together women writers who are Asian-American, black American, Chicana, and American Indian. The materials are excellent, but the anthology does little to interpret them, which is not surprising in view of its scope: the links between the "worlds" of the various writers and the "worlds" they project in their texts are missing. An earlier anthology edited by Naomi Katz and Nancy Milton, *Fragments from a Lost Diary and Other Stories* (Boston: Beacon, 1973; rpt. New York: Random, 1975), brings together stories by and about women from Asia, Africa, and Latin America. So far, there are no anthologies of black women playwrights and no anthologies with a thematic focus, such as black lesbians or violence against black women.

Writing by black women does appear in other anthologies—collections of black literature and of women's literature—but almost always as tokens, as nods toward affirmative action. Whether one is reading *By Women, Images of Women in Fiction, Feminist Literary Theory, The World Split Open, Psyche,* or *Shakespeare's Sisters,* the pattern is the same: an essay—sometimes two—by a black woman or the most frequently anthologized poem of Phillis Wheatley, Gwendolyn Brooks, or Nikki Giovanni. Naomi Long Madgett observed that her poem "Black Woman" may have been printed incorrectly ever since its first incorrect appearance in an Afro-American poetry anthology. Most poetry anthologies suggest that, at best, there are four recent black woman poets, and the four represented are usually chosen from Gwendolyn Brooks, Lucille Clifton, Mari Evans, Nikki Giovanni, Sonia Sanchez and sometimes include Audre Lorde.

The anthologies used in introductory and survey courses almost invariably omit the writings of black women, even though they contain those of black men and white women. And when teachers try to include black women's writings by distributing handouts, the fact that these are duplicated rather than printed in the text may reinforce the students' racist and sexist judgments about the quality of this literature and the need to study it. Literature by black women belongs in the textbooks that are used in writing, introductory, and survey courses and that define the "canon." Hurston and Petry as well as Hemingway and Faulkner reveal the nature of the short story, and the writing of these women has the additional value of not being racist or misogynistic.

What are the strategies and actions that will elevate black women's situation in publishing? While it is difficult to confront both the "literary-industrial complex" and the long tradition of white male cultural rule,[6] some publications and institutions show how change has been effected. The first step is to understand the problem—to acknowledge that black women have a particular relation to the publishing establishment and that there are political reasons for it. Understanding stimulates change.

The next step is to spread the word that black women writers have written books we need. Useful aids in this effort are Walter Schatz's *Directory of Afro-American Resources* (New York: Bowker, 1970), which still ranks among the most practical and easy-to-interpret guides available, and Ann Shockley and Sue Chandler's *Living Black American Authors: A Biographical Directory* (New York: Bowker, 1973), an invaluable source of information, especially for contemporary black American women.

Teachers of literature, women's studies, and black literature can alter publishing policies by reading and teaching black women writers. The more demand there is, particularly for course adoptions, the more likely are new titles and out-of-print books by black women to be published. Teachers can also criticize and refuse to order texts that exclude black and third-world women writers, informing publishers why they have done so, and they can assign books published by feminist presses. Women with decision-making power on journals and periodicals can give priority to publishing the creative and scholarly writings of black and third-world women, and sympathetic personnel at commercial and university presses can seek out black and third-world women writers, ensuring that in the processes of selection and publication their work is treated fairly.

Although we should continuously exert pressure to make the publishing industry accountable, perhaps the best way to effect change is to create our own autonomous means of publishing. We can thus produce the books we need but also have an impact on establishment publishing by furnishing examples of the books we want. We know that independent publishing can affect the industry because establishment publishers have, of late, been printing and distributing titles originally published by women's presses. Self-publishing must be understood in the light of cultural oppression: women publish themselves not from "vanity" but because establishment publishers reject them out of hand, not perceiving the value of their work or disagreeing with its political content.

Women are beginning to create their own resources. Naomi Long Madgett's Lotus Press publishes such black poets as May Miller. *Black Lesbians: An Annotated Bibliography,* edited by J. R. Roberts, a white feminist (Naiad Press, Box 10543, Tallahassee, FL 32302) includes an important section on literature and criticism and should encourage research and writing about black lesbians. *Sojourner: A Third World Women's Research Newsletter* has been providing an important communication network since 1977. *Truth: The Newsletter of the Association of Black Women Historians* began publication in Spring 1979 and, though it specializes in history, is a forum for women working in a variety of fields. *Azalea: A Magazine by Third World Lesbians,* the first publication of its kind, is committed to remaining autonomous; it publishes poetry, fiction, articles, and graphics. *Conditions: A Magazine of Writing by Women with an Emphasis on Writing by Lesbians* has demonstrated its commitment to the work of third-world women since its inception in 1977; the first four issues contain articles, poetry, and reviews by black and other third-world women, and the fifth issue is devoted to the writings of black women (*Conditions: Five,* 2, No. 2 [1979]). *Heresies: A Feminist Publication on Art and Politics* has produced a special issue on third-world women (2, No. 5 [1979]), as will *MELUS* (3, No. 7 [1981]) on ethnic women writers. A special issue of *Freedomways* (19, No. 4 [1979]) devoted to Lorraine Hansberry contains Adrienne Rich's challenging essay "The Problem with Lorraine Hansberry." Finally, a recent issue of *Signs* (6, No. 2 [Winter 1980]) contains my review of *Conditions: Five,* (2, No. 2). This issue is dedicated to black lesbians Audre Lorde and Mabel Hampton, and it includes Ann Allen Shockley's important essay "The Black Lesbian in American Literature: An Overview." These independent publications do not rely on the publishing industry for their existence. They represent the first wave of black feminist publishing, which is nevertheless not without its drawbacks. Many of these writings continue to suffer neglect because they have not enjoyed wide distribution: the self-published volumes of poet Gloria Oden (*The Naked Frame* [1952], *Resurrections* [1979], and *The Tie That Binds* [1980]), the small-press publications, and the work in the new journals.[7]

As black women, we have much to do to get ourselves into print and keep ourselves there—in literature, scholarship, pedagogy, and editing. But the key to success is a commitment to work for the fundamental social and political changes that will transform the process as well as the content of cultural production and will validate all women and their words.[8]

Notes

1. Kristen Hunter, *The Landlord* (New York: Scribners, 1966), p. 42.
2. The proscription of literacy is commonly acknowledged in records, histories, slave narratives, biographies, and many literary histories. Of course, it is from white-controlled institutions of education that blacks have been barred. For one account of black educational institutions, see Evelyn Brooks Barnett, "Nannie Burroughs and the Education of Black Women," in *The Afro-American Woman. Sturdy Black Bridges* and *The Third Woman* acknowledge the importance of oral forms and include transcribed conversations with writers (see the section on anthologies, pp. 102–04, for bibliographical information).
3. For a valuable discussion of racism and white women, see Adrienne Rich's "Disloyal to Civilization: Feminism, Racism, Gynephobia," *Chrysalis,* 7 (1970), 9–27 (rpt. in Adrienne Rich, *On Lies, Secrets, and Silence: Selected Prose, 1966–1978* [New York: Norton, 1979]).
4. See, e.g., the letters that Wheatley wrote to Obour Tanner, a black woman who was her confidante. They appeared in the *Proceedings of the Massachusetts Historical Society,* 7 (1863), 267–79, and have been reprinted in Phillis Wheatley, *Poems and Letters,* ed. Charles Fred Heartman (New York: C. F. Heartman Historical Society, 1915); *Letters of Phillis Wheatley, the Negro-Slave Poet of Boston,* ed. Charles Deane (Boston: J. Wilson, 1864); and more recently in Julian D. Mason, Jr., *The Poems of Phillis Wheatley* (Chapel Hill: Univ. of North Carolina Press, 1966). The availability of these letters allows us to compare Wheatley's poetry and epistolary conventions, as well as to study her interactions with her black and white, male and female correspondents in America and England.
5. Audre Lorde, *From a Land Where Other People Live* (Detroit: Broadside, 1973), *The New York Head Shop and Museum* (Detroit: Broadside, 1974), *Between Our Selves* (Pt. Reyes, Calif: Eidolon, 1976), *The Black Unicorn* (New York: Norton, 1978), *Uses of the Erotic: The Erotic as Power* (Brooklyn: Out and Out Pamphlet, 1978); Pat Parker, *Child of Myself* (Oakland, Calif.: Diana, 1972), *Pit Stop* (Oakland: Diana, 1973), *Womanslaughter* (Oakland: Diana, 1978), *The Collected Poetry of Pat Parker* (Oakland: Diana, 1978); Ann Allen Shockley, *Loving Her* (Indianapolis: Bobbs-Merrill, 1974; rpt. New York: Avon, 1978). The addresses of the alternative and feminist publishers of these writers are Broadside Press, 12651 Old Mill Place, Detroit, MI 48238; Eidolon Editions, Box 629, Pt. Reyes, CA 94956; Out and Out Pamphlet, 476 Second St., Brooklyn, NY 11215; and Diana Press, 4400 Market St., Oakland, CA 94608.
6. The "literary-industrial complex" is a phrase coined by Richard Kostelanatz, the "Grub Street Jeremiah." His *The End of Intelligent Writing* (1974) has been reprinted in paperback as *Literary Politics in America* (Mission, Kans.: Sheed, Andrews, and McNeel, 1978).
7. These publications may be obtained from the following addresses: *Black Lesbians,* c/o J. R. Roberts, The Women's Center, 46 Pleasant St., Cambridge, MA 02139; *Sojourner,* c/o Harriet G. McCombs, Dept. of Psycholo-

gy, Wayne State Univ., Detroit, MI 48202; *Truth,* c/o Darlene Clark Hine, Dept. of History, University Hall 212, Purdue Univ., West Lafayette, IN 47907; *Azalea,* c/o Joan Gibbs, 306 Lafayette Ave., Brooklyn, NY 11233; *Conditions,* P.O. Box 56, Van Brunt Station, Brooklyn, NY 11215; *Heresies,* Heresies Collective, Box 766, Canal Street Station, New York, NY 10013; *MELUS,* Dept. of English, Univ. of Southern California, Los Angeles, CA 90007; *Freedomways,* Freedomways Associates, 799 Broadway, New York, NY 10003; Gloria Oden's works, Box 1409, Olivant Press, Homestead, FL 33030.

8. I wish to thank Gloria T. Hull and Barbara Smith for their generous assistance with this essay.

Working-Class Women's Literature

An Introduction to Study

Paul Lauter

Writing—and indeed thinking—about working-class literature presents a number of unique problems. To begin with, what do we mean by "working-class literature"? Literature *about* working-class people, literature *by* them, or literature addressed *to* them? If we use the first definition, should we include works that are ignorant of or hostile to the working-class people they write about— like some turn-of-the-century "industrial" novels? If we focus on writing *by* working people, do we include pieces that do not deal with their lives or even with their real concerns, like some "popular" songs? Should we include, say, literature by people of working-class origins, like D. H. Lawrence? To complicate the issue still further, there is the question of audience or, perhaps more accurately, of the differing functions of works with differing audiences. Florence Reece's song "Which Side Are You On?" for example, urges miners to stick together in the union, whereas Edwin Markham's poem "The Man with the Hoe" calls on the "masters, lords and rulers in all lands" to right the wrongs of working people. Since both concern changing the condition of the working class, are both working-class literature? "Life in the Iron Mills," the first significant portrait in American literature of the lives of the industrial workers, clearly addresses a bourgeois audience, while many drugstore novels, like those of Mickey Spillane, attract a substantial working-class readership. Which would one want to retain in a "canon" of working-class fiction? Such questions cannot be answered categorically; we need a more adequate understanding of the techniques, functions, and distinctive qualities of working-class art.

Beyond these issues, there is the question of what defines the working class. Many such definitions exclude more people, especially women, than they include. The traditional image of the American industrial worker, for example, is male, in part because of ignorance about the role of women, historical and current, in United States industry. And the traditional image is also white, reflecting the racially segregated job structure that still persists in some industries.

It seems best to use relatively loose definitions and broad categories, but we must remain sharply aware of the difficulties involved, the manifestations within the culture of efforts to overcome (or to retain) class privilege, patriarchy, and white supremacy. Here I discuss literary works by *and* about working people, written and oral forms, "high," "popular," and "mass" culture. I designate as "working-class people" those who sell their labor for wages; who create in that labor and have taken from them "surplus value," to use Marx's phrase; who have relatively little control over the nature or products of their work; and who are not "professionals" or "managers." I refer to people who, to improve their lot, must either move in *solidarity* with their class or leave it (for example, to become managers).[1] I include those who work in homes, whose labor is sold although not for pay, as surely as is that of those who work in the mills or in the streets. I also include those who work on farms and those whose labor is extorted from them by slavery and peonage. Such categories, though admittedly blurred at the edges, give us at least a reasonable place from which to start.

In dealing with working-class culture, and especially with women's literature, we are confronted by a problem more fundamental than that of definition. It can be seen in a poem by Bertolt Brecht, "A Worker Reads History":

> Who built the seven gates of Thebes?
> The books are filled with names of kings.
> Was it kings who hauled the craggy blocks of stone?
> And Babylon, so many times destroyed,
> Who built the city up each time? In which of Lima's houses,
> That city glittering with gold, lived those who built it?
> In the evening when the Chinese wall was finished
> Where did the masons go? Imperial Rome
> Is full of arcs of triumph. Who reared them up? Over whom
> Did the Caesars triumph? Byzantium lives in some,

Were all her dwellings palaces? And even in Atlantis of the legend
The night the sea rushed in,
The drowning men still bellowed for their slaves.

Young Alexander conquered India.
He alone?
Caesar beat the Gauls.
Was there not even a cook in his army?
Philip of Spain wept as his fleet
Was sunk and destroyed. Were there no other tears?
Frederick the Great triumphed in the Seven Years war. Who
Triumphed with him?

Each page a victory,
At whose expense the victory ball?
Every ten years a great man,
Who paid the piper?

So many particulars.
So many questions.

Brecht's poem vividly illustrates that the workers of the world have been hidden from history—omitted from the chronicles, myths, sagas, and fictions that embody it. Less openly, the poem illustrates how much *more* hidden are the women of the working classes, appearing here fleetingly as those who weep for the drowned sailors of Philip's fleet, and, perhaps, as the haulers of stone and the slaves of Atlantis. The chronicles, sagas, fictions, and poems were seldom written by people who labored for their bread. Laborers did not have the leisure or, generally, the literacy to write books (though they did leave us the works of their hands, in materials like stone and wool). And if they were female, still other veils shrouded their lives and limited their creations.

But working people were by no means silent. On the contrary, they have always produced literature. Its forms, however—including the forms of its transmission—its structural elements, and its purposes have been quite different from the dominant written forms of the last twenty-five hundred years or so. To approach working-class culture, therefore, we must lay aside many of our presuppositions about what literature *is* and is *not.*[2] We must begin by asking in what forms, on what themes, in what circumstances, and to what ends working people spoke and sang to one another. How did they gather, examine, transmit, and renew their experiences?

First, we need a broader definition of what we can call "literature."

That working-class literature has often taken oral forms is not surprising, since many of its creators, along with their audience, did not read or write. (A theme of working-class art has been the struggle to gain access to the resources of culture and power, including literacy.) The study of working-class art must therefore include works that in the last fifty years have been generally displaced into courses called folklore and the like.[3] Today, when literature departments are more likely than they were a decade ago to include undergraduate folklore courses, as well as women's studies itself, we are better prepared for the interdisciplinary approach required for the study of folk culture. Similarly, since songs—for reasons I explain below—are one of the forms most widely used by working-class artists, we have to pay attention to their literary elements; many are significant creations of language. In addition, as is true in women's studies generally, we must pay more attention to the "fragmentary" or "incremental" genres—letters, diaries, and documents derived from oral sources.

As we move toward more inclusive definitions of "literature," certain issues that are largely submerged in the study of "high culture" become more critical. For example, it becomes necessary to distinguish between "folk" or "people's" ("popular") culture and what Dwight MacDonald characterized as "mass culture." Popular culture is what people who share class, ethnicity, and/or race produce in communicating with one another, as distinguished from what is produced for consumption by the "masses." There is, obviously, no clear-cut dividing line, and the distinction is particularly difficult for those of us brought up in the bourgeois cultural system, in which the norm is production by artists for consumption by consumers.

The distinction is only in part one of quality, although mass culture, which is often directed by the political imperative of shaping and dominating the consciousness of the masses, generally involves basically simplified ways of appealing to the lowest common denominator—as was illustrated by the sudden flourishing, a few years ago, of tv shows portraying the cop as hero. It is more important here, however, to understand the functions of "popular" art and its patterns of creation. Much working-class culture originates and exists in situations that do not absolutely distinguish between the active "performer/artist" and the passive "audience"; or, if that distinction is made, the artist's "product" is offered not for its *exchange* value (money for the song) but for its *use* in the lives of the people to whom it is directed. A fine example is provided by the Kentucky mountain songs sung with great majesty at the funeral of "Jock" Yablonski and recorded in the film "Harlan County, U.S.A."

This distinctive quality of popular culture becomes clearer when we consider more fully the processes of creation and the functions of working-class art. The creative process is nowhere better described and analyzed than in Lawrence Levine's *Black Culture and Black Consciousness,*[4] required reading for anyone concerned with this area. Levine has collected a number of vivid, firsthand descriptions of the creation of "sorrow songs," mainly in post–Civil War black churches, and he has examined the common features of these descriptions. One important observation is that new songs were most often based on old ones: a look at most labor songbooks shows that working-class artists were often concerned less with creating a work that would be unique than with building variations on tunes and themes well known in their communities. In many ways, working-class art, like other elements of working-class life, is highly traditional, even "conservative;" innovative form is certainly not a primary consideration. Similarly, working-class poetry and song—and to a lesser extent tales and the like—are often built around repeated elements—refrains, formulas, and commonly accepted assumptions about characters. Language, too, is often simpler, even commonplace, and less "heightened" than that of "high-culture" verse. These characteristics are, of course, common to oral art, made necessary by the exigencies of memory and improvisation.

But they also reflect a certain communal quality, which Levine finds exemplified in the creation of a song—different people chime in, a melody is picked up and carried forward by a new voice, or a chorus swells it spontaneously. In such situations, the individual creator is less important than the group, or rather, if the individual creator shapes a common stock to new group purposes, she or he does so without diminishing or expropriating that common stock. The song leader in church is not asked to provide new hymns (and would be looked at with suspicion for doing so) but is asked to point or enhance a hymn that is known, perhaps to add something especially appropriate to the situation.[5] Early jazz musicians may have been admired for a new melody, but probably more often for their ability to ring variations on melodies the listeners knew and followed. I emphasize the "folk" or communal elements of working-class art at the partial expense of work produced by self-conscious individual working-class artists because this approach helps to bring out distinctive qualities about working-class art that are not seen so easily when one focuses primarily on the production of individual artists. Yet a continuum obviously exists between works created primarily by individual imaginations and the songs, poems, and tales that are, so to speak, common property.[6]

Much working-class art is created and experienced in group situations—not in the privacy of a study, but in the church, the hall, the work site, the meeting hall, the quilting bee, or the picket line. It is thus rooted in the experiences of a particular group of people facing particular problems at a particular time. It is not conceived as timeless and transcendent, nor does it often function in such modes. Understanding this transitoriness is especially important in searching for working-class women's art. Many of the finest men's songs come from the prison chain gang or the work camp, and many women's songs have come from the communal experience of the church—but also from the loneliness of the solitary room often portrayed in the blues. More women's work songs have been located and recorded in recent years and doubtless as we come to understand more about female subcultures, we will discover more about songs and stories exchanged in the markets, mills, quilting rooms, and nurseries.[7]

Understanding the *instrumental* character of working-class art is also important to perceiving the aesthetic theory that informs it, a theory unfamiliar to most of us. Martha Vicinus has discussed the functions of working-class art in *The Industrial Muse* (the only full-length study in English of working-class [British] literature and, with Levine's book, required reading for anyone interested in this area). In a paper on the poetry of the Colorado miners, Dan Tannacito has addressed the same subject. Tannacito suggests that "the real value of the miners' poetry was the immediate use made of it by its local audience of miners and sympathizers" (p. 1). The writers' objectives in writing were inseparable from these goals toward which the lives of the workers directed them. Vicinus points out that working-class artists, themselves persuaded of the power of literature to "influence people's behavior," aimed to "persuade readers to adopt particular beliefs." Some artists recommended middle-class values and the culture of their "betters." Others, believing that social and political change was impossible, reassured readers of the worth of their own culture's values, providing at least entertainment and consolation in a fixed and largely oppressive world. More—certainly most of the poets discussed by Tannacito—aimed to produce change in the status quo. They wrote, Vicinus says, "to arouse and focus social tension in order to channel it toward specific political actions." By "clarifying" economic, social, and political relations between working people and those who held power, these artists helped to "shape individual and class consciousness" and to "imbue a sense of class solidarity that encouraged working people to fight for social and political equality" (Vicinus, pp. 1–3). Tannacito shows how miner poets accomplished such goals: poems of "praise," for example, "commemorate the heroic deeds of model individuals or important past struggles from which the community of workers takes its lessons." Other poems aimed to inspire workers to struggle in particular ways at specific moments. In general, the miner poets and "their allies produced poems for themselves about the realities they shared"—oppression by bosses, common work, the militia, scabs, and a heritage of struggle (Tannacito, pp. 2,3).

The fundamental points here are that "artists" and "audiences" shared a reality, a similar set of experiences and outlooks on the world. They saw artistic production within the context of that shared experience, the world here and now. Art was not a means of lifting people outside the world in which they lived, or a means of producing "catharsis" and thus achieving "stasis" (if art ever does produce whatever these are). Rather, it was a means of making working people conscious of their world and actions within it, of extending their experiences of that world, indeed of enlarging the world they could experience. Thus, even as sophisticated and artful an example of working-class fiction as Tillie Olsen's "Tell Me a Riddle" is directed to the problem of inspiring a new generation with the values, hopes and images that directed the actions of an earlier generation and that lie buried under forty years of daily struggle. Theories about the effects of art remain highly problematic, to be sure; I mention them here not to dispute them but to suggest that Aristotelian and other traditional notions will not be helpful in approaching working-class literature. Looking for the timeless and transcendent, for contemplation as an end, for metaphysical complexity of language, and for pastel ironies of tone can only obscure or demean the objectives and excellence of working-class art.

The next step, after developing a theory for an area of art, is to assemble examples and compile bibliographies. This work has begun to some extent for working-class literature in general, but rather little has been done with working-class women's literature. Appendix A lists the bibliographies I have come upon that will be helpful to anyone working in this area. But a word of warning is necessary: searching for examples of *women's* art in most of these bibliographies, like searching in collections, will be frustrating and slow. For example, the massive bibliography of German working-class songs assembled by a collective under the leadership of Inge Lammel lists perhaps a dozen songs by women in over two thousand entries. David Madden's *Proletarian Writers of the Thirties* (Carbondale: Southern Illinois Univ. Press, 1968), while it contains interesting background analyses, includes no woman writer as a subject—or, for that matter, as an author. The important collection *Folklore from the Working Folk of America* (ed. Tristram P. Coffin and Hennig Cohen [Garden City, N.Y.: Anchor-Doubleday, 1973]) focuses on men and presents women primarily as witches, running with wolves, and the like. Even collections from socialist nations provide little help; *Para un mundo amasado por los trabajadores,* selected by Roberto Retamar (La Habana: Editorial de Arte y Literatura, 1973) contains only works by and about men. The compilation of inclusive, annotated bibliographies is thus a priority, as is the writing of descriptive articles. A significant number of works deserve to be reprinted, but there are many, even by individual working-class women writers of the recent past, for which we must first locate copies.

Republication and fresh consideration of a small number of working-class American women fiction writers from the 1920s and 1930s (as well as from more recent times) are, in fact, under way. Harriette Arnow's *The Dollmaker* generally remains in print, and other works by Arnow are becoming available. Arno Press has republished two of Josephine Herbst's novels in the expensive series edited by Elizabeth Hardwick, and Elinor Langer's critical biography of Herbst will be out in 1983, as will a Feminist Press edition of one of her novels. Zora Neale Hurston, none of whose major works was available until quite recently, is the subject of a fine biography by Robert Hemenway (Urbana: Univ. of Illinois Press, 1977); and her best novel, *Their Eyes Were Watching God*, has also been reprinted (Urbana: Univ. of Illinois Press, 1978), as has her folklore classic, *Mules and Men* (Bloomington: Indiana Univ. Press, 1978). A Zora Neale Hurston reader, *I Love Myself When I Am Laughing*, is available from the Feminist Press (Old Westbury, N.Y., 1979). Edith Summers Kelley's *Weeds* and *The Devil's Hand* were originally reprinted by the Southern Illinois University Press (Carbondale, Ill., 1972, 1974), and the former is being reprinted by the Feminist Press (1982). West End Press has reissued a number of works by Meridel LeSueur, who is still writing; the Feminist Press will issue a LeSueur Reader, *Ripening*, in 1982. Agnes Smedley's *Daughter of Earth* (1927; rpt. Old Westbury, N.Y.: Feminist, 1973) has been in print now for a few years, as are a collection of her writings on Chinese women (Feminist, 1976) and her biography of Chu Teh (*The Great Road* [New York: Monthly Review, 1956]). Also, Jan and Steve MacKinnon are well advanced in their biography of Smedley. Two volumes by Anzia Yezierska, *Bread Givers* (New York: Persea, 1975) and *The Open Cage: An Anzia Yezierska Collection*, ed. Alice Kessler Harns (New York: Persea, 1979), are now in print. And of course, there is Tillie Olsen, the source for much of what we have learned about working-class literature—especially that by women—and the author of classics like *Tell Me a Riddle* (New York: Dell, 1960) and *Yonnondio* (New York: Delacorte, 1974). She remains a fount of inspiration and information.

While a few books by other working-class women fiction writers of the 1920s and 1930s (e.g., Tess Slesinger and Myra Page) are in print here and there, little has been done on most. Such writers include Sarah Henry Atherton, Sanora Bobb, Catherine Brody, Olive Tilford Dargan (Fielding Burke), Lallah S. Davidson, Josephine Johnson, Margerie Latimer, Josephine Lawrence, Grace Lumpkin, Grace McDonald, Ruth McKenney, Page and Slesinger, Anna Louise Strong, Gladys

Taber, Mary Heaton Vorse, Clara Weatherwax, Leane Zugsmith; these women were most prominent during the period in which left-wing literature flourished in the United States. Less is known about the women writers of a generation or two earlier who were concerned with the lives of working people, although they themselves seldom had working-class origins. In listing these I cite only a typical book or two for each: Estelle Baker (*The Rose Door,* 1912), Zoë Beckley (*A Chance to Live,* 1918), Helen Campbell (*Miss Melinda's Opportunity,* 1886), Florence Converse (*Children of Light,* 1912), Grace MacGowan Cooke (*The Grapple,* 1905), Amanda Douglas (*Hope Mills,* 1880), Mary Hallock Foote (*Coeur d'Alene,* 1894), Susan Glaspel (*The Visioning,* 1911; Glaspel continued to write fiction and drama well into the 1930s and was a significant figure in the *Masses* and *Liberator* as well as in the Provincetown Playhouse groups), Josephine Conger Kaneko (*A Little Sister of the Poor,* 1909), Myra Kelly (*Little Aliens*, 1910; *Little Citizens*, 1904), Alice Robbins (*Uncle Tom's Tenement,* 1886), Katherine M. Root (*The Stranger at the Hearth*, 1916), Vida Scudder (*A Listener in Babel*, 1903; more of a socialist discussion book than a novel, but fascinating nonetheless); Charlotte Teller (*The Cage*, 1907), and Marie Van Vorst (*Amanda of the Mill,* 1905). Among the interesting books that male authors have written about working-class women—apart from those by Dreiser, Crane, and Sinclair—are Arthur Bullard's *Comrade Yetta* (1913) and Reginald Wright Kauffman's *The House of Bondage* (1910). Not all these books are important works of fiction by any means, nor indeed are all sympathetic to working people, but they do cast light on the lives of workers in the early 1900s and on attitudes toward the working class. Given our inclusive definition of working-class literature, these books need to be reassessed.

Two earlier writers of considerable interest, Rebecca Harding Davis and Elizabeth Stuart Phelps Ward, have recently received attention in articles and dissertations. But only Davis' *Life in the Iron Mills* (1861; rpt. Feminist, 1972), which has an important afterword by Tillie Olsen, and Phelps Ward's *Story of Avis* (1879; rpt. New York: Arno, 1977), concerned with a woman artist not of the working-class, are readily available. Phelps's fascinating industrial novel, *The Silent Partner,* remains largely unknown, though it is, as Rideout suggests (App. A), the first American work of fiction after *Life in the Iron Mills* to treat a factory woman's life sympathetically and realistically. *The Silent Partner* is of great historical interest because it antedates most theoreticians in suggesting the importance of cross-class organizing of women; indeed, it implies that working women are organized less by the labor movement as such than by other women. Davis and Phelps are not, to be sure, women of the working class, but they are, as women, distinctively sensitive to working-class lives.

A rich and largely unexplored source of short working-class fiction is provided by the many labor, radical, and immigrant magazines and newspapers, particularly those of the decades immediately before and after the turn of the century. Most such periodicals that were published in English in the United States are listed in Black and Goldwater (see App. A). But there is also much in non-English-language journals and newspapers. Norma Fain Pratt has examined the work of Yiddish women writers (e.g., Celia Drapkin, Anna Margolin, Kadya Molodovski, Ester Schumiatcher, Rachel Holtman, Malcha Lee, Sara Barkin, and Aida Glazer) in periodicals like *Zukunft, Freiheit,* and *Frei arbeter shtime* (Norma Fain Pratt, "Culture and Politics: Yiddish Women Writers, 1900–1940," Jewish Studies Association Convention, Boston, 1978). Similar work could be done for other immigrant groups and with working-class publications from centers like Chicago, Milwaukee, and Minneapolis. (Tannacito provides a useful model, although he deals almost entirely with men.) The working-class world has, after all, never been restricted to "our fathers," however much foremothers have been ignored and submerged.

As one might expect, socialist countries, along with Finland and Sweden, have made more efforts to collect working-class fiction, songs, and poetry than have other countries, although women are not especially well represented in the anthologies I have located. For British working-class fiction, I know of no study equivalent to Martha Vicinus', which concentrates on ballads, broadsides, music-hall songs, and working-class poetry. But it is likely that in Britain, as in the United States, most such work is issued by feminist and radical journals and publishing houses and has simply not yet found its way into libraries here.

Autobiographies that reflect working-class life are a rich source of information. To be sure, many autobiographies, especially those by white women, were written after the authors had moved into other class circumstances. But taken as a whole, autobiographies constitute a significant body of working-class women's literature. I know of no comprehensive study of such works or even an adequate bibliography that includes both black and white women's autobiographies, much less those by women from other countries or those still in manuscript. Brigane, Fine, and Williams (App. A) provide useful basic bibliographies, which include such categories as slave narratives and immigrant autobiographies. Only a handful of prominent labor and radical organizers—"Mother" Mary Harris Jones, Emma Goldman, and Elizabeth Gurley Flynn—have published autobiographies, but many others probably exist in manuscript. There are at least three collections of interesting short autobiographies of British working-class people: *The Annals of Labor: Autobiographies of British Working-Class People, 1820–1920* (ed. John Burnett [Bloomington: Indiana Univ. Press, 1974]);[8] *Life as We Have Known It, by Cooperative Working Women* (ed. Margaret L. Davies, intro. Virginia Woolf, 1931; rpt. London: Virago, 1977); *Working Days: Being Personal Records of Sixteen Working Men and Women, Written by Themselves* (ed. Margaret A. Pollock [London: J. Cape, 1926]). A volume called *Women at Work* (Chicago: Quadrangle, 1972) includes both Dorothy Richardson's *The Long Day: The Story of a New York Working Girl* and Elinor Langer's *Inside the New York Telephone Company.* Probably, similar volumes, especially from the 1920s and 1930s, can be found in working-class libraries in English-speaking countries and elsewhere.

No comprehensive book about working-class women's songs and poems exists, nor is there any unified collection of them. I use the words "comprehensive" and "unified" to signify two basic requirements for work in this area. The first has to do with bringing together black and white working-class materials. Almost all writing produced by African-Americans is, by any definition, working-class literature: most of the authors have working-class origins, and their subjects and audiences are generally working-class people like themselves. Although some important collections of folk songs—notably those by socialist artists and collectors—do acknowledge that black literature is working-class literature, few secondary works in this area consider songs and poems of black and white working-class women together. The reason, in part, is that the two have different musical traditions: the black folk songs are largely "sorrow songs," or "spirituals," and the blues; the white songs are "country" and British-derived ballads. But separate treatment has obscured the commonalities of female experience as well as the interactions of the two traditions.

The second requirement is to integrate "folk," or "popular," songs with "high-culture" poetry. The two are almost invariably considered distinct. Most collections of women's poetry (with a few exceptions like Louise Bernikow, ed., *The World Split Open* [New York: Vintage, 1974]) ignore blues singers and songwriters like Aunt Molly Jackson. And while serious books on music carefully consider African-American influences on Western composers, starting with Dvorak, few books on formal poetry make even a gesture in that direction. For working-class women's art, such a separation is particularly harmful, whether one is talking of literature or the plastic and visual arts. Women of the past, generally excluded from formal schools and training, created works of art with what one might call "nonacademic" media like quilting, embroidery, and cutouts—works of art that were also useful in their daily lives.[9] Similarly, many women, especially those of working-class origins, were not familiar with academic traditions and academic forms in literature (e.g., the sonnet and blank verse) and used what was familiar or what came readily to hand—like songs that they learned from their grandmothers or in church, on the picket line, at quilting bees, or at other rituals of communal female experience. Such literature, which we generally designate as "song," must be read and studied together with the more academic or high-culture forms for which we usually reserve the term "poetry." And this union should be made *not* simply to show how, for example, Emily Dickinson transcends the banality of consolatory verse and tombstone poetry; rather, we need to become aware of the hierarchy of the categories themselves. Approaching works primarily in terms of their genre may provide the critic with useful, or at least convenient, lines of demarcation. But if we are interested less in literary typology and more in what literature reveals to us about the lives of women, and of working-class women in particular, then this approach is not useful. It implicitly places more value on the kinds of experiences with which "poetry" deals and the kinds of language (and the people who use it) in which it is expressed. Further, the categorization fragments what is continuous and distinctive in female experience, at least in Western societies, regardless of class—for example, labor that is undervalued or trivialized, the ever-threatening union of sexuality and childbearing, the power and limits of "sisterhood," the anger and waste in keeping one's "place." Further, working-class women's literature—by dealing with such concerns as work and especially work for wages, organizing with other women, and the fear of desertion and physical violence—completes the picture of women's lives that most bourgeois forms show only in fragments. Such female experiences, their commonalities and class-based distinctions, come into focus best when we base our work on women's historical reality rather than on the literary distinctions created primarily by male and bourgeois critics.

A "comprehensive" view of working-class women's poetry in the United States thus encompasses songs and more formal verse from both black and white traditions. We specifically need to reexamine the formal, often left-wing working-class poets. The names, though not generally the work, of a few such women, like Genevieve Taggard, are familiar to scholars, but others have been quite lost—for example, Lola Ridge, Hazel Hall, and Sarah N. Cleghorn. The major sources for studying their work are back files of such left-wing periodicals as *Masses, Liberator, Anvil, New Masses,* and *Mainstream* (see, e.g., Jayne Loader's bibliography). With the exception of *May Days,* edited by Taggard, anthologies of women's poetry have not included verse called "Comrade Jesus" (Cleghorn) or "Buttonholes" (Hall). Among the poets of "song" whose writing (or, in a few cases, interpreting) needs serious consideration are "Sis" Cunningham, Aretha Franklin, Sarah Ogan Gunning, Vera Hall, Billie Holliday, Mahalia Jackson, Aunt Molly Jackson, Ma Rainey, Florence Reece, Malvina Reynolds, Jean Ritchie, Bessie Smith, and Ella May Wiggins. For some black singers of the blues and gospel music, reasonably accurate bibliographies—or, more properly, discographies—exist, and often the text of at least one version of a song is in print. It is difficult to know whether even that much attention has been given to the work of women of the labor movement in the United States, although the collection *Hard Hitting Songs for Hard-Hit People* (App. C) does include works by writer-singers like Jackson and Gunning. I have not been able to locate any systematic treatment, like Alan Lomax' book on Vera Hall, of influential artists like the late Malvina Reynolds or "Sis" Cunningham.

I have included as Appendix C a list of sources for working-class women's poetry. This list is by no means definitive. In the first place, many songbooks are quite ephemeral, and the ones I list are those I happened on in the libraries to which I had access; different lists could probably be compiled from the holdings of libraries on the West Coast and in the South and from the personal collections of collector-activists like Mary Elizabeth Barnicle. Second, I have not included books contained in Vicinus' extensive bibliography, many of which I could not check (since they are available only in Britain) to see if they contain women's work. Finally, while extensive collections of working-class poetry and song have been published in Europe, particularly in the socialist countries (and some are included in App. C), these works are only erratically available in American libraries and, in some cases, the gender of writers cannot be ascertained.

In certain respects, bibliography will be the most useful resource to scholars working in this field. I have therefore included a number of appendixes as a means for sharing with readers what my own research has turned up. I have already mentioned Appendix A (a bibliography of bibliographies) and Appendix C (collections of working-class women's poetry). Appendix B lists collections of both prose and poetry, including some that consist primarily of "documents." Appendix D shows secondary works on working-class women's poetry and song, including a number of biographies of black women artists, a few major analyses of the blues and other expressions of black women's art, as well as the rather rare writings concerned with white working-class songwriters. Appendix E is a very selective list of secondary works that concern or can help inform the study of working-class women's literature. Finally, Appendix F is an even more selective list of magazines that publish, with some regularity, work of interest in this area. Wherever possible, I have examined the books to see whether they include works by or about women.

Notes

1. A most useful discussion of the distinctions between the working class and the bourgeoisie is that of Raymond Williams in *Culture and Society, 1780–1950* (New York: Harper, 1966), pp. 324–33.
2. See Martha Vicinus, *The Industrial Muse* (New York: Barnes, 1974): "What we call literature, and what we teach, is what the middle class—and not the working class—produced. Our definitions of literature and our canons of taste are class bound; we currently exclude street literature, songs, hymns, dialect and oral story telling, but they were the most popular forms used by the working class" (p. 1).
3. Note that the study of folk literature was once clearly a part of the literature and language profession; indeed, it was a field considered "appropriate" for female scholars. Louise Pound, the first female president of the Modern Language Association, specialized in the study of songs and ballads, and Mary Elizabeth Barnicle, an early life member of the MLA, was an important folklore collector and political activist.
4. Lawrence W. Levine, *Black Culture and Black Consciousness: Afro-American Folk Thought from Slavery to Freedom* (Oxford: Oxford Univ. Press, 1977), pp. 25–30.
5. See "The Burning Struggle: The Civil Rights Movement," an interview with Bernice Johnson Reagon, *Radical America,* 12 (Nov.–Dec. 1978), 18–20.
6. Dan Tannacito, "Poetry of the Colorado Miners: 1903–1905," *The Radical Teacher,* 15 (1980): "But the historical reality is that workers, like the Colorado miners, wrote poetry in order to share and express their feelings about their experiences as a class. They were creators of their culture as well as creators of their society" (p. 1).
7. Zoltan Kodaly, for example, wrote an entire opera, "The Spinning Room," based on songs exchanged among or sung to women working at their looms and spindles. I have come on pictures of women singing at quilting bees, but I have seen no detailed exposition of what they were singing.
8. In a useful review of this book, Catherine Gallagher discusses stylistic elements used by these and other working-class writers and the problem of an excessive concern, on the part of professionals, for the work lives of working-class people. See "Workers," *University Publishing*, 5 (Summer 1978), 1, 24.
9. See C. Kurt Dewhurst, Betty MacDowell, and Marsha MacDowell, *Artists in Aprons: Folk Art by American Women* (New York: Dutton, in association with the Museum of American Folk Art, 1979).

Appendix A

The following works either constitute or contain bibliographies useful to the study of working-class women's literature. Addresses are given for little-known publishers.

AMS Press, Inc., *Catalogue of the Labor Movement in Fiction and Non-fiction,* c. 1975. A useful publisher's catalog.

Anderson, Eleanor C. *A List of Novels and Stories about Workers.* New York: Woman's Press, 1938. Brief but helpful.

Arno Press. *Books by and about Women,* 1977. Publisher's catalog of several series of reprints. Arno also has a useful catalog of reprints dealing with American labor.

Batchelder, Eleanor, comp. *Plays by Women: A Bibliography.* New York: Womanbooks (201 W. 92nd St., NY 10025), 1977.

Black, Henry. *Radical Periodicals—Their Place in the Library.* Mena, Ark.: Commonwealth Coll., 1937. A brief essay justifying inclusion of such periodicals in library collections; the list of periodicals, with brief descriptions, includes some not listed in Goldwater's later bibliography.

Block, Adrienne Fried, and Carol Neuls-Bates. *A Bibliography of Women's Music.* Westport, Conn.: Greenwood, 1979.

Brignano, Russel C. *Black Americans in Autobiography: An Annotated Bibliography of Autobiographies and Autobiographical Books Written since the Civil War.* Durham, N.C.: Duke Univ. Press, 1974.

Chatham Book Seller (38 Maple St., Chatham, NJ 07928). *Radical Novels: Poetry and Drama in America,* No. 8; *The Political Novel in America,* No. 30; *Black Literature,* Nos. 34, 40; *Radical Novels, etc. in America,* No. 35; *Women's Rights and Liberation,* No. 43; and *Socialism, Communism, Anarchism, Pacifism in the U.S.,* No. 44. These catalogs not only list books for sale but record items not found in major libraries.

Collector's Exchange, comp. Frank Girard. This publication includes a list of periodicals, an index to articles, assorted notes of interest to collectors and anthologists. Write c/o Frank Girard, 4568 Richmond, NW, Grand Rapids, MI 49504.

Daims, Diva, and Janet Grimes. *Towards a Feminist Tradition: An Annotated Bibliography of Novels in English by Women, 1891–1920.* New York: Garland, 1980.

Dellinger, Harold R. "Notes on the Midwestern Literary Rebellion of the Thirties," *West End,* 5 (Summer 1978), 45–48. A genealogical and bibliographical essay, mainly about important left magazines of the 1930s.

Fine, David M. *The City, the Immigrant, and American Fiction, 1880–1920.* Metuchen, N.J.: Scarecrow, 1977. Useful bibliography of novels and stories, a number by forgotten women.

Foner, Philip S. *American Labor Songs of the Nineteenth Century.* Urbana: Univ. of Illinois Press, 1975. The excellent bibliography in this important book includes the locations of rare works.

Franklin, H. Bruce. *The Victim as Criminal and Artist: Literature from the*

American Prison. New York: Oxford Univ. Press, 1978. Includes works from slavery life and black life in general as well as works from prison.

George, Zelma. "A Guide to Negro Music: An Annotated Bibliography of Negro Folk and Art Music by Negro Composers. . . ." Diss. New York Univ. 1953. Mainly concerned with music, but helpful nonetheless.

Goldwater, Walter. *Radical Periodicals in America, 1890–1950.* New Haven: Yale Univ. Press, 1964. A list of 321 radical periodicals—dates, places published, editors, etc. Needs to be supplemented with black periodicals.

Greenway, John. *American Folksongs of Protest.* Philadelphia: Univ. of Pennsylvania Press, 1953. Apart from having an important text, the book contains a vital bibliography.

Grimes, Janet, and Diva Daims. *Novels in English by Women, 1891–1920: A Preliminary Checklist.* New York: Garland, 1980.

Guide to Working-Class History. Somerville, Mass.: New England Free Press, c. 1977. Includes novels, oral history, etc.

Humez, Jean. "Women Working in the Arts: A Bibliography and Resource List." Mimeographed, Women's Studies Program, Boston: Univ. of Massachusetts, c. 1976.

Janes, Louis. *Fiction for the Working Man, 1830–1850: A Study of the Literature Produced for the Working Classes in Early Victorian Urban England.* London: Oxford Univ. Press, 1963. Contains a list of penny-issue novels.

Jones, Hettie. *Big Star Fallin' Mama: Five Women in Black Music.* New York: Viking, 1974. Useful brief bibliography and discography and a list of notable women in black music.

Ladyslipper Music (Box 3124, Durham, NC 27705). *Catalogue and Review.* Extensive list of records, tapes, etc., by women singers and some writers.

Lammel, Inge, et al. *Bibliographie der deutschen Arbeiterliedblätter, 1844–1945.* Leipzig: Deutscher Verlag für Musik, 1975. Massive list of 2,000 songs, almost none by women.

Loader, Jayne. *Women on the Left, 1906–1941: A Bibliography of Primary Resources, University of Michigan Papers in Women's Studies,* 2 (Sept. 1975), 9–82. Contains much useful information on journals, reportage, autobiographical writings, poems, and the like.

McBrearty, James G. *American Labor History and Comparative Labor Movements.* Tucson: Univ. of Arizona Press, 1973. Has a section devoted to a list of novels, which is uneven but helpful.

Michigan Dept. of Education, State Library Services. *Michigan Women: Biographies, Autobiographies and Reminiscences.* Lansing, Mich., 1975. A bibliography.

Ogden, Jean Carter. *Annotated List of Labor Plays.* Rev. ed. New York: American Labor Education Service, 1945.

Porter, Dorothy B. *North American Negro Poets: A Bibliographical Check-List of Their Writing (1760–1944).* 1945; rpt. New York: Franklin, 1963.

Prestridge, Virginia W. *The Worker in American Fiction.* Champaign: Univ. of Illinois, 1954. Inst. of Labor and Industrial Relations. The most extensive bibliographical work on the subject; describes fiction that, from any point of view, has "authentic working-class problems and conditions as the central theme."

Reuben, Elaine, and Deborah Rosenfelt. "Affirmative Interactions in Literature and Criticism: Some Suggestions for Reading and Research" (Mimeographed). MLA Commission on the Status of Women in the Profession, Dec. 1974. Among other items this contains Tillie Olsen's invaluable reading lists from the *Women's Studies Newsletter* (Vol. 1, No. 1 [1972], Nos. 3, 4 [1973]; Vol. 2, No. 1 [1974]); Sonny San Juan's "Provisional Listing for Third-World Literature/Culture Courses," a bibliography from the *Radical Caucus Newsletter,* 10 (July–August 1973); and the useful (for background) but almost entirely male reading list from an M.A. course—Literature and Society, 1910–1945 from the same *Radical Caucus Newsletter.*

Rideout, Walter. *The Radical Novel in the U.S., 1900–1945.* New Haven: Yale Univ. Press, 1956. The bibliography, arranged chronologically, is one of the most helpful.

Skowronski, Jo Ann. *Women in American Music: A Bibliography.* Metuchen, N.J.: Scarecrow, 1978. Annotated bibliography of secondary sources—not of collections or anthologies—covering 1776–1976 and including every possible subject relating to women in American music.

Soltow, Martha Jane, and Mary K. Wery. *American Women and the Labor Movement: An Annotated Bibliography.* Metuchen, N.J.: Scarecrow, 1976. Useful for background and for bibliography of archival sources.

Steiner-Scott, Elizabeth, and Elizabeth Pearce Wagle. *New Jersey Women, 1770–1970: A Bibliography.* Rutherford, N.J.: Fairleigh Dickinson Univ. Press, 1978.

Vicinus, Martha. *The Industrial Muse.* New York: Barnes, 1974. The bibliography, which, like the text, is extraordinarily rich and comprehensive, may be considered definitive for the British work it covers.

Williams, Ora. *American Black Women in the Arts and Social Sciences: A Bibliographical Survey.* Revised and expanded ed. Metuchen, N.J.: Scarecrow, 1978. The basic bibliography on the subject, with lists of other bibliographies, anthologies, novels, autobiographies, poems, etc.

Women's Soul Publishing, Inc. (Box 11646, Milwaukee, WI 53211). *My Sister's Song: Discography of Women-Made Music.* 1975. Mainly folk and popular, but separate sections on jazz, blues, etc.

Appendix B

The following books contain prose (some of it more documentary than imaginative) and/or poetry by working-class women.

Baxandall, Roslyn, Linda Gordon, and Susan Reverby. *America's Working Women: A Documentary History, 1600 to the Present.* New York: Vintage-Random, 1976.

Blassingame, John W., ed. *Slave Testimony.* Baton Rouge: Louisiana State Univ. Press, 1977.

Cole, Josephine, and Grace Silver, comps. *Socialist Dialogues and Recitations.* Chicago: Kerr, 1913.

Conroy, Jack, and Curt Johnson. *Writers in Revolt: The Anvil Anthology, 1933–40.* New York: Lawrence Hill, 1973.

Courlander, Harold. *A Treasury of Afro-American Folklore.* New York: Crown, 1976.

Foner, Philip S., ed. *The Factory Girls,* Urbana: Univ. of Illinois Press, 1977.

Handler, Esther, ed. *The Pavement Trial: A Collection of Poetry and Prose from the Allis-Chalmers Picket Lines.* Foreword by Meridel LeSueur. West Allis, Wisc.: Local 248 United Auto Workers, 1946.

Hicks, Granville, et al., ed. *Proletarian Literature in the United States,* New York: International, 1935.

Hoffman, Nancy, and Florence Howe, eds. *Working Women: An Anthology of Stories and Poems.* Old Westbury, N.Y.: Feminist, 1979.

Keating, P. J. *Working-Class Stories of the 1890's.* London: Routledge and Kegan Paul, 1971. No stories by women but a number about them.

Kornbluh, Joyce. *Rebel Voices: An IWW Anthology.* Ann Arbor: Univ. of Michigan Press, 1964.

Lerner, Gerda. *Black Women in White America.* New York: Pantheon, 1972.

———. *The Female Experience—An American Documentary.* Indianapolis: Bobbs-Merrill, 1977.

Loewenberg, James, and Ruth Bogin, eds. *Black Women in Nineteenth Century American Life.* University Park: Pennsylvania State Univ. Press, 1976.

Münchow, Ursula. *Frühe deutsche Arbeiteraubiographie.* Berlin: Akademie–Verlag, 1973.

North, Joseph, ed. *New Masses: An Anthology of the Rebel Thirties.* New York: International, 1969.

Voigtländer, Annie, ed. *Hierzulande, heutzutage: Lyrik, Prosa, Graphik aus dem werkkreis, "Literatur der Arbeitswelt."* Berlin: Aufbau-Verlag, 1975.

Wenzel, Karl Heinz, Marianne Schmidt, and Konrad Schmidt. *Körnchen Gold: Eine Anthologie Schreibender Arbeiter.* Berlin: Tribüne, 1969.

Appendix C

Collections (or articles) containing at least some songs or poems by working-class women writers.

Abelson, Walter. *Songs of Labor.* Newburgh, N.Y.: Paebar, 1947.

Allen, William Francis, Charles Pickard Ware, and Lucy McKim Garrison. *Slave Songs of the United States.* 1867; rpt. Freeport, N.Y.: Books for Libraries, 1971.

Alloy, Evelyn. *Working Women's Music: The Songs and Struggles of Women in the Cotton Mills, Textile Plants, and Needle Trades.* Somerville, Mass.: New England Free Press, 1976.

Althoff, Arneliese, et al. *Für eine andere Deutschstunde, Arbeit und Alltag in neuen Texten.* Ed. Arbeitskreis Progressive Kunst. Oberhausen: Asso Verlag, 1972.

Amalgamated Clothing Workers. *Song Book.* New York, 1940.

Amalgamated Clothing Workers, Local #489. *Picket Line Songs.* Andalusia, Ala., c. 1967.

American Music League. *March and Sing.* New York, 1937.

Arbeiterdichtung: Analysen, Bekenntnisse, Dokumentationen, comp. Österreichischen Gessellschaft für Kulturpolitik. Wuppertal: Hammer, c. 1973.

Arbeiter und Freiheitslieder, No. 1 (1973). Hannover: Arbeiter-Musik-Assoziation.

Bab, Julius. *Arbeiterdichtung.* Berlin: Volksöuhnen-Verlags-und-Vertriebs, 1924.

Balch, Elizabeth. "Songs for Labor," *Survey,* 31 (1914), 408–12, 422–28.

Benet, William Rose, and Norman Cousins. *The Poetry of Freedom.* New York: Random, 1945.

Bogorad, Miriam, et al., comps. *Songs for America.* New York: Workers Library, 1939.

Bold, Alan. *The Penguin Book of Socialist Verse.* Baltimore: Penguin, 1970.

Busch, Ernst, ed. *Internationale Arbeiterlieder.* Berlin: "Lied der Zeit" Musikverlag, 1953.

Carpenter, E. *Chants of Labor: A Song-book of the People.* London: 1897; rpt. Allen and Unwin, 1922.

Cheyney, Ralph, ed. *Banners of Brotherhood: An Anthology of Social Vision Verse.* North Montpelier, Vt.: Driftwood, 1933.

Clark, Thomas Curtis, comp. *Poems of Justice.* New York: Willett, Clark and Colby, 1929.

Collinson, Francis. *The Traditional and National Music of Scotland.* London: Routledge and Kegan Paul, 1966.

Commonwealth Labor Songs: A Collection of Old and New Songs for the Use of Labor Unions. Mena, Ark.: Commonwealth Coll., 1938.

Conroy, Jack, and Ralph Cheyney, eds. *Unrest, 1931.* New York: H. Harrison, 1931.

Davis, N. Brian. *The Poetry of the Canadian People, 1720–1920: 200 Years of Hard Work.* Toronto: N C Press, 1976.

Denisoff, R. Serge. *Sing A Song of Social Significance.* Bowling Green, Ohio: Bowling Green Univ. Popular Press, 1972.

Druskin, Mikhail Semenovich. *Russkaia revoliutsionnaia pesnia.* Moscow, 1954.

Every-day Songs for Labor Festivals. London: Labour Party, n.d.

Federal Music Project. *Folk Songs from East Kentucky.* Washington, D.C.: Works Project Administration, c. 1939.

Folksongs of Peggy Seeger. New York: Oak, n.d.

Folk Songs of the Southern Appalachians (as Sung by Jean Ritchie). New York: Oak, n.d.

Foner, Philip S. *American Labor Songs of the Nineteenth Century.* Urbana: Univ. of Illinois Press, 1975.

Fowke, Edith, and Joe Glazer. *Songs of Work and Freedom.* New York: Dover, 1973.

Friedman, Perry, ed. *Hör zu, Mister Bilbo: Lieder aus der Amerikanischen Arbeiterbewegnung, 1860–1950.* Berlin: Rütten und Loening, 1962.

Friedrich, Wolfgang, ed. *Im Klassenkampf: Deutsche revolutionäre Lieder und Gedichte aus der zweiten Hälfte des 19 Jahrhunderts.* Halle: Verlag Sprache und Literatur, 1962.

Glazer, Tom, ed. *Songs of Peace, Freedom and Protest.* New York: David McKay, 1970.

Heisden, Marcel Charles Antoon van der, comp. *Werkmansbrekje.* Utrecht: Het Spectrum, 1971.

Heller, H. *Oesterreichisches Proletarier-Liederbuch.* Wien: Wiener Volksbuchhandlung, c. 1900.

Highlander Folk School. *Songbook.* Monteagle, Tenn.: Highlander Folk School, 1943.

———. *Songs: Labor, Folk, War.* Monteagle, Tenn.: Highlander Folk School, 1944.

Hille, Waldemar, ed. *The People's Song Book.* New York: Oak, various dates.

Industrial Workers of the World. *Songs of the Workers (To Fan the Flames of Discontent).* Chicago: IWW, many dates and editions.

International Ladies Garment Workers Union. *Dixie Union Songs.* Atlanta, Ga.: ILGWU, n.d.

———. *Everybody Sings.* New York: ILGWU, 1942.

———. *Let's Sing.* New York: ILGWU, 1934.

Köpping, Walter, ed. *Unter Tage, über Tage: Gedichte aus der Arbetswelt unserer Tage.* Frankfurt a.M.: Europäische Verlags-anstalt, 1966.

Kriselkreisel: Lieder und Texte. Berlin: Arbeitskreis Musik im Klassenkampf, 1974.

Kuhnke, Klaus, comp. *Lieder der Arbeiterklasse, 1919–1933.* Arhensburg: Damokle Verlag, 1971.

Kürbisch, Friedrich G., comp. *Anklage und Botschaft: Die lyrische Aussage der Arbeiter seit 1900.* Hannover: Dietz, 1969.

———. *Arbeiterdichtung: Versuch einer Standortbestimmung.* Wien: Sozialistiche Bildungszentrale, c. 1972.

Lazarus, Emma. *Emma Lazarus: Selections from Her Poetry and Prose,* ed. M. U. Schappes. New York: Book League, Jewish People's Fraternal Order of the International Workers Order, 1947.

Leuchtkugeln: Ernste und heitere Vortragsgedichte für Arbeiterfeste. Berlin: Verlag Vorwärts, 1905.

Levenstein, Adolf, comp. *Arbeiter—Philosophen und Dichter.* Berlin: E. Frowe, 1909.

Lloyd, Albert Lancaster. *Come All Ye Bold Miners: Ballads and Songs of the Coalfields.* London: Lawrence and Wishart, 1952.

Lomax, Alan. *American Ballads and Folk Songs.* New York: Macmillan, 1934.

———. *The Folk Songs of North America.* Garden City, N.Y.: Doubleday, 1960.

———. *Our Singing Country.* New York: Macmillan, 1941.

Lomax, Alan, Woody Guthrie, and Pete Seeger. *Hard Hitting Songs for Hard-Hit People.* New York: Oak, 1967.

Lowenfels, Walter, ed. *For Neruda, for Chile: An International Anthology.* Boston: Beacon, 1975.

MacColl, Ewan, ed. *The Shuttle and the Cage: Industrial Folk Ballads.* London: Workers' Music Association, 1954.

MacColl, Ewan, and Peggy Seeger. *I'm a Freeborn Man and Other Original Ballads and Songs.* New York: Oak, 1968.

Marcus, Shmuel, ed. *An Anthology of Revolutionary Poetry.* New York: Active Press, 1929.

Mühle, Hans, ed. *Das Lied der Arbeit, selbstzeugnisse der schaffenden.* Gotha: Leopold Klotz Verlag, 1930.

———. *Das proletarische Schicksal.* Gotha: Leopold Klotz Verlag, 1929.

Münchow, Ursula, ed. *Stimme des Vortrupps: Proletarische Laienlyrik, 1914 bis 1945.* Berlin: Dietz Verlag, 1961.

Nechaev, Egor Efimovich. *U istokov russkoi proletarskoi poezil.* Leningrad, 1965.

Offenburg, Kurt, comp. *Arbeiterdichtung der Gegenwart.* Frankfurt a.M.: Mitteland-Verlag, 1925.

Olivier, Paul. *Les Chansons de Métiers.* Paris: Charpentier et Fasquelle, 1910.

Palmer, Roy, ed. *Poverty Knock: A Picture of Industrial Life in the 19th Century through Songs, Ballads, and Contemporary Accounts.* New York: Cambridge Univ. Press, 1974.

Poslední bitva uzplála: Vybor z veršů a písní dělnických bás níku. Praha: Československý spisovatel, 1951.

Reynolds, Malvina. *Little Boxes and Other Handmade Songs.* New York: Oak, 1965.

———. *The Malvina Reynolds Songbook.* Berkeley, Calif.: Schroder Music, various editions and dates.

———. *There's Music in the Air.* Berkeley, Calif.: Schroder Music, n.d.

Riddle, Almeda. *A Singer and Her Songs.* Baton Rouge: Louisiana State Univ. Press, 1970.

Salzman, Jack, and Leo Zanderer. *Social Poetry of the 1930's: A Selection.* New York: Burt Franklin, 1978.

Schramm, Godehard, and Bernhard Wenger, comps. *Werkkreis Literatur der Arbetswelt.* Frankfurt a.N.: Fischer-Taschenbuch-Verlag, 1974.

Schwachhofer, Rene, and Wilhelm T. Kaczyk, comps. *Spiegel unseres Werdens: Mensch und Arbeit in der deutschen Dichtung von Goethe bis Brecht.* Berlin: Verlag der Nation, 1969.

Silber, Irwin, ed. *Lift Every Voice! The Second People's Song Book.* New York: People's Artists Publication, c. 1953.

Smith, Lewis Worthington, ed. *Women Poets Today.* New York: George Sully, 1929.

Songs of the Southern School for Workers. Asheville, N.C.: Southern School for Workers, c. 1940.

Taggard, Genevieve, ed. *May Days: An Anthology of Verse from Masses-Liberator.* New York: Boni and Liveright, 1925.

Trask, Willard R. *The Unwritten Song: Poetry of the Primitive and Traditional Peoples of the World.* 2 vols. New York: Macmillan, 1966–67.

Trent, Lucia, and Ralph Cheyney. *America Arraigned! (Poems on Sacco and Vanzetti).* New York: Dean, 1928.

Vi Viltaende: Ukjente nord-norske arbeiderdikt, 1780–1920. Oslo: Pax, 1975.

Vincent, Leopold. *The Alliance and Labor Songster: A Collection of Labor and Comic Songs.* 1891; rpt. New York: Arno, 1975.

White, Newman I., ed. *American Negro FolkSongs.* Cambridge: Harvard Univ. Press, 1928.

Woolridge, Dorothy, comp. *The Poetry of Toil: An Anthology of Poems.* London: Faber, 1926.

The Worker Looks at the Stars. Vinyard Shore, Mass.: n.p., 1927.

Yearsley, Ann (a milkwoman of Bristol). *Poems, on Several Occasions.* London: T. Cadell, 1785.

———. *Poems, on Various Subjects.* London: Robinson, 1787.

Appendix D

Secondary books and articles mainly on working-class women's songs and poetry.

Albertson, Chris. *Bessie.* New York: Stein and Day, 1972.

Armstrong, Toni L., and Sally G. Newbury. "Women's Songbooks: An Introduction and Survey." *Paid My Dues,* 3, No. 1 (1978), 34–36.

Baraka, Imamu Amiri (LeRoi Jones). *Blues People.* New York: Morrow, 1963.

Barry, Phillips. "The Factory Girl's Come-All-Ye." *Bulletin of the Folksong Society of the Northeast,* 2 (1931), 12.

Charters, Samuel. *Poetry of the Blues.* New York: Oak, 1963.

Chilton, John. *Billie's Blues: A Survey of Billie Holiday's Career, 1933–1959.* London: Quartet, 1975.

Cunningham, Agnes "Sis." "Sis Cunningham: Song of Hard Times" (as told to Madelaine Belkin Rose). *Ms.,* 2 (March 1974), 29–32.

Denisoff, R. Serge. *Great Day Coming: Folk Music and the American Left.* Urbana: Univ. of Illinois Press, 1971.

Drew, Caroline. "Remember Ella May!" *Equal Justice (Labor Defender),* (Sept. 1930), 181.

Feldman, Eugene P. Romayn. "Union Maid Revisited: The Story of Ella Mae Wiggins." *ABC–TV Hootenanny,* 1, No. 3 (1964), 25–26.

Green, Archie, ed. "Aunt Molly Jackson Memorial Issue." *Kentucky Folklore Record,* 7, No. 4 (1961), 129–75.

Greenway, John. *American Folksongs of Protest.* Philadelphia: Univ. of Pennsylvania Press, 1953.

Harrison, Daphne Duval. "Black Women in the Blues Tradition." In *The Afro-American Woman: Struggles and Images.* Ed. Sharon Harley and Rosalyn Terborg-Penn. Port Washington, N.Y.: Kennikat, 1978.

Heath, Colin. "Bessie Smith: Empress of the Blues." *Heritage,* No. 17 (1970), 2–5; No. 18 (1970), 2–5.

Heilbut, Tony. *The Gospel Sound, Good News and Bad Times.* Garden City, N.Y.: Anchor-Doubleday, 1975.

Higginson, Thomas Wentworth. *Army Life in a Black Regiment.* New York: Macmillan, 1962.

Jackson, Aunt Molly. "I Am from Kentucky Born." *Equal Justice (Labor Defender),* 8 (Jan. 1932), 8.

Japenga, Ann. "Women of the Blues." *Paid My Dues,* No. 5 (1975), 12–14.

Jones, Hettie. *Big Star Fallin' Mama: Five Women in Black Music.* New York: Viking, 1974.

Kahn, Kathy. *Hillbilly Women.* Garden City, N.Y.: Doubleday, 1973.

Korson, George. *Coal Dust on the Fiddle.* Philadelphia: Univ. of Pennsylvania Press, 1943.

Larkin, Margaret. "Ella May's Songs." *Nation,* 9 Oct. 1929, pp. 382–83.

Lomax, Alan. *The Rainbow Sign* (on Vera Hall). New York: Duell, Sloan and Pearce, 1959.

Lovell, John, Jr. *Black Song: The Forge and the Flame*. New York: Macmillan, 1972.
Lynn, Loretta. *Loretta Lynn: Coal Miner's Daughter.* Chicago: Regnery, 1976.
Mitchell, George. *Blow My Blues Away.* Baton Rouge: Louisiana State Univ. Press, 1971.
Monahan, Kathleen. "Women's Songs of the American Labor Movement," Master's thesis Univ. of Pittsburgh, 1975.
———. "Union Maid," *Paid My Dues.* No. 4 (March 1975), 24–26, 36.
Odum, Howard W., and Guy B. Johnson. *Negro Workaday Songs.* 1926; rpt. New York: Negro Univ. Press, 1969.
Oliver, Paul. *Bessie Smith.* New York: Barnes, 1961.
———. *The Meaning of the Blues.* New York: Collier, 1963.
———. *Screening the Blues: Aspects of the Blues Tradition.* London: Cassell, 1968.
———. *The Story of the Blues.* New York: Chilton, 1969.
Ritchie, Jean. *The Singing Family of the Cumberlands.* New York: Oxford Univ. Press, 1955.
Rosen, David M. *Protest Songs in America.* Westlake Village, Calif.: Aware, 1972.
Rushing, Andrea Benton. "Images of Black Women in Afro-American Poetry." In *The Afro-American Woman: Struggles and Images.* Ed. Sharon Harley and Rosalyn Terborg-Penn. Port Washington, N.Y.: Kennikat, 1978.
Russell, Michele. "Slave Codes and Liner Notes." *Radical Teacher*, No. 4 (1977), 1–6.
Ryder, Georgia A. "Black Women in Song: Some Sociocultural Images." *Negro History Bulletin,* 39 (May 1976), 601 ff.
Seeger, Pete. *The Incompleat Folksinger.* New York: Simon, 1972.
Sing Out! 25 (1976), esp. No 1: *Songs of the Labor Struggle,* No. 2: *Songs of American Women,* No. 3: *Music of La Raza—Songs of the Puerto Rican Nation,* and No. 5: *Immigrant Traditions in America.*
Southern, Eileen. *The Music of Black Americans: A History.* New York: Norton, 1971.
Southey, Robert. *The Lives and Works of the Uneducated Poets.* Ed. J. S. Childers. 1831; rpt. London: H. Milford, 1925.
Stanford, Ron. "Which Side Are You On? An Interview with Florence Reece," *Sing Out!* 20, No. 6 (1971), 13–15.
Stewart-Baxter, Derrick. *Ma Rainey and the Classic Blues Singers.* New York: Stein and Day, 1970.
"Successful Women Song-Writers." *Literary Digest,* 13 (Oct. 1917), p. 87.
Watson, Edward A. "Bessie's Blues." *New Letters,* 38 (Winter 1971), 64–70.

Appendix E

Secondary books and articles especially helpful to the study of working-class women's literature.

Adickes, Sandra. "Mind among the Spindles: An Examination of Some of the Journals, Newspapers and Memoirs of the Lowell Female Operatives." *Women's Studies,* 1 (1973) 279–87.

Dundes, Alan. *Mother Wit from the Laughing Barrel: Readings in the Interpretation of Afro-American Folklore.* Englewood Cliffs, N.J.: Prentice-Hall, 1973.

Farrer, Claire R. Introd. to special issue on women in folklore, *Journal of American Folklore,* 88 (Jan.–March 1975).

Fine, David M. *The City, the Immigrant, and American Fiction.* Metuchen, N.J.: Scarecrow, 1977.

Franklin, H. Bruce. *The Victim as Criminal and Artist: Literature from the American Prison.* New York: Oxford Univ. Press, 1978.

Greiner, Bernhard. *Die Literatur der Arbeitswelt in der DDR.* Heidelberg: Quelle und Meyer, 1974.

Hull, Gloria, Patricia Bell Scott, and Barbara Smith, eds. *But Some of Us Are Brave: Black Women's Studies.* Old Westbury, N.Y.: Feminist, 1982.

Levine, Lawrence W. *Black Culture and Black Consciousness: Afro-American Folk Thought from Slavery to Freedom.* New York: Oxford Univ. Press, 1977.

Lipsitz, George. "Working Peoples Music," *Cultural Correspondence,* No. 2 (1976), 15–33.

Ragon, Michel. *Les Ecrivains du peuple: Historique, biographies, critique.* Paris: J. Vignau, 1947.

———. *Histoire de la littérature ouvrière du moyen âge à nos jours.* Paris: Éditions Ouvrières, 1953.

———. *Histoire de la littérature proletarienne en France: Littérature ouvrière, littérature paysanne, littérature d'expression populaire.* Paris: A. Michel, 1974.

Randall, Margaret. "Truth Is a Convincing Answer . . . !" (conversations with three Vietnamese women writers). *Left Curve,* No. 3 (1975), 30–35.

Runnquist, Åke. *Arbetarskildare från Hedevind till Fridell.* Stockholm: Bonnier, 1952.

Tannacito, Dan. "Poetry of the Colorado Miners: 1903–1905." *Radical Teacher,* No. 15 (1980), 1–8.

Unwin, Rayner. *The Rural Muse: Studies in the Peasant Poetry of England.* London: Allen and Unwin, 1957.

Vicinus, Martha. *The Industrial Muse.* New York: Barnes, 1974.

Walker, Alice. "In Search of Our Mother's Gardens: The Creativity of Black Women in the South," *Ms.,* 2 (May 1974), 64–70, 105.

Wertheimer, Barbara. *We Were There: The Story of the Working Women in America.* New York: Pantheon, 1977.

Appendix F

A very selective list of magazines that regularly run material of interest in the study of working-class women's literature.

Frontiers: A Journal of Women's Studies, esp. 2, No. 2 [Summer 1977], on women's oral history.
Paid My Dues: A Journal of Women and Music.
People's Songs. 4 vols., 1946–49.
Radical Teacher, esp. Nos. 4, 6, 10, 15.
Sing Out! esp. 25, Nos. 1, 2, 3, 5.
West End, esp. 5, No. 1 (1978): *Midwest People's Culture Anthology.*

Women in German Language and Literature

Susan L. Cocalis, Kay Goodman, and Sara Lennox

In the field of German, opportunities for research and publishing in women's studies have been limited by the prevailing double standards. Many Germanists, both male and female, have traditionally regarded feminist criticism as a separate and secondary activity and have completely ignored it in making editorial, tenure, and promotion decisions. But this situation is gradually changing. In the past five years, the general recognition accorded the women's movement in America and England has encouraged feminist scholars to challenge the canon of German literature in special sessions at national conferences, in special issues of American scholarly journals, and in their own organizations and publications. These efforts are creating a new awareness of literature about women writers and of feminist criticism within the discipline.

Literary Histories and "Frauenliteratur"

Professional resistance to feminist criticism can be traced to a preconception of German literary scholarship, that women's writing (*Frauenliteratur, Frauendichtung*) is confined to limited, subjective literary forms (short lyric poems, letters, autobiographies, popular romances) and to sentimental or domestic themes that "even women" can master.[1] German literary historians of the nineteenth century

(Schmidt, Treitschke, Hillebrand, Barthel, Gervinus, König) postulated that the literary genres they considered "serious" (the historical novel, the drama, epic poetry, the novella)—genres that form the basis of the literary canon—were beyond the literary and artistic capabilities of women.[2] Hence literary histories either did not mention women poets at all (Gervinus) or classified all women together, regardless of style, genre, and period (Barthel, Weber, Kirchner, Engel, Kluge, Gottschall), so that writers associated with romanticism (Bettina von Arnim), poetic realism (Marie von Ebner-Eschenbach), the *Vormärz* (Fanny Lewald), and popular best-selling literature (Eugenie Marlitt) were arbitrarily condemned to the ranks of a separate, purportedly homogeneous and inferior *Frauenliteratur*.

The only woman the German literary historians exempted from this condemnation was Annette von Droste-Hülshoff, whose style, in contrast to that of other women writers, was described as curt, hard, dry, ironic, powerful, vigorous, and objective and was thus praised as "masculine" (Gottschall, Engel, Leixner, Howald, E. Arnold, Vogt, Barthel) (Brinkler-Gabler, pp. 23–25). Droste-Hülshoff violated current standards of feminine behavior, but her writing was accepted by male critics as part of the literary canon because she did not explicitly challenge traditional sex roles in her life or her work. Like the few other women writers who found their way into the annals of nineteenth-century German literature, Droste-Hülshoff regarded herself, and was regarded by critics, as atypical of her sex. But when women novelists like Louise Aston and Fanny Lewald addressed their literary talents to the social and economic emancipation of women, Jews, and other oppressed groups, the critical establishment regarded their vigor and objectivity as blemishes and used "unfeminine" as a term of censure (Brinkler-Gabler, pp. 24–25). Whether considered traditionally feminine or unfeminine, most German women writers were denied the stature of serious poets and were condemned to the literary ghetto of *Frauenliteratur*. This classification also effectively neutralized women writers as topics of literary scholarship, and this neutralization, in turn, perpetuated the fallacy that they were inferior to their male counterparts. As a result, the literary canon that emerged in nineteenth-century Germany, in contrast to the Anglo-American or French tradition, refused a priori to acknowledge women as writers.

Bibliographies, Reference Works, and Student Handbooks

Bibliographies, reference works, and student handbooks of German literature reflect and perpetuate the concept of a separate and secondary *Frauenliteratur*. Although women are represented in the most comprehensive bibliographies (Goedeke, Kosch, Körner), they are usually grouped together as *Frauendichtung* when entries are nonalphabetical. In biographical and bibliographical reference works dealing with modern literature (e.g., *Handbuch der deutschen Gegenwartsliteratur* and Rowohlt's *Literaturlexikon des 20. Jahrhunderts*), contemporary writers like Irmtraud Morgner, Christine Brückner, Gisela Elsner, Ursula Erler, and Eva Strittmatter are ignored, while lesser-known male authors are included. There are, however, two specialized bibliographies of German women writers of the nineteenth and early twentieth centuries: Sophie Pataky's *Lexikon deutscher Frauen der Feder* (*Eine Zusammenstellung der seit dem Jahre 1840 erschienenen Werke weiblicher Autoren nebst Biographien der Lebenden und einem Verzeichnis der Pseudonyme*), reprinted in Bern in 1971, catalogs all works written by women in the latter half of the nineteenth century, and Hans Sveistrup and Agnes von Zahn-Harnack's *Die Frauenfrage in Deutschland: Strömungen und Gegenströmungen 1790–1930* contains bibliographical information, although it is incomplete. While both bibliographies are necessary research tools for feminist criticism, they are not considered standard reference works and hence are not easily accessible to interested scholars.

Reference works that provide definitions of literary terms and explanations of literary movements, periods, and genres (Kruger, Merker-Stammler, Kindermann and Dietrich, Wilpert) tend to perpetuate the concept of *Frauenliteratur* as defined in the literary histories cited above. Although some reference works, like Merker-Stammler's *Reallexikon der deutschen Literatur*, have dropped the term in later editions, popular student handbooks like Wilpert's *Sachwörterbuch der Literatur* and Georg Ried's *Wesen und Werden der deutschen Dichtung* have retained it (Szépe, pp. 12–13). At present, the pejorative connotations of this concept are so widely accepted that many contemporary women writers have been reluctant to identify themselves with the current women's movement or to discuss gender-specific elements in their work because they are afraid their writing will be classified as *Frauenliteratur* (Szépe, pp. 13–14). Since the standards of literary taste advanced by such reference materials generally determine what authors are read, what works are published, and what literary topics of study are acceptable, the legitimation of both feminist criticism and women's writing would seem to demand the removal of the term *Frauenliteratur* from the basic reference works.

Primary Texts and Secondary Material

Women's works cannot be read, studied, and fairly reevaluated if they are not easily accessible to readers and if the materials necessary for locating those works in a historical context are lacking. We therefore need collected editions, editions of single works, anthologies, biographical and bibliographical monographs, feminist criticism of women's works, and editions of German texts in English translation. We also need to research and publish the noncanonical literary forms (letters, diaries, memoirs, and autobiographies), not only because they would provide essential secondary information about women writers but also because, excluded from other literary channels, women have traditionally cultivated and developed these forms. The problem of adequate texts and secondary materials is a critical one for Germanists, since the holdings of many German libraries were either destroyed or misplaced during World War II and since many of the texts by women are currently out of print.

Collected Editions

Research on women authors such as Luise Gottsched, Sophie La Roche, Fanny Lewald, Luise von François, Hedwig Dohm, Ilse Aichinger, Luise Rinser, and Marie-Luise Kaschnitz would be greatly facilitated by complete editions of their works. Feminist scholars wishing to edit the complete works of the earlier writers would probably have to apply to West German foundations like the Deutsche Forschungsgemeinschaft for financial support, although such foundations have never been sympathetic to projects outside the canon. It might be easier to convince West German publishing houses of the need for complete editions of modern writers like Aichinger, Rinser, and Kaschnitz, since comparable volumes have already appeared: the collected works of Ricarda Huch (Kiepenheuer and Witsch), Franziska zu Reventlow (Langen Mueller), Ingeborg Bachmann (Piper), Anna Seghers (Luchterhand), Marieluise Fleisser (Suhrkamp), Marie von Ebner-Eschenbach (Winkler), Annette von Droste-Hülshoff (Hanser), and Else Lasker-Schüler (Kösel). Publishing houses like Hanser, Nymphenburger, and the Wissenschaftliche Buchgesellschaft appear to be the most receptive to the possibility of editing collected editions of women writers from the eighteenth and nineteenth centuries.

Individual Editions

Individual works by women authors from earlier periods do exist in older editions, but these are difficult or sometimes impossible to locate in libraries. Since women's works were either classified as *Frauenliteratur* or included in nonliterary genres, many libraries treated them negligently or failed to order them at all. For similar reasons, such works have not been reprinted or reissued, so that there are virtually no modern West German editions of Sophie Mereau, Henriette von

Paalzow, Therese Huber, Louise Aston, Ida von Hahn-Hahn, Fanny Lewald, and Gabriele Reuter. If West German publishing houses were aware of a new demand for such texts, however, they would probably respond favorably, for there have been recent editions of selected works by Luise Gottsched (Reclam and other presses), Sophie La Roche (Winkler, Wissenschaftliche Buchgesellschaft), and Luise von François (Manesse). Smaller feminist presses have also reprinted works by Hedwig Dohm (Verlag Arndtstrasse) and Anna Weirauch (Lesbenselbstverlag). Apart from dealing with the explicitly feminist presses, scholars wishing to issue new editions of older works by women might approach publishing houses like Reclam, which has inaugurated a series Neue Frau, dealing with texts by women; Fischer, which has a series of paperbacks entitled Die Frau in der Gesellschaft; and the Wissenschaftliche Buchgesellschaft. Still needed are works like Karoline von Wolzogen's *Agnes von Lilien,* more of Luise Gottsched's plays, Ida von Hahn-Hahn's *Gräfin Faustine,* Fanny Lewald's *Jenny,* Luise von François' *Die letzte Reckenbürgerin,* and Gabriele Reuter's *Aus guter Familie* and *Tränenhaus.*

Anthologies of German Literature in German

Because *Frauenliteratur* existed apart from the traditional canon, very few women authors have been represented in untranslated literary and popular anthologies of German literature, readers intended for students of German, or in textbooks. Although anthologies of recent literature do represent some modern women writers, women included in anthologies of older writing are usually those exceptional authors whose works were accepted by male literary historians (Catharina von Greiffenberg, Bettina von Arnim, Annette von Droste-Hülshoff, Marie von Ebner-Eschenbach, and Ricarda Huch). To correct the impression that only these women are worthy of notice, feminist critics should demand revisions of extant anthologies or should themselves publish alternative collections of women's writing. Gisela Brinkler-Gabler's *Deutsche Dichterinnen vom 16. Jahrhundert bis zur Gegenwart* (Fischer) and Elke Frederiksen's forthcoming collection of texts from the German women's movement (Reclam) are important steps in this direction.

Critical Studies and Books

In addition to the problem of inadequate and inaccessible texts, the paucity of secondary material about women writers further complicates research. Although the major West German publishing houses (Fischer, Rowohlt, Suhrkamp, Luchterhand, Metzler, Kiepenheuer and Witsch, Beck) have published a variety of German and foreign works on the history, sociology, psychology, and politics of women and the women's movement, corresponding works of literary scholarship have not appeared, perhaps because German feminism originated in the social sciences and has shown greater concern with the issues in those fields. Whatever the reason, the publication of Renate Möhrmann's *Die andere Frau: Emanzipationsansätze deutscher Schriftstellerinnen im Vorfeld der 48'er Revolution* (Metzler) and Gisela Brinkler-Gabler's *Deutsche Dichterinnen* suggest that the opportunity for publishing feminist literary criticism in German does exist, at least insofar as manuscripts otherwise conform to the standards of a particular series like Metzler's Abhandlungen zur Germanistik or Studien zur allgemeinen und vergleichenden Literaturwissenschaft, Böhlau's Literatur und Leben, or the Edition Beck. Manuscripts that do not follow the guidelines of the series sponsored by the major West German presses or that are written in English might be published by author-subsidized presses like Lang or Bouvier. Much of the opprobrium attached to author-subsidized publication has disappeared in German scholarship, since a number of German publishing houses (Beck, Kohlhammer, Erich Schmidt) not formerly known as subsidy presses now require financial contributions from potential authors. The publication of feminist literary criticism in West Germany might thus depend less on the receptivity of the publisher than on the author's ability to secure financial support for a feminist project from an American or West German source.

Critical works in German may also be submitted to the smaller leftist or feminist presses, but these presses are generally not recognized by the academic community as legitimate scholarly enterprises. Rotbuch, Roter Stern, and Merve have all published nonliterary socialist-feminist studies and they would probably be receptive to socialist-feminist literary criticism. Small feminist presses like Frauenoffensive, Frauenselbstverlag, Verlag Frauenpolitik, and the Amazonenverlag might also welcome manuscripts, although these houses have not been primarily concerned with academic literary criticism. Frauenoffensive seems to be interested in analyses of the physical and psychological oppression of women; Frauenselbstverlag has published several empirical studies dealing with sexism in Marxist theory; Verlag Frauenpolitik has offered Marxist analyses of sexuality and politics; and the Amazonenverlag is interested in lesbian literature.[3]

Finally, if the editorial boards of the various West German biobibliographical monograph series could be persuaded to incorporate critical works on women writers into their programs, they would create entirely new opportunities for scholarly publishing, while facilitating future research in feminist literary criticism. At present, the Rororo

Bildmonographien and the Reihe Hansers Literaturkommentar include no works on German women writers; the Sammlung Metzler Realienbücher für Germanisten has alloted 1 of 175 volumes to a woman, Annette von Droste-Hülshoff; and the *Autorenbücher* have a volume on Christa Wolf. Only the series Text + Kritik, whose volumes provide critical essays as well as biobibliographical information, has devoted several issues to women (Ingeborg Bachmann, Nelly Sachs, Anna Seghers, and Christa Wolf). Before we can adequately reassess the literary canon, for the eighteenth and nineteenth centuries, for instance, we need modern monographs on women like Luise Gottsched, Anna Luise Karsch, Sophie La Roche, Therese Huber, Luise Mühlbach, Louise Aston, Luise von François, Gabriele Reuter, Hedwig Dohm, Marie von Ebner-Eschenbach, Eugenie Marlitt, and Hedwig Courths-Mahler.

The publication of feminist critical studies of German literature in America entails other but no less complicated problems. Commercial presses in this country have displayed little interest in German literary criticism, feminist or otherwise. Many university presses, however, will consider manuscripts dealing with any aspect of German literature (Princeton, Yale, Harvard, North Carolina, California, Chicago, Indiana, Wisconsin, Stanford, Johns Hopkins), provided that the studies are written in English and seem likely to interest a broad readership. Problems arise when feminist scholars submit manuscripts on previously neglected women writers that editors may not have heard of; publishers may doubt that writers ignored in their own country will appeal to an American audience. Translation of primary sources creates additional problems for feminist scholars: they may be forced to present in translation works that are not available to readers in the original. Furthermore, analyses of gender-specific semantic or syntactic usage in the works of women writers must attempt to devise English equivalents for the German original that do not distort the main argument. The inherent limitations of working in translation may thus be prohibitive for certain kinds of feminist criticism.

Critical Studies: Articles and Essays

Opportunities for publishing shorter feminist studies in the leading professional journals have also not been great. According to our own survey of articles printed in these periodicals since 1945, each journal published an average of less than one article every second year dealing with German women as authors, characters, or historical figures.[4] Contrary to our expectations, journals of the 1970s display approximately the same number of contributions on women as do those from the 1950s, although a few American journals, like *Monatshefte, German*

Quarterly, and *Unterrichtspraxis*, seem to be making an effort to include more articles on women.

Of the articles we surveyed on women, roughly two-thirds treat women authors; the rest deal with female characters, traditionally woman-related themes such as love and marriage, women as correspondents, and women as personalities. Apart from the studies of Annette von Droste-Hülshoff, clearly the most popular woman author, the articles primarily concern modern women writers like Christa Wolf, Marie-Luise Kaschnitz, Ingeborg Bachmann, Nelly Sachs, Ricarda Huch, Gertrud Kolmar, Gabriele Wohmann, Else Lasker-Schüler, and Ilse Aichinger. Women of earlier periods are represented by occasional articles on Catharina von Greiffenberg, Bettina von Arnim, Marianne von Willemer, Rahel Varnhagen, Caroline von Günderode, Dorothea Schlegel, Anna Luise Karsch, Anna Owena Hoyers, Victoria Gambara, and Johanna Kinkel. The scope of articles accepted by the professional journals also reflects the assumption of German literary historians that women master only certain genres. Since drama is a traditionally nonfeminine genre, dramatists like Hroswitha von Gandersheim, Luise Gottsched, Marieluise Fleisser, and Gerlinde Reinshagen are ignored. Similarly, although some women have written dramatic works as well as poetry or fiction (Annette von Droste-Hülshoff, Marie von Ebner-Eschenbach, Ingeborg Bachmann, Else Lasker-Schüler, and Nelly Sachs), their plays are generally neglected in favor of their other works.[5] Emphasis of this sort may be an expression of editorial policy, or it may simply indicate that even feminist scholars have accepted the prevailing stereotypes. In any case, the relation of women to traditionally "nonfeminine" literary genres is one that warrants investigation.

Furthermore, most articles from the journals we examined seem to approach women writers in a sex-neutral manner; that is, they fail to examine the self-image of the author in question, her image of other women, and the problems she may have encountered because of her sex. Since women historically have been neither raised nor treated sex-neutrally, "objective" criticism of this sort often perpetuates the prevailing stereotypes and prejudices associated with women.

We need further examination of women writers as women—studies on the reception of women writers like Rahel Varnhagen and Eugenie Marlitt by women readers, on female literary circles like those of Fanny Lewald in Berlin and Marie von Ebner-Eschenbach in Vienna, on the traditions and relationships of women writing in German, and on feminist aesthetics.

Finally, many of the journal articles we examined rely on traditional stereotypes for their analyses of female literary characters. Only recent articles appearing in American journals like *Monatshefte*, *Ger-*

man Quarterly, and *Unterrichtspraxis* seem to display a new tendency to treat these images critically. Critical analyses of the literary portrayal of a broader range of figures—educated women, prostitutes, lesbians, and mothers and daughters—are therefore still needed.

As a rule, the length of study, the language in which it is written, and the type of content determine where one should submit a manuscript. Most West German journals now accept articles in English, and many American journals, though no British ones, print papers in German. In general, American periodicals intended specifically for Germanists will contain both languages, while those concerned with comparative literature or a mixed audience insist on contributions in English. The American journals are also more receptive to critical feminist topics than are their British or German counterparts. Of the American journals, *Monatshefte* and *German Quarterly* have accepted feminist analyses of literary or philological problems, while *Unterrichtspraxis* favors short papers on pedagogical questions. Some German periodicals like *Euphorion* and *Merkur* have also printed occasional pieces on women, the former (in English) on images of women or on neglected German women writers and the latter on cultural aspects of the women's movement. The other journals we surveyed tend to avoid the issue of women, unless articles deal with traditional images of women or with canonical women writers in a "scholarly"—that is, sex-neutral—manner.

Despite the scarcity of women-related articles in regular issues of scholarly journals, some publications have devoted entire issues or parts of issues to feminist criticism. *Unterrichtspraxis* has included material for a feminist pedagogy in a section of one issue, while leftist journals like *New German Critique* in America and *Kursbuch, Alternative,* and *Aesthetik und Kommunikation* in West Germany[6] have published articles on a variety of historical, social, political, economic, and aesthetic feminist topics in their special issues. Similarly, a few professional conferences have been devoted to the topic of women. The Lessing Akademie in Wolfenbüttel sponsored a convention on the theme Frauen und Frauenbildung in der Aufklärung, and the topic of the Tenth Amherst Colloquium was Die Frau als Heldin und Autorin. The proceedings of these sessions have subsequently been published.[7] Other American colloquiums, however, such as the Wisconsin Workshop, the University of Texas Symposium, Washington University's International Symposium, and the Kentucky Foreign Language Conference have not been as receptive to women's issues. Contributions for such special feminist issues or colloquiums are usually solicited in American professional journals, the *AATG Newsletter,* and the *WiG* (Women in German) *Newsletter.*

A number of West German journals, conferences, and organizations with a specifically feminist focus also provide opportunities for publishing articles, but such opportunities are more limited in Germany than in the United States. No academic feminist journal of the stature of *Signs* exists there, nor does anything approximating the focus on literature and aesthetics provided by *Women and Literature* or *Feminist Studies.* The West German journals that publish articles on feminist aesthetics and women writers (*Courage, Emma, Frauenoffensive Journal, Die schwarze Botin, Mamas Pfirsiche,* and *Frauen und Film*) have a limited circulation and, often, an explicitly antiacademic bias; they are not regarded as scholarly publications by the academic community. The only academically recognized outlet for feminist criticism, the annual Sommeruniversität für Frauen held in West Berlin since 1976, is primarily concerned with topics drawn from the social sciences (Frauen und Wissenschaft, Bezahlte und unbezahlte Arbeitskräfte, and Mutterschaft: Ideologie, Wirklichkeit oder Utopie). Papers and workshops dealing with literary analysis, feminist aesthetics, or the reception of women writers would, however, be welcomed, and the Berliner Dozentinnengruppe, which organizes the Sommeruniversität, encourages American feminists to submit proposals for such works. Many of the papers presented at the Sommeruniversität are published in *Beiträge zur Berliner Sommeruniversität für Frauen.*[8] In this country, recognized feminist journals like *Signs, Feminist Studies,* or *Women and Literature* report a lack of contributions in the area of German literature—a lack reflected in their offerings.

Translations

The availability in English of the works of German women writers and the opportunities for publishing such translations are of particular interest to American and English teachers of German and the modern languages. At present, only limited bibliographies of literature by German women writers in translation are available, and a more comprehensive bibliography is being developed to facilitate research, to aid in the compilation of texts for women's studies courses, and to avoid duplication of efforts.[9] As might be expected, the works of German literature chosen for translation generally correspond to the traditional standards of German literature discussed above, as do the anthologies in translation. In the twenty volumes of Kuno Francke's *The German Classics: Masterpieces of German Literature,* for example, only eight entries are by women (Bettina von Arnim, Annette von Droste-Hülshoff, Isolde Kurz, Lulu von Strauss und Torney, Agnes Miegel, Ricarda Huch, Helene Böhlau, and Clara Viebig). In less comprehensive anthologies of German prose, few women appear: Annette von Droste-Hülshoff and perhaps Marie von Ebner-Eschenbach or Ricarda Huch from the nineteenth century and Ilse Aichinger or Christa Wolf from the twentieth. In poetry the situation is not as bleak, but it still leaves much to be desired. Anthologies of older poetry may include poems by Catharina von Greiffenberg, Annette von Droste-Hülshoff, and Ricarda Huch, while those of modern poetry may list poems by Hilde Domin, Else Lasker-Schüler, Nelly Sachs, Gertrud Kolmar, Ingeborg Bachmann, Marie-Luise Kaschnitz, and Elisabeth Langässer. Some German women writers, however, have become either popular or critical successes in America, and their books have been translated and published here in separate editions (Vicki Baum, Gertrud von Le Fort, Anna Seghers, Ilse Aichinger, and Christa Wolf). But much work remains to be done to make available to a larger American audience the prose and poetry of lesser-known but critically acclaimed modern women writers like Sarah Kirsch, Christa Reinig, Elisabeth Borchers, Barbara Frischmuth, Gabriele Wohmann, Luise Rinser, Gertrud Leutenegger, Irmtraud Morgner, Gisela Elsner, Ursula Erler, Verena Stefan, Helga Novak, and Angelika Mechtel. The special issue of *New German Critique* and the two new anthologies of modern German women writers are the first steps in this direction.[10]

The major forum for translations of modern German writers is *Dimension,* a journal published by the German Department at the University of Texas, Austin. Smaller poetry reviews like Stanford University's *Sequoia* and the *Massachusetts Review* have also accepted occasional short translations from the German. In the past, one or two stories by German women have even found their way into *Ms. Magazine.* Such periodicals are, however, primarily interested in modern literature, so that scholars concerned with translating works of the eighteenth and nineteenth centuries would probably have to design their own anthology projects, call for translations, and then approach publishers who have previously demonstrated an interest in German literature (Grove, Dell, Penguin, New Directions, Ungar, Schocken, and Pergamon). University presses like Indiana, Chicago, and Massachusetts have also shown an interest in printing translations of German women writers.

Of all feminist publishing possibilities in the field of German literature, the liveliest and most regular forum for German women's studies in America has been created by feminist Germanists themselves through the organization Women in German (WiG), founded in 1975. A newsletter, published four times annually at the University of Wisconsin, Madison, informs subscribers of the latest trends in German feminism, reminds them about professional meetings and publications of interest, and prints pedagogical material relevant to women's studies in German. In addition to the newsletter, WiG regularly sponsors special sessions at national and regional MLA and AATG conventions and has held its own annual conference and retreat since 1976. Active members of WiG have also petitioned to have feminist topics included in the regular divisions of the MLA and AATG. All WiG's functions and projects are publicized well in advance and all interested feminists are encouraged to submit contributions.

Thus, despite the ingrained prejudices of many Germanists against women's writing, opportunities for feminist research and publishing in German literary scholarship do exist. A general recognition of the legitimacy of feminist concerns, a growing interest in women's issues, and the pressure of feminists themselves have combined to create a climate more favorable than ever before, even in this recalcitrant discipline, to the publication of feminist scholarship. There is every indication that the situation will continue to improve.

Since the summer of 1979, when we wrote this report, many works have appeared to alleviate the sense of severe shortage in the area of women's studies in German. But apart from Silvia Bovenschen's study of the image of women in literature around 1800, monographs have fared less well than collections of critical essays. Anthologies of primary sources have also begun to appear, and Gisela Brinker-Gabler is editing a series (Die Frau in der Gesellschaft [Fischer Verlag]) that includes autobiographical writings by women.[11] Both this series and the new journal *Beiträge zur feministischen Theorie und Praxis,* launched in 1978 by Sozialwissenschaftliche Forschung und Praxis für Frauen e.v. (Munich: Frauenoffensive Verlag), confirm the tendency in West German women's studies to emphasize the social sciences rather than literature. We are therefore still in need of monographs on individuals and themes in German women's literature. Although there has been a slight increase in the number of journal articles, the smaller, more radical presses continue to lead the publishing industry as a whole in exploring and reprinting women's literature. We still have no indication, however, that any serious revision of basic handbooks or resource materials is forthcoming.[12]

Notes

1. See Helena Szépe, "The Term *Frauendichtung,*" *Unterrichtspraxis,* 9, No. 1 (1976), 11–14.
2. Gisela Brinkler-Gabler, "Die Schriftstellerin in der deutschen Literaturwissenschaft: Aspekte ihrer Rezeption von 1835 bis 1910," *Unterrichtspraxis,* 9, No. 1 (1976), 15–27.
3. For a more detailed description of the policies of these presses, see Miriam Frank, "Feminist Publications in West Germany Today," *New German Critique,* 13 (1978), 181–94, from which we have taken the information we provide here. The article also lists the addresses of feminist presses.
4. Our survey covered *Deutsche Vierteljahresschrift, Euphorion, German Life and Letters, German Quarterly, Germanic Review, Jahrbuch der deutschen Schiller Gesellschaft, Jahrbuch des freien deutschen Hochstifts, Merkur, Modern Language Review, Monatshefte, Neophilologus, Publications of the English Goethe Society, PMLA, Sinn und Form, Weimarer Beiträge, Wirkendes Wort,* and *Zeitschrift für deutsche Philologie.*
5. Sigrid Novak's dissertation on nineteenth-century female dramatists, "Images of Womanhood in the Works of German Female Dramatists: 1892–1918" (Diss. Johns Hopkins 1971), has begun this reexamination.
6. See *Unterrichtspraxis,* 9, No. 1 (1976); *Alternative,* Nos. 108–109 (1976); *Aesthetik und Kommunikation,* No. 25 (1976); *Kursbuch,* No. 47 (1977); *New German Critique,* No. 13 (1978) and No. 23 (1981).
7. *Wolfenbüttler Studien zur Aufklärung,* Vol. III, ed. G. Schulz (Wolfenbüttel: Jacobi, 1977); *Die Frau als Heldin und Autorin,* ed. W. Paulsen (Bern: Francke, 1978).
8. *Frauen und Wissenschaft: Beiträge zur Berliner Sommeruniversität für Frauen, Juli 1976* (Berlin: Courage Verlag, 1977); *Frauen: Bezahlte und unbezahlte Arbeitskräfte* (Berlin: Courage Verlag, 1978).
9. See the bibliography of the Indiana Collective, *WiG Newsletter,* No. 6 (1976); *GDR Bulletin,* 4, No. 1 (1978); Edna Huttenmaier Spitz, "German Women Writers of the Twentieth Century: An Introductory Course in English Translation," *Unterrichtspraxis,* 9, No. 1 (1976), 30–38; *Female Studies IX: Teaching about Women in the Foreign Languages,* ed. Sidonie Cassirer (Old Westbury, N.Y.: 1975) pp. 202–25; and *Women Writers in Translation: An Annotated Bibliography, 1945–1980,* ed. Margery Resnick and Isabelle de Courtivron (New York: Garland, 1982).
10. These anthologies have been edited by Naomi Stephan and Jeanette Clausen, who are still looking for a publisher, and by Edna Huttenmaier Spitz and Elizabeth Rütschi-Hermann, *German Women Writers of the Twentieth Century* (New York: Pergamon, 1978).
11. Bovenschen's work is called *Die imaginierte Weiblichkeit: Exemplarische Untersuchungen zu kulturgeschichtlichen und literarischen Präsentationsformen des Weiblichen* (Frankfurt a. M.: Suhrkamp, 1979). Recent collections of critical essays include Marianne Burkhard, ed. *Gestaltet und Gestaltend: Frauen in der deutschen Literatur* (Amsterdam: Rodopi, 1980); Barbara Becker-Cantarino, ed., *Die Frau von der Reformation zur*

Romantik (Bonn: Bouvier, 1981); Susan L. Cocalis and Kay Goodman, eds., *Beyond the Eternal Feminine: A Collection of Critical Essays on Women in German Literature* (Stuttgart: Akademischer Verlag Heinz-Dietrich Heinz, 1982); *Modern Austrian Literature: Special Issue on Austrian Women Writers,* 12, Nos. 3–4 (1979); and Gabriele Dietze, ed. *Die Überwindung der Sprachlosigkeit: Texte aus der neuen Frauenbewegung* (Darmstadt: Luchterhand, 1979). Two new anthologies of primary sources are *Frauenemanzipation im deutschen Vormärz: Texte und Dokumente,* ed. Renate Möhrmann (Stuttgart: Reclam, 1978), and *Die Frauenfrage in Deutschland 1865–1915: Texte und Dokumente,* ed. Elke Frederiksen (Stuttgart: Reclam, 1981).

12. This is not to say that there has been no progress in this area. Elisabeth Friedrichs, *Die deutschsprachigen Schriftstellerinnen des 18. und 19. Jahrhunderts: Ein Lexikon* (Stuttgart: Metzler, 1981) has appeared, and other major bibliographical projects on women writers in the medieval era and in the eighteenth century are now in progress.

Women's Studies in Russian Literature

Opportunities for Research and Publication

Barbara Heldt

with

A Selective Bibliography

Sandra M. Thomson

Russian literature presents a fertile field for the study of the way men view women. Rather than the Other, a woman character in Russian fiction by a male writer often turns out to be the Self, a better or worse self, perhaps, but always one more fully or intensely realized. One might hypothesize that male-centeredness, whether woman-hating or woman-worshiping, becomes more solipsistic the further we move away from realism in Russian fiction. Above all, the Russian realistic tradition is deeply moral, and one set of moral standards applies to men and women alike. Tolstoy expects his men to lead family lives in the country along with his women; both can fall prey to false social values. If Dostoevsky's men are often imperfect saints and his women rebellious acolytes, the roles can also be reversed. With Chekhov, women characters are more likely than men to have a heightened perception of both emotions and surrounding physical data. The pregnant heroine of "A Name-Day Party" (who obviously could not have been a man) stands for other female characters who are pregnant with the awareness of reality, Chekhov's essential moral good. The convention of female understanding extends beyond realism: Pasternak's modernistic masterpiece "The Childhood of Luvers" centers on a girl who has just reached puberty, who perceives the world as a poet does, and who builds her bridges to other people through those primary sensations. But the Russian realistic aesthetic especially is free of sexist deformations, and not by chance. Russian realistic novels, novellas, or short stories place women characters at their center, since these works aspire to be fully human, beyond Western materialism and derivative social mores. The aesthetic implies an ethic.

Of course, Russian literature is not without a tradition of misogyny, much of it cruel and much highly comical, which betrays, as it usually does, male anxieties. This motif goes back to the original sources of the literature, the folk and the church traditions. Chants like bridal laments bitterly reflect the fate of the young bride, going to live with her husband's family. In the written literature, Daniel the Exile rails against "evil women" and conjures up images of the threatening female slob, later elaborated by Fonvizin, Gogol, Saltykov-Shchedrin, Zamyatin, Biely, Olesha, and other writers of the grotesque. In the three early twentieth-century writers Zamyatin, Biely, and Olesha, the mother who devours boys becomes the sexual pit that engulfs men. But in the earliest Russian texts, from the medieval *Primary Chronicle,* the clever avenger Olga sets standards of heroic fidelity for Russian womanhood (e.g., Tatyana, the Decembrist wives, and the Soviet woman faithful to revolution rather than to husband). While fidelity to a man or a cause may be low on the scale of contemporary virtues in the West, in Russia it may be seen as somewhat equivalent to the Western virtue of fidelity to self.

Outside the realistic tradition we often find interesting reversals of conventional sex roles. The sentimentalist hero of the prerealist Karamzin wants to cultivate his sensibilities. In the symbolist world of the postrealist Aleksandr Blok, a world split into two, the man in the lower sphere waits passively for something active and female from the higher sphere to happen.

Given these patterns, some of which are peculiarly Russian, how important is the study of Russian women writers? Do they provide an alternative perspective or constitute a literary subculture that shares the values and attitudes of the male culture? Here almost no work has been done, probably because of the "greatness" obstacle. Unlike another East Slavic literature, Ukrainian, which has a woman as one of its three greatest writers (Lesia Ukrainka), Russian literature has no women writers to equal the best men writers before the advent of the poets Akhmatova and Tsvetaeva in the twentieth century. But it does have a great many very good female authors. Bunina, Dashkova, Zhadovskaya, Pavlova, Rostopchina, Kokhanovskaya, Tur, Gan, and Khvoshchinskaya (to mention a few who wrote before the late nineteenth century, after which there was a profusion of women writers to the present day) have been totally neglected outside Russia and slighted within Russia. They have never been translated. My own study of Karolina Pavlova led to the discovery of an extraordinarily interesting biography: slanders by most male contemporaries, private letters full of despair, a bold show of valor and perseverance that enabled her to write excellent poetry, and a novel that translated very well into English.

When more women writers are studied, certain common patterns in their lives and writings will surely emerge. For example, when we investigate the writing of three female authors in the eighteenth, nineteenth, and twentieth centuries, we find that all repeatedly protest their ordinariness. Dashkova in her memoirs stresses the fulfillment of her domestic obligations (which included administering her estates and supervising the education of her children). Pavlova writes to a prominent editor that she cannot help being a writer, as much as she would like to be an ordinary woman. In her lyric poetry Akhmatova assumes the persona of an ordinary woman courted by somewhat predatory males; in her epic poetry, that of a Russian wife and mother with husband dead and son jailed, waiting in line for news like so many other Russian women. Yet these three women in particular were aware of themselves as cultural and literary powers, despite their protestations of female modesty and womanly dutifulness. Reflected directly or indirectly in the writing of other Russian women, does this paradox lend a special coloring to their works? What are the other repeated themes and latent conflicts that inform women's writings in particular?

The first step in attempting to answer these questions is to establish the texts. Soviet archives are full of women's writings that are either unpublished or published obscurely. Although Soviet scholars have made good beginnings in sifting through them, there have been fewer editions of women writers in recent years than in past decades. The most extensive bibliography of women writers (Golitsyn) dates from 1889. Soviet bibliographies occasionally list "women" under subject headings. Often, criticism of women writers and women characters is copious for a time and then negligible or nil. Some of the best contemporary Soviet criticism of women writers (e.g., Bukhstab and Iezuitova) does not have "women" in the title and can therefore be discovered only in the course of pursuing other critical reading. This last consideration is perhaps the most compelling reason for producing a continually updated bibliography.

These difficulties notwithstanding, many ancient translations of Russian writers, even lesser ones, exist and could be unearthed and updated. New translations continue to appear in journals like *Russian Literature Triquarterly.* These provide scattered material for an anthology, which could demonstrate continuity in the Russian–Soviet time span. For example, Natalya Baranskaya's recent story "A Week Like Any Other" portrays in detail the work-and-home week of a Soviet woman who lives out many of the hypotheses of prerevolutionary times. Critical reaction to the story in the Soviet press reflects some facets of the nineteenth-century "woman question."

The nineteenth-century "thick journals" are a gold mine for seeking out writings by or about women, both because the "woman question" was a general intellectual issue and because women readers wanted to read about women. My study of *Rassvet,* the first journal seriously devoted to a female readership, produced innumerable leads into areas of debate on women writers, female characters, and social questions regarding women—areas not always kept distinct in Russia. Journals specializing in translated works could be combed with a view to discovering which works by foreign women novelists (like the Brontës, George Sand, and George Eliot) were translated, what reviews they received, and which Russian authors they may have influenced.

Polemical writings on women in Russian literature constitute an established tradition that dates from the beginning of Russian criticism, in the second half of the eighteenth century, and we must read these materials with a critical eye. From Belinsky to Briusov, women writers have been discussed by their contemporaries as *women* writers. Female "types" in literature were grouped and compared in and out of context, the latter not a totally invalid procedure, since male writers like Turgenev, Goncharov, Ostrovsky, and Pisemsky consciously employ female characters as variations of a type. Some types, like the Female Nihilist, appear and disappear within a twenty-year span; they are clearly tied to a limited social debate. Others, like the Russian "strong woman," arise in medieval Russia and continue straight into the Soviet present.

This character type, whom Russians view as more real than fictional, needs closer scrutiny because she has often been regarded in both the nineteenth and the twentieth centuries as a sort of historical "given." The strong female is a young girl of marriageable age, fresh from the parental nest and uncorrupted by society, who is willing and able to act to establish her independence, to enact the ideals of her older and more experienced beloved, and to improve Russian society in general. She is intense and "whole" in spirit (to use a favorite Russian adjective). She was probably a literary type before she became a historical reality, since Russian writers saw it as their mission to articulate incipient reality. She usually belonged to the upper classes, but women in peasant dress, perhaps by analogy to the upper-class female image, were endowed with the same traits. She was the stable element longed for by citizens of an oppressively willful and unpredictable patriarchal autocracy. She was the idealized mother for sons of remote and often, at best, benignly negligent actual parents (see Herzen's memoirs for a classic instance). She was the idealization of a childhood that never existed, that these men carried into adulthood (see Oblomov's dream). And yet, perhaps because literary documentation is so abundant, both Russian and Western critics past and present have largely confined themselves to cataloging the strong woman's numerous appearances rather than criticizing her functions. She is so *good* that Russians are proud of her!

But a more dispassionate feminist critic might well conclude that in most works the strong woman is of secondary importance, that she merely serves as a contrast for the real (male) heroes of the work—the Byronic Eugene Onegin and his friend the narrator, the imaginatively slothful Oblomov, the neoromantic modern Raskolnikov—all of whom need Tatianas, Olgas, and Sonias to point the way toward a wisdom that these superfluous men are incapable of attaining on their own. "On their own" is perhaps too Western a notion, and we might relate the female character to a more Russian notion of communality. In any case, most of these female strong characters, who have been traditionally discussed as if they were central, function stylistically not as pivotal forces but rather as foils to set off male characters. A good way to begin investigating this thesis would be to analyze the language these women speak and the language used to characterize them. Do our authors depend on the feelings of their readers about such maidens and rely on clichéd codes to transmit their messages? How do the relevant passages differ from those used to characterize the men, and from others in the work as a whole?

The social and economic background of Russia has been used heavily in Russian literary criticism, but we should not overreact here and neglect it entirely. Social and literary currents rarely run exactly parallel before the 1930s. The "woman question" that was prominent in the 1860s was anticipated in the literature of the 1830s and 1840s—in the society tales of Odoevsky and in the writings of Pavlova, Gan, Nestroeva, Herzen, Druzhinin, and others. It was one of many literary-philosophical questions of one generation that became political programs of another. Thus, in novels written by men in the 1860s and 1870s, we see a literary reaction to the literary type become political reality: the structurally unnecessary but polemically obligatory insertion of the chain-smoking, short-haired nihilist woman. By the 1880s, when political action by women was even more evident, this particular crude literary type disappears or becomes transmuted, as in Turgenev's more subtle studies of populist women in *Virgin Soil* or in Tolstoy's final agonized coming to grips with marriage in *Kreutzer Sonata* or in the more generalized antibourgeois attitudes of the naturalist or symbolist writers. To say that writers lagged behind radical critics or that writers never understood the woman question is to reverse the truth. They wrote about women earlier and better than the critics did and, often when taking a politically conservative position, they could not help creating apolitical characters that carried their own weight. Tolstoy's women speak for women, as his men speak for men, in the social sphere of his works; but in the larger natural sphere of his novels and stories the men and women characters are highly interdependent. They involuntarily reveal to each other truths about how to live. Because Ivan Ilych decides to be a careerist and cuts himself off from his wife, she—the female counterpart such a husband deserves and often gets—dissociates herself from him when he is dying. Russian retributional interaction—the deep morality typical of realism—prevails even in a story about isolation. This proposition, like many others that might be made about Russian literature, strongly suggests that feminist criticism must play a decisive role in future interpretations.

Selective Bibliography

REFERENCE

Berkov, P. N., ed. *Istoriia russkoi literatury XVIII veka: Bibliograficheskii ukazatel'.* Leningrad, 1968.

Foster, Ludmilla A. *Bibliography of Russian Emigré Literature, 1918–1968.* 2 vols. Boston: Hall, 1970.

Golitsyn, Prince N. N. *Bibliograficheskii slovar' russkikh pisatel'nits.* St. Petersburg, 1889; rpt. (with Ponomarev) Leipzig: Zentralantiquariat, 1974.

Gul'binskii, I. V. [I. V. Vladislavlev]. *Russkie pisateli: Opyt bibliograficheskogo posobiia po russkoi literature XIX–XX st.* Moscow, 1924.

Iazykov, D. D. *Obzor zhizni i trudov pokoinykh russkikh pisatelei.* Moscow, 1885–1916. (13 issues, covering writers who died between 1881 and 1893.)

Kandel', B. L., L. M. Fediushina, and M. A. Benina. *Russkaia khudozhestvennaia literatura i literaturovedenie: Ukazatel' spravochno-bibliograficheskikh posoboi s kontsa XVIII veka po 1974 god.* Moscow, 1976.

Muratova, K. D., ed. *Istoriia russkoi literatury XIX veka: Bibliograficheskii ukazatel'.* Moscow, 1962.

———. *Istoriia russkoi literatury kontsa XIX-nachala XX veka: Bibliograficheskii ukazatel'.* Moscow, 1963.

Ponamarev, S. I. *Nashi pisatel'nitsy.* St. Petersburg, 1891. (2 secs.: a critical review of Golitsyn's bibliography and a supplementary bibliography); rpt. (with Golitsyn) Leipzig: Zentralantiquariat, 1974.

Russov, S. V. *Bibliograficheskii katalog rossiiskim pisatel'nitsam.* St. Petersburg, 1826.

GENERAL (Excluding Most Criticism of Single Authors)

In Russian

Avdeev, Mikhail V. *Obshchestvo 1820–1870 gg. v. geroiakh i geroiniakh literatury.* St. Petersburg, 1874.

———. *Zhenshchiny russkikh pisatelei.* St. Petersburg, 1879.

Beletskii, A. I. "Ocherednye voprosy izucheniia russkogo romantizma." *Russkii romantizm: Sbornik statei.* Leningrad, 1927, pp. 5–25.

———. "Turgenev i russkie pisatel'nitsy 30–60-kh godov." *Tvorcheskii put' Turgeneva: Sbornik statei.* Ed. N. L. Brodskii. Petrograd, 1923, pp. 135–66.

———. "Do pytannia pro vplyv Pushkina na rosiis'ku literaturu XIX viku: Pushkin i rosiis'ki pysmennytski 1830–1860-kh rokiv." *O. S. Pushkin: Statti i materialy.* Kiev, 1938, pp. 116–49. (In Ukrainian.)

Belinskii, V. G. "Sochineniia Zeneidy R-voi." *Polnoe sobranie sochinenii.* Vol. VII. Moscow, 1955, pp. 648–78.

Briusov, V. Ia. "Zhenshchiny-poety." *Sobranie sochinenii.* Vol. VI. Moscow, 1975, pp. 318–21.

Bukhshtab, B. Ia. Pref. *Poety 1840–1850-kh godov.* Biblioteka poeta. Leningrad, 1972.

Chernyshev, K. *Lishnie liudi i zhenskie tipy v romanakh i povestiakh I. S. Turgeneva: Opyt razbora literaturnogo tipa russkikh lishnikh liudei, kak material dlia kharakteristiki razvitiia obshchestva.* St. Petersburg, 1896, rpt. 1913.

Davidovich, M. T. "Zhenskii portret v russkikh romantikov pervoi poloviny XIX veka." *Russkii romantizm: Sbornik statei.* Ed. A. I. Beletskii. Leningrad, 1927, pp. 88–114.

Iezuitova, R. V. "Svetskaia povest." *Russkaia povest' XIX veka: Istoriia i problematika zhanra.* Leningrad, 1973, pp. 169–99.

Mordovtsev, Daniil. *Russkiia zhenshchiny novago vremeni: Biograficheskie ocherki iz russkoi istorii.* 3 vols. St. Petersburg, 1874.

Pisarev, D. I. "Zhenskie tipy v romanakh i povestiakh Pisemskogo, Turgeneva i Goncharova." *Sochineniia v chetyrekh tomakh.* Vol. I. Moscow, 1955, pp. 231–73.

Portugalov, Mikhail V. *Zhenshchina v russkoi khudozhestvennoi literature XIX veka (1823–1876): Vstupitel'naia stat'ia i izbrannye otryvki iz proizvedenii.* St. Petersburg, 1914.

Shaskov, S. S. *Istoriia russkoi zhenshchiny.* 2nd ed. St. Petersburg, 1879.

Shchepkina, E. N. *Iz istorii zhenskoi lichnosti v Rossii.* St. Petersburg, 1914.

In English

Atkinson, Dorothy, Alexander Dallin, and Gail Worshofsky Lapidus, eds. *Women in Russia.* Stanford, Calif.: Stanford Univ. Press, 1977.

Benson, Ruth Crego. *Women in Tolstoy: The Ideal and the Erotic.* Urbana: Univ. of Illinois Press, 1973.

De Maegd-Soëp, Carolina. *The Emancipation of Women in Russian Literature and Society.* Trans. and adapted Carolina De Maegd-Soëp and Jos Coessens. Ghent, Belgium: Ghent State Univ., 1978.

Dunham, Vera S. "The Strong-Woman Motif." *The Transformation of Russian Society.* Ed. Cyril E. Black. Cambridge, Mass.: Harvard Univ. Press, 1960, pp. 459–83.

Gasiorowska, Xenia. *Women in Soviet Fiction, 1917–1964.* Madison: Univ. of Wisconsin Press, 1968.

Grossman, Joan. "Feminine Images in Old Russian Literature and Art." *California Slavic Studies,* 11 (1980), 33–70.

Monter, Barbara Heldt. Introd. *A Double Life,* by Karolina Pavlova. Trans. and intro. Barbara Heldt Monter. Ann Arbor, Mich.: Ardis, 1978.

———. "*Rassvet* (1859–1862) and the Woman Question." *Slavic Review,* 36 (1977), 76–85.

Nielsen, Marit Bjerkung. "The Concept of Love and the Conflict of the Individual versus Society in Elena A. Gan's *Sud Sveta.*" *Scando-Slavica,* 24 (1978), 125–38.

Pachmuss, Temira, trans., ed., and introd. *Women Writers in Russian Modernism: An Anthology.* Urbana: Univ. of Illinois Press, 1978.

Russian Literature Triquarterly, No. 9 (1974). (Issue devoted to Women in Russian Literature.)

Selivanova, Nina. *Russian Women.* New York: Dutton, 1923; rpt. Westport, Conn.: Hyperion, 1976.

Schneidman, N. N. "The Controversial Prose of the 1970s: Problems of Marriage and Love in Contemporary Soviet Literature." *Canadian Slavonic Papers,* 18 (1976), 400–14.

Siegel, George. "The Fallen Woman in Nineteenth-Century Russian Literature." *Harvard Slavic Studies,* 5 (1970), 81–107.

Stites, Richard. *The Women's Liberation Movement in Russia: Feminism, Nihilism, and Bolshevism, 1860–1930.* Princeton: Princeton Univ. Press, 1978.

Opportunities for Women's Studies in the Hispanic Field

Jean Franco

Any discussion of women's studies in Hispanic literatures comes up against the problem of definition. To begin with, we are dealing with the literature of nineteen Spanish-speaking countries of the Western Hemisphere, as well as the literature of Spain and that of the Spanish-speaking minorities of the United States. In each country and area, the women's movement is at a different stage. In some, like Peru, the traditional upper- and middle-class family structures are still extremely rigid. In other countries, repressive military regimes not only prevent free discussion of women's issues but also create a climate that makes any publishing difficult, curtails literary creativity, and generally discourages (or actively suppresses) the criticism and dissent without which the women's movement cannot develop. Even in countries like Cuba, where the government has directly encouraged the women's movement, and, to a lesser extent, Mexico, where International Women's Year gave some publicity to women's rights, there are often external conditions that adversely affect literary production in general and limit women writers and critics in particular. In Mexico, for instance, the recent outpouring of texts by new writers has far outstripped the capabilities of publishing outlets, and women writers will inevitably suffer the most from this discouraging situation. In Cuba, especially in the late 1960s, the economic condition severely curtailed even government-sponsored publication. In contrast, post-Franco Spain underwent a euphoric period in publishing, and publications by and about women shared somewhat in the bonanza. Furthermore, some parts of Spain, especially in Catalonia, have a long tradition of feminism.

When surveying women's studies in Latin America, we must recall Marysa Navarro's warning in *Signs:* she reminds us that Latin American scholarship in the social sciences is not specifically feminist. After noting that in the United States, scholarship on women has been connected to the women's liberation movement, she points out, "Some Latin American scholars engaged in research on women are feminists—or at least they do not make a point of declaring their anti-feminism. However, most do not consider themselves feminists and resent being seen as such because the subject of their research is women" ("Research on Latin American Women," *Signs,* 5, No. 1 [1979], 113–14). This repudiation may be tactical: the military regimes in power in many Latin American countries ban all forms of political activity. Then, too, "the North American origins of feminism render it implicitly tainted or suspicious, a perception that must be viewed in light of the complex and tense relationship that unites the United States and Latin America" (Navarro, p. 114). These considerations help to explain why feminist theory is apparently not keeping pace with the increasing importance of literature by women. They also explain a notable difference between Latin America and Spain in this respect: in Spain, despite the fragmentation of the women's movement, many women do acknowledge themselves to be feminists.

The differences between the feminist movements of Spain and Latin America are rooted in history. Feminism was already an important issue in Spain by the nineteenth century, not only in early socialist and liberal circles but even among more traditional women, such as the Catholic novelist Emilia Pardo Bazán and the Catalonian writers Marie Aurèlia Campmany and Teresa Pámies. During the Civil War and the Franco regime, however, all such manifestations of feminism were forced underground or extinguished. Thus, though post-Franco feminism was something of a fresh start, it did have important antecedents. Contemporary Spanish feminism has been distinguished by the emergence of the journal *Vindicación feminista* and by the appearance of an active group of feminist critics and writers, one of whom, Carmen Conde, has become the first woman elected to the Spanish Academy. Two other major writers, Carmen Martín Gaite and Lidia Falcón, are active feminists.

In Latin America, by contrast, there is little in the way of a specific feminist tradition despite the achievement of such individuals as the seventeenth-century Mexican nun Sor Juana Inés de la Cruz and the twentieth-century Chilean writer Gabriela Mistral. The strong social censorship of any female activity outside the convent or home—which has, in some areas, lasted well into the twentieth century—has inhibited open discussion of feminist issues. Even in the upper classes women have been hindered by their rudimentary education, as the novelist Rosario Castellanos points out in her article "Mujer que sabe latín" (published in the collection under the same title, 1973). Literature has been a male preserve not because women were specifically prevented from writing but because it involved activities—polemic, travel, study, debate—that were beyond their scope. At best, they might become hostesses or patronesses. Clorinda Matto de Turner, for instance, a nineteenth-century Peruvian novelist, would cast herself in the role of protectress of the poor. Until comparatively recently, it was still easier for a woman to present herself as a patroness—as did Victoria Ocampo, the founder of the influential Buenos Aires journal *Sur*—than to confront directly the solitude of female authorship.

Poetry was the genre most commonly chosen by women writers, although the seventeenth-century nun Sor Juana, who wrote both sacred and profane drama, is a notable exception. In addition to the few women poets who were recognized during their lifetimes, there must have been a great many who wrote occasionally, without hope of publication. Even Sor Juana wrote a great deal of verse for private rather than public circulation—verse intended as a tribute to a patroness. In the nineteenth and early twentieth centuries the vast majority of women writers turned to poetry, among them Julia de Burgos (Puerto Rico), Delmira Agustini (Uruguay), Gabriela Mistral (Chile), and Juana de Ibarbourou (Uruguay). All encountered the problem of male-defined creativity, but they had neither the tradition nor the movement to deal with it. Gabriela Mistral, for instance, was convinced that motherhood was the only real vocation for a woman and that her life as a teacher and poet was secondary and somewhat sterile. One of the first women to confront female authorship was the Mexican writer Rosario Castellanos, who included in a collection of essays called *Mujer que sabe latín* a lighthearted, indeed a desperately humorous, attempt to describe her situation as a writer, which she confessed to feeling was ridiculous. The fear of ridicule has been a strong deterrent to women writers.

And yet, despite the limitations on female creativity, certain Latin American countries—Argentina, Uruguay, and Chile—have a rich tradition of writings by women. In Argentina, for instance, talented women writers such as Norah Lange emerged with the avant-garde movements of the 1920s. By the 1940s and 1950s there was a constellation of women novelists, such as Silvina Bullrich, Marta Lynch, Beatriz Guido, Gloria Alcorta, and María Angélica Bosco, as well as Victoria Ocampo, one of the first consciously feminist writers. In Uruguay, women made outstanding contributions to poetry (Sara Ibañez and Idea Vilariño) and the short story (Giselda Zani and Armonía Sommers), and in Chile, such women writers as Marta Brunet, María Luisa

Bombal, Margarita Aguirre, and Mercedes Validivieso broke new ground in subject matter. Many women writers of the past have been underestimated because their work has not been placed within its historical and social context or studied in relation to the obstacles they faced. For all these countries, research is needed on the contexts in which women writers interacted and developed if we are to dispel the notion that these women are isolated and exceptional.

In recent years, the international women's movement has given encouragement to Latin American women writers, especially through the convocation of International Women's Year in Mexico. A young generation now openly expresses a feminine, if not a feminist, point of view. The novels and stories of Rosario Ferré of Puerto Rico; Elena Poniatowska, Josefina Hernández, Elena Garro, and Julieta Campos of Mexico; Carmen Naranjo of Costa Rica; Cristina Peri Rossi of Uruguay; Luisa Valenzuela, Marta Traba, Marta Lynch, and Griselda Gambarro and Tununa Mercado of Argentina, and many others represent a totally new stage in the development of feminist literature, one in which the problems of female authorship can become the central topic of the poem or novel itself, as in Julieta Campos' *Tiene los cabellos rojizos y se llama Sabina* (1974).

The study of Hispanic and particularly Latin American women's literature remains very much under the influence of scholars working in the United States. Because women's studies has not been and cannot be established in many Latin American countries, this situation is likely to prevail until these countries are democratized. Mexico is the exception. Not only is the journal *Fem* published there but Mexico was the site of the first Mexican-Central American symposium on research on women, which included papers by the writer Carmen Naranjo and the Latin American critics Margo Glantz, the late Alaíde Foppa, Margarita Peña, María Luisa Erreguerra, and Georgina García. In June 1981, Mexico also hosted the congress of Latin American women writers. It is interesting, however, that during the congress several women writers (notably Julieta Campos) refused to take a feminist position and, indeed, argued that writing has no gender.

North American scholarship in Latin American women's literature has so far followed the pattern set by women's studies in English and North American literatures: first an analysis of the portrayal of women in male literature, then an attempt to discover neglected women authors, and finally theoretical work. Women's literature in Latin America, however, is not confined to the written texts and genres that are recognized in the English and North American traditions. We must broaden the definition of literature to include both the traditional, orally transmitted popular forms, such as song and storytelling, which now survive mainly in rural areas, and the newer mass culture, including film, radio, television, romances, comics, and photonovels (i.e., fiction narrated as a series of photographs, resembling a comic book). By including these forms we can gain insights into the cultural activity of women who do not belong to the privileged social classes. Regarding orally transmitted literature, the novelists Rosario Castellanos and Miguel Angel Asturias have both acknowledged the importance of the women storytellers who passed along traditional tales, which, as we know from Bruno Bettleheim's *Uses of Enchantment,* are important modes of cognition and education in traditional societies. The first scholars to use the tape recorder extensively—for instance, Oscar Lewis in *The Children of Sánchez*—opened up new possibilities for the study of women's popular culture, even if their work was controversial. The tape recorder made it possible to collect women's oral biographies, especially those of working-class women. June Nash and Manuel María Rocca's *Dos mujeres indígenas* (1976) and Moema Viezzer's *Testimonio de Domitila* (1977) not only record the lives of their subjects but also upset the stereotypes about such women.

A significant portion of the new mass culture—especially comics, photonovels, and soap operas—is directed at women, both to reinforce traditional morality and, as Michèle Mattelart has shown, to help promote a consumer culture and hence "modernization." Her article "Apuntes sobre lo moderno: Una manera de leer la revista feminina" (*Casa de las Americas,* No. 77 [1973]) points out the ideology of modernization underlying fiction of this sort written during the Allende regime in Chile; her work is applicable to other countries as well. There are also studies of the photonovel, a genre read by hundreds of thousands of Latin Americans, such as Cornelia Butler Flora and Jan L. Flora's "The Fotonovela as a Tool for Class and Cultural Domination" (*Latin American Perspectives,* Winter 1978), and Marie Claire Acosta's "Los estereotipos de la mujer mexicana en las fotonovelas" (*Diálogos,* No. 53 [1973]).

Although there has been some preliminary research on women's literature, most of it by North American women scholars who have concentrated on the images of women and on women writers, much remains to be done. What follows is intended not as a survey of the priorities in research and publication but simply as an indication of some areas that have been neglected and of others in which progress has been made.

Opportunities for Research on Women and Hispanic Literature

Meri Knaster's *Women in Spanish America: An Annotated Bibliography from Pre-Conquest to Contemporary Times* (Boston: Hall, 1977) has listings under the headings "Biography and Autobiography," "Arts and Literature," and "Mass Media and Folklore." The "Literature" entries are limited to "publications of a more personal nature rather than those which are strictly literary criticism." This section is highly selective in the choice of authors and does not include Spain. Diane Marting has compiled and circulated three bibliographies: *Bibliography of Women Writers of Spain, Bibliography of Women Writers of Spanish America,* and *Bibliography of Hispanic Women Writers of the Caribbean.* Garland Press is planning to publish an annotated bibliography of translations of works by Spanish American women writers. Maureen Ahern of Arizona State University has completed but not yet published an annotated bibliography of the writings of Rosario Castellanos. Similar tasks could be undertaken for many other women writers, particularly for those who, like Gabriela Mistral, contributed to many newspapers or for the "forgotten" women writers of the nineteenth century, like Clorinda Matto de Turner and Gertrude Gómez de Avellaneda.

There is an urgent need for basic texts, especially the complete works of particular women writers. One has only to contrast the amount of textual and critical work done on Virginia Woolf, for example, with the paucity of material on Gabriela Mistral to be aware of the opportunities for scholarly work on the Chilean writer. Of course there are many articles and some books on aspects of her work, but there is no edition of her complete writings. The Aguilar edition of her poetry, published in 1958, is awkwardly arranged by theme, and a full edition of her prose has yet to appear. We need, first of all, a preliminary survey of the field of Hispanic women's literature and of the availability of the works of women writers. Then we need a series of guides to the critical writings on women in each of the Hispanic countries or societies. Diane Marting of Rutgers University has made a start by compiling a checklist of Latin American women writers with the aim of establishing what writers most need to be reedited, translated, and published. Any extensive survey, however, will require funding from a foundation. One possible source is UNESCO, which published *América Latina en su literatura* (1970); because this survey made no explicit mention of women writers or feminist criticism, a case might be made for a supplementary volume.

Women writers have been poorly represented in anthologies, as Beth Miller pointed out in her article "Less than Tokenism" (*Latin American Writers Today,* a special issue of the *Latin American Literary Review,* 11 [1977], 11–17). The older Latin American anthologies of women poets are often pathetic compilations that purvey false ideas of "femininity." June E. Hahner has edited an anthology about important women in history, *Women in Latin American History: Their Lives and Views* (Los Angeles: Univ. of California Press, 1976). As for literary anthologies, it is time to think of something more ambitious than a collection of poems or stories. There is a need for annotated anthologies that treat women's writings in their social frameworks and for anthologies that include letters, memoirs, plays, and journalism as well as poetry and narrative.

One impediment to incorporating Latin American women writers into women's studies courses in the United States has been the lack of good translations. There are now some promising beginnings in this field. Maureen Ahern's *Looking at the Mona Lisa* is an excellent collection of translations of poems by Rosario Castellanos (Rivelin, 1981), which, unfortunately, has appeared only in a very limited edition in England. The Binghamton Drama Center is undertaking a much needed translation of some women dramatists' work, including that of such hitherto unpublished writers as Pilar Campesino. A seminar on the translation of writing by Latin American women met in San Miguel Allende, Mexico, in 1978 under the sponsorship of the Mexican government. Such meetings may give translators practical assistance and encouragement. Under the direction of Sandra Dijkstra, a project is planned for translating the works of women writers from Europe and Latin America; if funded by the National Endowment for the Humanities, it will commission translations of the works of Sor Juana Inés de la Cruz, Rosario Castellanos, and perhaps some of the nineteenth-century women writers, like Gertrudis Gómez de Avellaneda.

The field of literary criticism and scholarship offers many opportunities for work by Hispanic scholars and students. In general, Latin America is poor in autobiography and memoirs. This historical gap can be partially filled by collecting oral histories, especially of the women who have had central roles in literary culture and artistic movements. An example of such a history is Margaret Randall's *Somos millones . . .* (Mexico, 1978; trans. as *Doris Tijerino: Inside the Nicaraguan Revolution* [Vancouver: New State, 1978]), the life of the Nicaraguan militant, Doris María. Full biographies of some important women writers are now in progress. Parts of Octavio Paz's life of Sor Juana Inés de la Cruz have appeared in *Vuelta,* and a translated portion has been published in *Signs.* Yvonne Guillén Barrett is preparing a biography of Gabriela Mistral, and Gabriela Mora is writing a full-length study of the Mexican writer Elena Garro and her work.

Literary historians pay lip service to the writings of Juana de Ibarbourou, Delmira Agustini, and other women poets but not the serious scholarly attention normally accorded male writers. Moreover, the lists of completed dissertations, in Carl Deal's *Latin America and the Caribbean* and in *Hispania,* show no increase, over the past decade, in the research on women writers or on topics of interest to women's studies scholars. Of the more than one thousand titles listed by Deal, only about thirty-seven relate either to women writers or to women in literature. The 1976 listing in *Hispania* contained seven titles pertinent to women's studies. Although that listing is based on an admittedly cursory check, it does indicate the need for scholarship and criticism in Hispanic women's studies. There is a wealth of material for the revision of male-authored criticisms of such women writers as Sor Juana and Gabriela Mistral, and there is room for textual study of every female writer I have mentioned.

Though there is little feminist criticism as such in the field of Hispanic studies, a start has been made. *The Theory and Practice of Feminist Literary Criticism,* edited by Gabriela Mora and Karen Van Hooft, includes two theoretical essays by Gabriela Mora, "crítica feminista: apuntes sobre definiciones y problemas" and "Narradoras hispanoamericanas; vieja y nueva problemática en renovadas elaboraciones." In addition, there are articles on individual women writers; still, a number of possibilities exist for critical works of a large scope. We lack a sociology of Hispanic women writers that might provide a framework for research. Such a study would have to go beyond the recognized modes of creativity, that is, the writing of poetry, drama, and fiction, to review other modes of female creativity that society has permitted, such as oral and popular literary forms and the permissible roles of patroness, mother figure, and teacher. The sociology would also have to discuss the infrastructure of illiteracy and education in Hispanic countries. We need works along the lines of Gilbert and Gubar's *The Madwoman in the Attic,* works that show how women writers have used irony, allusion, parody, and fantasy. Such studies might be part of a larger effort to examine the ways in which women writers relate to the dominant ideology, whether it is religious or nationalistic, and the choices women make in genre, theme, imagery, and linguistic euphemism when they are externally or self-repressed. It would be useful to have studies of the "unconscious" of the literary text that makes women the bearers of meaning; Laura Mulvey's article "Visual Pleasure and Narrative Cinema" (in *Women in the Cinema,* ed. G. Peary and K. Kay [New York: Dutton, 1978]) is the first example of this kind of work. There are no studies yet of women's popular literature in nineteenth- or twentieth-century Latin America. Mexico and Argentina, in particular, offer possibilities for this work. Finally, a number of critical approaches might be explored and tested for insights into women's literature. For example, semiotics, the study of the ways sign systems are encoded and organized to produce meaning, has provided a valuable instrument for the analysis of literary discourse and other kinds of representation. This approach might be taken with Hispanic women's literature, perhaps most fruitfully in analyzing how sign systems are encoded by women writers and used to reinforce traditional female roles. Another challenging approach is offered by neo-Freudianism, the method that Laura Mulvey has employed in her article on cinema. More work could be done in the area of reception theory, that is, empirical studies of audiences and textual studies aimed at identifying implied readers. Such studies may refute the notion that mass culture unilaterally manipulates its recipients. All these efforts, however commendable, are still very far from providing a comprehensive theoretical base, and one reason, as scholars in every field of women's studies realize, is that more interdisciplinary work is needed first. All too often political and social studies furnish empirical data on women's condition without considering the important cultural aspects of their situation, as is true of the two-volume work *La mujer en América Latina* (ed. María del Carmen Elu de Leñero [Mexico: Sepsetenta, 1975]); conversely, literary studies traditionally ignore social and political contexts.

Conferences

Conferences on Hispanic women writers now offer the best opportunities for fostering research papers, readings, and other activities by Hispanic women writers and scholars. Several congresses have been held in recent years: the first in Pittsburgh, at Carnegie-Mellon University, in 1975; the second in San José in 1976; the third in Ottawa in 1978; and a fourth in Mexico in 1981. The history of these congresses on women writers is instructive. The first, on Latin American women writers, was sponsored by the *Latin American Literary Review,* which published the proceedings of the conference, and supported by the National Endowment for the Arts. The *Review* (ed. Yvette Miller) is one of the few scholarly publications that encourages writing by and about women. The second conference, organized by Celia Zapata of San José State University, was broader in its scope. Many women writers came from Latin America to participate, and the sessions dealt with North American women poets as well as Hispanic women writers. Unfortunately, funding could not be obtained to publish the proceedings of this conference. The third congress, held under the auspices of the Canada Council in Ottawa, brought together women from Latin America, Spain, and francophone Canada. The Canada Council will fund the publication of the proceedings. Papers from the Mexico 1981 congress have been appearing in journals such as the *Revista de la Universidad* and *Fem,* but publication of the complete proceedings seems unlikely.

Latin American scholars and regional branches of the Modern Language Association have organized a number of smaller-scale events. For instance, Lucía Guerra Cunningham and Julia Palley of the University of California, Irvine, organized an interdisciplinary symposium on women and society in Latin America, held in Tijuana, Mexico, in March–April 1978, and a second conference, in Enseñada, Mexico, in March–April 1979, which welcomed papers in "any field of inquiry which may pertain to the role of Hispanic women in Latin America." A colloquium on literary analysis at York College, City University of New York, on 11 May 1979, took as its main topic An Interdisciplinary Approach to Feminism. The May 1979 California Conference on Regionalism and Women's Studies, held at Sonoma State University, was of particular interest to Chicanas. Finally, the meeting of the Latin American Studies Association in October 1980 at Bloomington, Indiana, included a session called Feminist Alternatives: Reconsidering Ideology and Criticism. These conferences provide a useful basis for future research in Hispanic women's literature and in interdisciplinary approaches to Hispanic women's studies. Work in these areas must not depend on single events, however: ways must be found to enable scholars to work together on a continuous basis and to facilitate publication of their research.

Opportunities for Publishing Work on and by Women Writers in the United States

Apart from the *Latin American Literary Review,* standard academic journals and publishers (the *Revista Iberoamericana, Hispania, Hispanic Review, MLR*) and newer publications (e.g., *Hispamérica* and *Ideologies and Literature*) have shown little interest in feminist criticism. This situation may result less from editorial policy than from a paucity of materials. But it does suggest that any advance in women's studies in the Hispanic field will require individual initiative in commissioning the materials, organizing the work, and persuading a publisher to take it. One such effort was made by Beth Miller of the University of Southern California, who has gathered materials for the volume *Images: Essays on Women in Hispanic Literature.* Rosario Sánchez of San Diego recently coedited *Essays on La Mujer,* a series of studies of the Chicana. Some magazines do provide a forum for discussing the interests and problems of Hispanic women minorities in the United States. The New York–based *Areito,* for instance, although not exclusively feminist in perspective, includes three women on its editorial board and encourages female creativity in various forms and fields—literature, film criticism, and graphics. On the West Coast, an active group of Chicana writers and critics based at the University of California, San Diego, have contributed to *Aztlan*'s special issue on the Chicana. A second special issue of *Aztlan* is being planned by Chicanas at the University of California, Los Angeles.

Opportunities for Publishing in Spain and Latin America

In addition to the opportunities for publication in this country, an expanding spectrum of periodicals in Spain and Latin America are promising vehicles for feminist work. It has not been possible to compile a list of editors and publishers sympathetic to feminist criticism and women writers, for much depends on the overall focus of the particular journal and often on personal contact. Journals rarely devote entire issues to women, but two have done so, though both are now defunct: *Libre* and *Cuadernos para el diálogo.* The only feminist journal I know of in Spanish America is *Fem,* published in Mexico.

In Spain, *Vindicación feminista* provided a forum for feminist criticism. Of the other established journals run by women, the best known are *Sur* (ed. Victoria Ocampo), which has now ceased publication, and *Sin Nombre* (ed. Nilita Vientos Gastón). Other journals and reviews (e.g., *Siempre* and *Nexos* of Mexico) consistently give space to women writers, women critics, and discussions of women's interests. Because so much depends, as I have said, on the personal contact between authors and editors, the need for detailed information about potential publishers is evident; we have to identify the editors who are receptive to women's studies scholarship and keep informed about new journals that will open their pages to women writers and critics—and also about the demise of periodicals that had offered publishing opportunities.

Women and the Profession

The many lacunae in research and publication in the the study of Hispanic women's literature, lives, and contexts are part of a long history of exclusion and discouragement. It is not accidental that the term most widely used to mean aggressively male—"macho"—should be Hispanic. Departments of Spanish in this country generally accept women professors only insofar as these women can prove their worth in already established fields. The overwhelming majority of women employed in our profession hold one-year temporary appointments, lectureships, or assistant professorships. To advance, they must produce research and publications, but research and publication in women's studies do not weigh heavily in the tenure and promotion decisions made in many universities. Furthermore, women's studies programs are often the first to suffer the effects of financial cuts. The limitations placed on the profession are thus particularly oppressive to women.

There have, however, been some advances for women in the profession, mostly made by women on their own behalf. At the annual conferences of the Latin American Studies Association its Committee on Women organizes panels on the methods and findings of feminist research in history, sociology, and political science; much of the committee's work is relevant to literary studies. The newsletter circulated by the committee and coordinated by its chairwoman, Jane Jaquette, provides job information, encourages contacts between researchers in this country and Latin America, and serves as a clearinghouse of information on the work in progress in various disciplines. In addition, the association annually awards a prize to an essay on women.

At the 1980 meeting of the Modern Language Association, an association of women in Spanish was integrated with the Chicano-Hispanic-Luso-Brazilian Feminist Caucus to form a single organization. Information will be sent to participants through the newsletter of the Women's Caucus for the Modern Languages. Finally, the Women's Caucus, the Division of Women's Studies in Language and Literature, and the Commission on the Status of Women in the profession organize sessions at the annual conferences of the Modern Language Association and are eager to offer selections of women's literatures and topics representative of various cultures.*

Note

*I wish to thank the people I consulted while I was preparing this paper—Bridget Aldaraca, Susan Kirkpatrick, Beth Miller, Yvette Miller, Diane Marting, Elizabeth Ordoñez, Martha Paley Francescato, Rosaura Sánchez, and Celia Zapata. The article was originally written in 1979. I have partially revised the original but have not been able to take into account all the individual contributions to criticism and the many younger writers who are now beginning to publish.

Directions in French Women's Studies

Christiane P. Makward and Sylvie Weil

The need to justify French women's studies has slowly subsided in the past five years. Feminist thought has blossomed, and the indisputable brilliance of some of the women on the Parisian scene has made French women's studies a major forum for feminist debate. By the mid-1970s names such as Luce Irigaray, Hélène Cixous, Julia Kristeva, and Catherine Clément began to be introduced in the United States as major exponents of a new feminist philosophy and aesthetics. At that time, a landmark of feminist criticism in the United States, *Les Femmes en France,* had just been published.[1] Presenting texts by French feminists, many of which (especially those written during the 1789–92 and the 1848 revolutions) were reprinted for the first time, this book made courses in French women's studies a practicable endeavor. Designed for classroom use, this critical anthology combines feminist documents with excerpts from well-known fiction writers, both female and male. Thus readers can gain a perspective on the evolution of feminism and compare the evidence with artists' representations of women of the same period. Selected for their potential to generate discussion, the texts constitute an exciting reader for students and instructors alike.

The wealth of materials available for examination is virtually inexhaustible. In Paris abundant texts by women still gather dust in the Bibliothèque Nationale and the Archives. Few researchers are aware of the facilities of the Bibliothèque Marguerite Durand, founded in 1934, which is a collection of some twelve thousand volumes, manuscripts, and graphic documents.[2] The Laruelle Collection in the Cabinet des Estampes of the Bibliothèque Nationale is another little-known collection of graphics solely devoted to women. Since 1975, French feminists have been reprinting a number of texts, especially by women famous for their participation in various revolutionary movements, such as Louise Michel (1830–1905), the "Red Virgin" of the 1871 Paris Commune, and Flora Tristan (1803–44), the major socialist figure of the 1840s.[3] Interest in them was reawakened by the events of May 1968.

The role of the French feminist press Editions des femmes cannot be overestimated in the fundamental task of spreading women's words and writings, of retrieving from oblivion—or from repression, in the case of contemporary writers—the outstanding intellectual and political works of French women. Recently two novels by Germaine de Staël were edited by Claudine Herrmann, one of the better-known Franco-American feminist critics and one of the pioneers of feminist literary criticism (see her *Voleuses de langue* [Paris: Editions des femmes, 1976]). About the time of International Women's Year, several French publishers founded "women's" collections that continue to thrive, so that a feminist scholar in quest of a French publisher might approach Grasset, Stock, Denoël-Gonthier, or Flammarion if she cannot induce Des femmes to publish her manuscript. Des femmes is the only major publisher in France entirely owned and run by women. It is the only uncompromisingly feminist press, even though it sometimes disowns the label "feminist" because the term has become tame and acceptable in many circles. Although it started on a very amateurish and self-trained basis, Des femmes became a resounding success once it resigned itself to using regular distribution and advertising channels. Within eight years (1972–80) it became omnipresent and remarkably diversified, publishing children's literature, paperback collections, and reprints as well as nonfiction collections (herstories, philosophical essays, political diaries, and translations from Mediterranean, Latin-American, and Anglo-Saxon countries).[4]

Until quite recently, French feminist criticism dealt mostly with the major writers of the eighteenth and nineteenth centuries: Zola, Rousseau, Balzac, Sade, and the like. In other words, there was a renaissance of an ageless academic tradition, the "gynocentric" tradition of "images of women" or feminine archetypes in canonical literature, usually with commendable results: for example, Pierre Fauchery's *La Destinée féminine* or Jeannette Rosso's *Montesquieu et la féminité*.[5] Much remains to be done in this tradition, one of genuine concern with "the woman question" in culture and literature. Our ideas about the sixteenth century, for instance, are still largely determined by the writings of giants such as Rabelais and Montaigne; feminist scholars must assume responsibility for analyzing how women saw themselves in any given period. Because there is no modern edition of Marie de Gournay's *Traité de l'égalité des hommes et des femmes* (1622), readers without training in Renaissance French are essentially barred from this important feminist statement. There are several other prestigious and inaccessible monuments as well, including Christine de Pisan's *Cité des dames* and *La Mutacion de fortune* (an ancestor, thematically, of Virginia Woolf's *Orlando*).

The "woman question" was the subject of an ongoing debate throughout the Middle Ages and in every major period in French literature, as MLA President Jean A. Perkins recalled in her entertaining and inspiring address at the 1979 convention in San Francisco.[6] The breadth and vivacity of the *Querelle* have not yet been fully assessed. Unlike other major European literatures, French literature has had at least one "major" woman writer in every period and movement. While German women writers emerge only in the nineteenth century and the continuity of women writers in Spanish did not begin until the late nineteenth century, in France the very first "professional writer" to debate the doctors of the University was Christine de Pisan in the late fourteenth century. After her, sexist prejudice notwithstanding, Marguerite de Navarre (1492–1549), Louise Labé (1526–66), Marie-Madeleine de La Fayette (1634–93), Marie de Sévigné (1626–96), Germaine de Staël (1766–1817), Marceline Desbordes-Valmore (1786–1859), and Colette (1873–1954) have been viewed as "major" even though misrepresented—that is, overfeminized or defeminized—if at all possible. French women writers thus have a strong tradition to invoke, and the feminine intellect, though sometimes ridiculed, sometimes unduly exalted, remains present in literary history. Upper-class women consistently enjoyed social and intellectual power although they were deprived of political rights until 1945. Many convincing defenses of the female sex were written, by both men and women. The paramount question of women's education was posed by Erasmus in the early sixteenth century, taken up by exponents of the women's cause in the seventeenth century, and thoroughly probed by eighteenth-century essayists such as the contributors to *Le Journal des Dames* (1759), Stéphanie de Genlis, and Albertine Necker de Saussure. Some of these essays on women's education should be systematically reviewed and reprinted in toto or in excerpts.

In her excellent study on French women in the seventeenth century, *Le Paradis des femmes*, Carolyn Lougee gives much information on the composition of the Parisian salons and the family background of the "salonnières," thus opening an area for research.[7] Publishing the correspondence of the secondary figures in the Précieuses' circles would help modern scholars to develop a more accurate idea of this innovative but not homogeneous group of women. There is still much to discover about illustrious figures like Mlle de Montpensier (1627–93), who fought in La Fronde, the Aristocrats' rebellion of the mid-century, and Antoinette des Houlières (1638–94), who was associated with the "Libertine Poets." To date, Pascal's sisters remain obscure figures, much like Marx's daughters until 1980,[8] and most definitely should be researched. More women's diaries and correspondence need to be unearthed. Writing well-documented biographies is an important priority. Françoise Mallet-Joris's biography of Jeanne Guyon (1648–1717), who is best known for her influence on Fénelon and for her popular prayer book, still in use in Switzerland and the United States, is an outstanding example of the kind of research that has to be done on a great many writers whose lives remain shrouded in obscurity, including some very popular writers of recent times: Daniel Lesueur (1860–1921), for example, and Victorine Monniot (1825–88), a novelist from the Réunion Island. Not enough information is easily accessible about famous figures like Ninon de Lenclos (1620–1705), the extraordinary grand lover and free spirit of the seventeenth century, or about the Duchesse du Maine (1676–1753), remembered for her salon and her part in political conspiracies. Another scholarly project would be to unravel the life of Marie-Catherine d'Aulnoy (1650–1705), the fairy-tale writer who conspired to have her husband executed and then disappeared from the Parisian scene for three decades.

Women have played important roles in the revolutions that shook France after 1789. Edith Thomas' books, *Pauline Roland* and *Les Pétroleuses,* could serve as models for more detailed investigation of the personalities of women who were involved in the 1848 and 1871 revolutions; and Laure Adler's *A l'aube du féminisme* is another substantial contribution to a comprehensive assessment of periods of intensive feminist activity.[9] There are no readily available editions of the correspondence of Pauline Roland, who was probably the most sensitive and remarkable of the "Saint-Simoniennes," along with Suzanne Voilquin, whose *Mémoires d'une Saint-Simonienne en Russie* was published in 1979 by Des femmes. Some of the most original work of the women of 1848 has been ignored because of their radical positions; they were ridiculed by the very men who should have supported them as socialists—Proudhon being the best known. Included in this category are the correspondence and the witty essays of Jeanne Deroin, a militant socialist and founder of *La Voix des femmes* (1848) and *L'Opinion des femmes* (1848–49). These are at the Bibliothèque Nationale together with another feminist monument published in 1848 by the Vésuviennes: *Constitution politique des femmes.* The Vésuviennes, as the most visible and "eccentric" feminist socialist group of that period, were the favorite subject of Daumier's satirical cartoons.

In France, much as in any other culture and throughout history—not herstory—the male has had the privilege of defining all things. At the beginning of the seventeenth century, the Christian tradition of a duality between the physical and the spiritual realms, which great mystics, from the Cathars to Teresa de Avila, have tried to resolve, was firmly established. So was woman's association with the nonspiritual lower order of things. Despite social and political upheavals and the passage from Christian tradition to a moral system based on a new concept of Nature, largely to be credited to eighteenth-century philosophers like Rousseau, the respective positions of men and women in French society changed very little. Whereas the Russian revolution produced authentically radical feminists like Alexandra Kollontai, in France an upper-class feminist like Daniel Lesueur (Jeanne L. Lapauze) could not conceive that sexuality and men's sexual repression of women were at the root of the "woman question." In her novels Lesueur recognized the status of women as objects of exchange between men. Although in her 1905 report on the status of women workers to the International Convention of Commerce and Industry she denounced the double exploitation of the working-class woman and advocated what amounted to a homemaker's salary, her arguments ultimately rested on the principles of the preservation of the "race" and on the "sacredness" of motherhood.[10] Similar ambiguities and reticences about women's emancipation can be found in George Sand and Colette: both acted out a sexual emancipation they did not deem available to women in general. Colette declined to make nonfictionalized statements on such an issue as the advisability of equal sexual roles, and the male establishment efficiently passed her on to posterity as a singer of motherly love and nature. Colette's radical stance on sexuality, as it is developed in *The Pure and the Impure,* had to wait for the development of contemporary feminist criticism to be fully understood. In this collection of autobiographical texts written around 1930, Colette celebrates one lesbian relationship, in "The Ladies of Langollen," but she almost berates other homosexual experiences and certainly avoids clear references to her own. Her relationship with "Missy," the "Chevalière" of *The Pure and the Impure,* had nonetheless inspired her most accomplished love prose poems in "The Tendrils of the Vine" (1907).

In a recent paper Elaine Marks underlined a lack of reliable tenets for feminist theory and the problematic distinctions among "theory," "fiction," and subjective expression in women's writing. Even Simone de Beauvoir's *Second Sex,* the pivotal theoretical document of modern feminism, comes under the category of works that attempt "to insert the undeniable and overwhelming evidence of women's oppression and repression into pre-existing theories and systems. *We continue to be in search of theory.*"[11] Because "theory" is comparable to gold as the most highly valued commodity on the scholarly marketplace, we continue for the most part to function on the ageless paradigm of "masculine" versus "feminine," although Colette tried to resolve this opposition in *The Pure and the Impure* and in her numerous androgynous characters. Fascinating developments in the area of a "theory of the feminine" deserve attention.[12] The time is ripe for some ambitious feminist critic to assess the current literary movement sometimes labeled "writing in the feminine." Only partial analyses have emerged so far, and no comprehensive synthesis of psychoanalysis, feminism, and the philosophy of language has been attempted.

American feminists may be aware that one crucial difference between the French and the American movements is that, unlike NOW, the Mouvement de Libération des Femmes is not nationally organized. It was not until October 1979 that the designation MLF was officially registered, and thereby legally appropriated, by the "Politics and Psychoanalysis" group (names reversed from earlier usage). For a decade the movement has comprised relatively small groups with no formal membership, varying from a dozen participants to several hundred. "La Spirale," for example, gathers some thirty Parisian artists interested in feminist aesthetics, while "Choisir" is widely known for its mass demonstrations and its work on rape and reproduction legislation. Sometimes a group emerges or disintegrates because of a leading figure. In the aftermath of 1968 this was true of "The Red Dykes," organized around Monique Wittig; then "Psychoanalysis and Politics" became *the* radical lesbian group in Paris. Presumably Wittig was not involved enough in theory to accept some of the tenets of the new group. Anonymity in publishing, for instance, to signify the rejection of "the name of the father" or of the phallic principle was for a time one of the most controversial issues.

In connection with the "Psychoanalysis and Politics" group led by rebellious students of Lacan around 1970, who soon gave birth to Editions des femmes, Luce Irigaray undertook a thorough critique of Western "phallogocentrism," philosophical discourse from Plato to Freud. Marx was spared, as Marxist feminist philosopher Catherine Clément succeeded in maintaining a fruitful dialogue between the feminist heiresses of Freud and Marx. Irigaray's *Speculum de l'autre femme* appeared in 1974, the year when *La Quinzaine Littéraire,* a respected literary bimonthly, polled a number of writers of both sexes on the question of "the sex of writing." For the first time the relation of gender to the experience of writing was given serious attention outside feminist circles. Numerous pamphlets, essays, dialogues, and collective statements on this subject punctuate the following years.

The agitation focused on the issue of "difference," a key word in poststructuralist France. French feminists chose to assert the difference of the feminine and postulated a nonmasculine relation of women to language. This vindication was primarily made in feminist and nonsystematic critiques of Lacan and Freud: by Hélène Cixous in *La Jeune née* and "The Laugh of the Medusa" (trans. for *Signs* [Summer 1976]), by Luce Irigaray in articles collected as *Ce sexe qui n'en est pas un* (1977), and by contributors to special issues of the journal *L'Arc* (No. 58 on Lacan and No. 61 on Simone de Beauvoir). Excellent, albeit brief, overviews of these debates are available in English: Elaine Marks's "Review Essay: Women and Literature in France" (*Signs* [Summer 1978]) and Marks's and Isabelle de Courtivron's Introductions I and III in *New French Feminisms.* This recent and most timely anthology enables American critics to become acquainted with the important French feminist texts of the past decade.

It would be impossible to analyze these developments in the proper perspective without taking into account the antipsychiatry and antipsychoanalysis movement that developed in the past two decades in the wake of Deleuze, Guattari, and Lyotard. Equally crucial is an awareness of Derrida's critique, or "deconstruction," of philosophy and language, which had a tremendous impact on feminist "theory" and feminist writing. For feminists trying to communicate across the Atlantic, a near insoluble problem must be confronted: to reflect in standard language a writing-in-the-feminine movement that functions against certain Lacanian tenets—and is therefore deeply involved in Lacanian theory—and that equally functions on the Derridian notions (nonconcepts) of "differ*a*nce" (delay-dissemination of meaning), linguistic closure (phallogocentrism), and "trace" (the unnameable essential embedded in the text).

Perhaps we are still too close to these debates to argue that the writing-in-the feminine movement has entered a second phase, but the "theorizing" fermentation appears to have subsided, fragmentary and cautious though it was. Luce Irigaray's latest publications are not essays but creative texts dominated by incantation, fluidity of imagery, and a determination to shun the stereotypes of philosophical discourse and its—typically masculine?—delusions: the "system" and the "theory," or "thesis."[13] The first model for this new "woman language" was Cixous' "Laugh of the Medusa." From the early 1970s on, Cixous' texts have functioned on the principles of avant-garde poetics after Mallarmé and Joyce, that is, on the disruption of univocal meaning. Her own historical impact on writing is to have integrated into writing, through subconsciouslike material, the exploration of the female experience of the body. The liberation or delivery of the text, then, consists in circumventing censorship and disrupting language at all levels while maintaining some measure of significance. Cixous asserts primarily the feminine and in her most recent texts (*Là, Préparatifs de noces au-delà de l'abîme, Ananké, Illa, Ou l'art de l'innocence*) the love of women as well.

On a different Parisian stage Julia Kristeva was for a couple of years considered a "theoretician" of the woman question. Her one feminist essay, *About Chinese Women* (1974), and various articles and interviews around 1975 reflected the more conservative conception of the feminine as that which cannot be verbalized or codified in the symbolic order (also designated "the law of the father"). In this respect Kristeva's position paralleled Catherine Clément's, both in the wake of structural anthropology and Lévi-Strauss's analyses of the structures of kinship in natural societies. For Kristeva in the mid-seventies, the feminine was on the negative and therefore potentially disruptive side of power. But, argued Kristeva, any access of women to power implies a process of virilization, an entry into the phallic order. In *About Chinese Women*, Kristeva discusses the exceptional figure of Empress Wu, who waged a delicate war against male power in order to acquire the title of emperor. Kristeva does not, however, account for the fact that Wu's "virilization" strategy partly rested on promoting the cult of the mother. Wu seems to have succeeded in establishing herself as both the holy mother and the divine emperor.[14] The relative importance of Kristeva's pronouncements on the feminine should be viewed within her general theory of language and of the subject of writing as it is primarily expounded in *The Revolution of Poetic Language* (1974). Her distinction between the "semiotic" (associated with the "genotext," or the nonverbal, disruptive dimension of creativity) and the "symbolic" (explicit discourse) seemed to concur with the feminist intuition of writing in the feminine as a new mode of exploration of the feminine, one that permits the feminine to be captured in the symbolic of the text regardless of the writer's gender. Kristeva's position may be related to the Freudian postulate of psychological bisexuality, but the question remains largely unexplored.[15] The new terminologies—whether inspired by Lacan, Kristeva, or Derrida—enabled feminists to postulate "the inscription of the body" as the privileged difference and the mark of the feminine. It is impossible to account briefly for these approximations and ambiguities, which aim at destroying previously accepted concepts in order to achieve a new language. A symptom, perhaps, of modern consumerism, neologisms fascinate but wear out quickly.

Other feminists, such as Wittig, not having graduated from the same schools as Cixous, Irigaray and Kristeva (notably the "free" University of Vincennes), strove all along to do away with the yoke of "masculine/feminine," together with a number of abused terms referring to gender and sexual preference. In her pursuit of a new language, Wittig excluded any entries in the masculine from her "draft for a dictionary of lesbian lovers," recently translated as *Lesbian People: Material for a Dictionary.* In the short story "Un jour mon Prince viendra" ("One Day My Prince Will Come")—a text in the science-fiction mode—Wittig does away with gender references altogether; the four species involved are nurturing giant bees, helpless "creatures" having penes but no limbs, the subservient gorillas, and the divine and free "beings."[16] Wittig has stayed clear of abstract pronouncements and, like Colette, leaves to her readers the responsibility of inferring the theory from the fiction. Today sustained creativity and theoretical quiet seem to characterize the French movement on its literary front. Criticism, meanwhile, has gathered momentum, especially around the work of Marguerite Duras. In 1969 a "feminine" critic, Edmée de la Rochefoucauld, remarked, "Literary feminism does not exist; women do not gather in schools like men: they are isolated."[17] Fortunately, the most important acquisition of the movement is the joy and comfort of togetherness, of pluralistic functioning, of collective effort, which is the only possible answer to some of the most pressing needs in women's studies.

Beyond making forays into French women's literary heritage, many of which have already taken place, and beyond trying to recover vast amounts of material, feminist scholars must emancipate their efforts from the weight of old criteria. "Women must dare," to quote Hélène Cixous; they must overlook certain traditional values in research and publication. In particular they must not be paralyzed by the hierarchy of "prestige" publishing houses. A good essay will not become mediocre if turned down by Gallimard or Seuil. Gallimard, preeminent in the publishing world in France, has published less than first-rate fiction and criticism as well as many intellectual landmarks of the century. Any publisher can be misled by financial considerations. Rather objectionable anthologies of women's writings have appeared in print alongside the best efforts of feminist research. We have Jeanine Moulin's *Huit siècles de poésie féminine* as an example of gynocentric research, but we also have M.-C. Fleury's *Femmes poètes de notre temps.*[18] In between, the Larousse paperback *Femmes écrivains* sometimes reprints the most conservative and tedious excerpts from authors and apparently makes no effort to investigate the concept of femininity in women writers.

To avoid wasted publishing opportunities, we need to work relentlessly and to develop better communication strategies. Whether manuscripts are to be published in the United States or in France, we have to learn to sell them efficiently. Practical steps are to solicit interviews with writers, to attend meetings in which they participate,[19] to endure literary parties and dinners, to listen to publishers' and writers' guesses and impressions, and to elect mentors and support groups—in other words, to come out of isolation, to dare and to share, to give and to request information. In 1975, inspired by a feminist-criticism collective and by the example of the *Women in German Newsletter*, a *Bulletin de Recherches et d'Etudes Féministes Francophones* (*BREFF*) was started at the University of Wisconsin, Madison. This bulletin has proved useful to hundreds of feminist scholars in the United States, France, and elsewhere. Its primary goal is to record current publications in French by women and on women and to stimulate interest and research in French women's studies. Because it depends on the work of volunteers, *BREFF* has not resolved some of its shortcomings: its circulation remains limited, and only a rare feminist scholar will send in a book review, since it will add little luster to her publication record. Only altruists will take the time to share information that they are not sure anybody else needs. But through such collective efforts *BREFF* has survived, even though it has not reached its full potential audience. A grant from the College of Liberal Arts at Pennsylvania State University has made it possible to compile computerized indexes of *BREFF*, so that most of the relevant publications can be easily identified within a few months of their appearance.[20]

Another crucial aid to research in women's studies and teaching is the ongoing bibliography of women's texts translated from the French. Isabelle de Courtivron (MIT) is the coordinator of this monumental project, part of the general inventory of women's texts in English translation sponsored by the MLA division for women's studies. This list will provide French women's studies with a precious reference tool, and individual researchers will save hundreds of hours when starting projects or preparing syllabi. Another important collective undertaking of some fifty participating critics, *Ecrits de femmes* (cited in n. 10) accounts for all major and for most really significant women writers in the French language from the Middle Ages to the present. Over a hundred articles that include biographical information, comprehensive bibliographies, and selected secondary sources constitute the bulk of the book. It also contains an introduction retracing the history of women and education—and therefore of women's writing—in the various areas of the francophone world; a review of traditional criticism of feminine writing; a review of contemporary feminist poetics; and as comprehensive a bibliography as could be compiled in four years for some four hundred additional women writers in French. Furthermore, it has a name and thematic index that should enable researchers to identify quickly the most promising texts for comparative thematic analysis.

Neither *Ecrits de femmes* nor any of the previously mentioned projects is classroom material. Perhaps French women's studies should devote more energy to developing adequate pedagogical tools. We must transcend the justified fear that pedagogical materials bring limited rewards from paternalistic institutions. To specialize in women's studies materials compounds this fear. Unfortunately *Les Femmes en France* has now gone out of print, but *New French Feminisms* has been published in paperback (New York: Schocken, 1981). *Ecrits de femmes,* because of its format, will probably be less expensive for undergraduates. The inadequacy of the available teaching tools suggests that we should develop new kinds of classroom materials and talk publishers into supporting them or else found our own feminist press; again, daring collective work and funding are the only answers. For classroom use we need cheap short monographs and reprints that will allow flexibility in selecting genres, including nonfiction texts, and in planning our courses according to our institutional schedules, the levels of our students' skills, and our own inclinations. French paperbacks are not cheap or durable and are reported "out of print" when they are simply not in stock in New York; one has to order them at least three months before they are needed. Moreover, some of the most significant women's texts in French are not available in paperback: Sand's *Lélia* is a case in point. Then, these significant texts are often too long—if not too difficult for undergraduate studies—to be assigned in their entirety or to be analyzed in depth. The solution is to develop a series of no-frills (no-illustrations) monographs that will include the essentials: annotations for lexical problems, biographical and bibliographical information, and texts reduced to a hundred pages, with careful plot summaries and important quotations provided where cuts have been made. Plays by women could be printed in groups of three or four or organized by theme or author. Such a format would be particularly helpful for poetry: currently no more than four or five women poets in French are available in paperback, at a cost of $6 to $8 to the American consumer. This situation puts intolerable limits on the sort of literature our students have access to. We should be able to convince some American or perhaps Quebecois publisher to undertake a new monograph series for classroom use in French women's studies and in French studies at large. Most of the volumes would probably warrant translation and marketing for wider undergraduate and high school use. Some of these short monographs could be anthologies—for example, of surrealist women poets, 1848 journalists, eighteenth-century pedagogues, seventeenth-century letter writers, fairy-tale writers, or post-1968 feminists. Short-story anthologies are sorely needed, both in French and in English translation. In addition, we should have cheap short monographs that would allow us at least to introduce our students to the unknown excellence of many nonmetropolitan writers from Africa, Quebec, the Caribbean islands, Switzerland, and Belgium. French women's studies outside France are still in their infancy. The advantage of a monograph series is of course that each volume would not need to be advertised separately once the series was launched. Needless to add, there is more than enough talent in Franco-American educational circles to prepare such a series: we can imagine a hundred of these monographs available for classroom use within a year.[21]

A few positive notes are in order. French women's studies may well fare better than French studies as a whole. The past ten years have established several women writers and essayists as "major" and internationally recognized: Nathalie Sarraute, Marguerite Duras, Hélène Cixous, Monique Wittig, and Marguerite Yourcenar. Important feminist research has been carried out, if not theoretically clarified. "Masters" of contemporary French thought have had to address the "woman question." Feminist philosophers have emancipated themselves from their mentors, whose work they read with sharp and "different" eyes. French women's studies have been developed in several French universities, while numerous courses were created in the United States.[22] Two MLA presidents have been "women in French": Germaine Brée, who also directed an NEH summer seminar on French women writers in 1979, and Jean A. Perkins, who spoke to the membership as a feminist scholar. Dozens of French women's studies papers and special sessions are arranged every year in the United States and in France. Special colloquiums also take place frequently. The most prestigious French feminists visit this country on a regular basis. All these undertakings will be sustained, for women's studies as a whole is not a fashion but an academic mutation. Women in modern languages will not cease to invest their energies but will rather multiply the bridges they have built between their lives and their works. Like their Hispanic and English counterparts, French women's studies have an international dimension.

The work to be carried out has no limits: research in cultural aspects of women's lives in the various francophone countries; the herstory of education; the implications of the colonial heritage; research on popular women writers, humorists, filmmakers, and mystics—all these have not yet emerged. We have witnessed a Sand revival, a Colette revival, a Beauvoir reassessment; a retrieval of nineteenth- and seventeenth-century women's movements is under way; an exploration of lesbian literature is maturing. The least developed areas of research seem to be poetry and drama by women,[23] nonmetropolitan writers,[24] and untranslated contemporary writers who continue to be ignored because their temperaments or their situations isolate them from literary women's groups.[23] It is our hope that *Ecrits de femmes* will begin to reveal the written riches of Chantal Chawaf, Emma Santos, Catherine Colomb, and Corinna Bille, to name only a few as yet unrecognized women who live(d) to write the feminine.

Notes

1. Marie Collins and Sylvie Weil-Sayre, *Les Femmes en France* (New York: Scribners, 1974).
2. See *Bulletin de Recherches et d'Etudes Féministes Francophones* (hereafter *BREFF*), No. 5 (1977), 5.
3. Louise Michel, *La Commune* (Paris: Maspéro, 1975) and *Mémoires* (Paris: Maspéro, 1978). Flora Tristan, *Pérégrinations d'une paria* (Paris: Maspéro, 1979). See also the biography by Pierre Leprohon: *Flora Tristan* (Paris: Corymbe, 1979).
4. Editions des femmes runs a feminist bookstore located in the Quartier Latin: 74 rue de Seine, Paris 75006 (Tel. 329-5075) and will mail current catalogs on request. It has also published several periodicals: *Le Quotidien des Femmes* (which was a very sporadic "daily" in the early 1970s), then *Des Femmes en Mouvements* (a monthly published for one year; Nos. 1–13 [Dec. 1977–Jan. 1979]), and currently, *Des Femmes Hebdo* (a weekly; No. 1[9–16 Nov. 1979]).
5. Pierre Fauchery, *La Destinée féminine dans le roman européen du XVIIIe siècle, 1713–1807* (Paris: Armand Colin, 1972); Jeannette Geffriaud Rosso, *Montesquieu et la féminité* (Pisa, Italy: Lib. Goliardica, 1977).
6. Jean A. Perkins, "Presidential Address 1979: E Pluribus Unum," *PMLA*, 95 (1980), 312–18.
7. Carolyn Lougee, *Le Paradis des femmes* (Princeton: Princeton Univ. Press, 1976).
8. *Les Filles de Marx, lettres inédites* (Paris: Albin Michel, 1980) is a volume of correspondence by Marx's daughters, recently translated from the German. See the substantial review in *La Quinzaine Littéraire,* No. 320 (March 1980).
9. Edith Thomas, *Pauline Roland: Socialisme et féminisme au XIXe siècle* (Paris: Marcel Rivière, 1956) and *Les Pétroleuses* (Paris: Gallimard, 1963). Laure Adler, *A l'aube du féminisme: Les Premières Journalistes (1830–1850)* (Paris: Payot, 1979).
10. See "Daniel Lesueur: 1860–1921," in C. Makward, M. Hage, et al., *Ecrits de femmes* (forthcoming).
11. Elaine Marks, "We Come to Praise and Deconstruct," New York University colloquium: *The Second Sex*—Thirty Years After, 27–29 Sept. 1979. See *BREFF,* 15 (Nov. 1979), 5.
12. See Elaine Marks and Isabelle de Courtivron, Introd. III and Selected Bibliography, in their *New French Feminisms* (Amherst: Univ. of Massachusetts Press, 1980).
13. Luce Irigaray, *Speculum de l'autre femme* (1974) and *Ce sexe qui n'en est pas un* (1977) are collections of essays. *Et l'une ne bouge pas sans l'autre* (1979) and *Amante marine* (1980) are "texts in the feminine." All were published in Paris by Editions de Minuit. See also Christian Delacampagne's review of *Amante marine* in *Le Monde,* 25 April 1980.
14. See Diana Paul, "Empress Wu and the Historians: A Tyrant and a Saint of Classical China," in *Unspoken Worlds: Women's Religious Lives in Non-*

Western Cultures, ed. Nancy Falk and Rita M. Gross (New York: Harper, 1980).

15. See Christiane Makward, "To Be or Not to Be . . . a Feminist Critic," in *The Future of Difference,* ed. Hester Eisenstein and Alice Jardine (Boston: Hall, 1980).
16. Monique Wittig, *Lesbian People: Material for a Dictionary,* trans. David Le Vay (New York: Avon, 1979). See a review in *New Women's Times,* 9 (Feb.–March 1980), and an interview with Christine Delphy in *Off Our Backs* (Jan. 1980). "Un jour mon prince viendra" appeared in *Questions Féministes,* 2 (Feb. 1978), 31–39.
17. Edmée de la Rochefoucauld, *Femmes d'hier et d'aujourd'hui* (Paris: Grasset, 1969), p. 52.
18. Jeanine Moulin, *Huit siècles de poésie féminine* (Paris: Seghers, 1975); Marthe-Claire Fleury's anthology (Paris: Grassin, 1976) has about the same number of pages and represents about as many poets but leaves out *all* the best-known women poets: Hébert, Prassinos, Chedid, Lasnier, and so on.
19. An international association of women writers was founded in 1975. For information on membership and on the biennial conventions in Paris, write Association Internationale des Femmes Ecrivains, 38 rue du Faubourg Saint-Jacques, Paris 75005. This is not a feminist organization.
20. For information write to *BREFF,* Dept. of French, Pennsylvania State Univ., University Park 16802.
21. Technology makes it feasible, as demonstrated by PaperBook Press (Mass.), to publish "disposable textbooks that sell for less than $1."
22. See *Teaching about Women in the Foreign Languages,* ed. Sidonie Cassirer, Female Studies, No. 9 (Old Westbury, N.Y.: Feminist, 1975), and the "Enseignement" section of *BREFF.* For women's studies in France and a recently created French feminine studies newsletter (*BIEF—Bulletin d'Information des Etudes Féminines*), see *BREFF,* 7 (1977), 3–4; 11 (1978), 4; 13 (1979), 2; and 16 (1980), 6.
23. Drama studies are under way: the 1981 NEMLA convention (Québec) offered a French program on "the woman playwright." C. Makward and Judith Miller (Univ. of Wisconsin, Madison) will complete an anthology in translation in 1982.
24. Resource persons to address for nonmetropolitan writers are, for Quebecois, Paula Lewis (Howard Univ.); for Arab and Middle Eastern writers, Evelyn Accad (Univ. of Illinois, Urbana); for Caribbean writers, Clarisse Zimra (through *BREFF*); and for African and Swiss writers, Christiane Makward (Pennsylvania State Univ.). In general, *BREFF* coeditors will channel requests for information. There is to date no identifiable specialist in Belgian writers.

Opportunities for Scholarship in Eighteenth-Century British Literature

Katharine M. Rogers

To discuss the limitations of current scholarship on women in English literature and the opportunities for better coverage, one must select a part of this vast field, and perhaps the eighteenth century provides the clearest examples. This was the first period in which women wrote and published in significant numbers. They produced poems, plays, children's books, educational and moral treatises, travel books, political pamphlets, reviews, criticism, and even radical history. In the later eighteenth century, they dominated the new form of the novel, as both readers and writers. And yet, because none of these women, before Jane Austen at the end of the century, was indisputably a writer of the first rank, it was easy for contemporary and later critics to patronize and stereotype them.

Social institutions affecting women, such as marriage law and exclusion from formal higher education, remained traditional throughout the period. But it seems clear that attitudes toward women were changing significantly. Many women acquired a good education informally and earned the intellectual respect of influential men. These developments were reflected not only in the unprecedented number of women writers but in the widespread interest, by the end of the century, in the nature, education, and role of women. This was expressed directly in feminist manifestos, which first appeared in England at this time, from Mary Astell's *Serious Proposal to the Ladies* (1694) to Mary

Wollstonecraft's *Vindication of the Rights of Woman* (1792). While most of Wollstonecraft's contemporaries considered her too radical, a surprising number admired her; and most thinking people agreed with her that the education of women had to be improved for the good of society.

Attitudes of the past, however, are hard to define. Literature (written in a male tradition) offers some indications, but one wonders how close the literary representations were to reality. Were good young women as preoccupied with filial duty as Sophia Western and Clarissa Harlowe? What really happened when a woman lost her chastity? Were the sentimental, superdelicate, constantly fainting heroines of late eighteenth-century novels at all like real young women, or were they fantasy ideals? When the witty independent coquette of Restoration comedy became the weepy, abjectly dependent heroine of sentimental comedy, did this transformation reflect an actual change in women's behavior? Or did it merely mean that women were being told to behave differently? Or were the literary ideals unconnected with what was happening in real life? If so, why should literary ideals have changed if reality did not? The whole ambiguous relation between sentimentalism and feminism—predominantly negative in the drama, predominantly positive in the novel—should be explored.

We need more direct evidence of how women felt and thought, how they interacted with one another and with men. Since intelligent women of leisure spent much of their time writing letters or journals, there must be a great deal of unpublished material. Few radical women, apart from Wollstonecraft, have had their letters published, nor has any woman not attached to a recognized literary circle. The letters of Elizabeth Inchbald, Charlotte Smith, and Amelia Opie (in the Bodleian, Huntington, Yale University, and other libraries) should be collected to throw light on their works and their working conditions, their reading of other women, and their relationships with William Godwin's circle. Joanna Baillie's letters, which richly illuminate the literary life of her time, have been partially collected (Chester Lee Lambertson, Diss. Harvard 1956); the collection should be completed and published.[1]

Many papers of the Bluestockings and other members of Samuel Johnson's circle have been published, but apart from such obvious exceptions as Katharine Balderston's *Thraliana* (Oxford: Clarendon, 1951) and Joyce Hemlow's ongoing *Journals and Letters of Fanny Burney* (Oxford: Clarendon, 1972–), most have appeared only in bowdlerized nineteenth-century editions. They might be reedited, or at least restudied, in terms of modern feminist awareness. We need a book on the Bluestockings that would evaluate their contributions and limitations, their relationship to earlier developments in England and France, and their influence on the nineteenth century.

Study of such material would provide vivifying personal detail to fill out the bald outlines of the social condition of women. We know that they had virtually no legal rights in marriage, but we do not know how much voice the average wife had in running her household, or how she felt about constant childbearing, or whether she longed to get outside the home and do something else, or how much she thought about general political and social questions. Above all, we need women's views to balance the dominant, male-created image. For example, it was a commonplace in the eighteenth century that England was a paradise for wives. But when English women compared their own lot with that of women in other countries, they found women more fortunate in Italy, in the wilds of North America, even in Turkey. In describing unfamiliar cultures, the innumerable travel writers of the period, both English and foreign, sometimes throw incidental light on the position of women at home. They often contrast English and French ladies in status, education, and morality, although it is yet to be determined how much these contrasts revealed actual differences and how much they reflected mere national prejudices. We need a bibliography of English women's travel books and those of foreign women who reported on England, as well as modern translations of such works as Madame du Boccage's *Lettres d'Angleterre* (written in the 1750s).

Just as we must reconsider social history, we must reevaluate women authors. We should study their lives—their education, their response to other women writers, their relation with family and patrons, and so forth—to find out how they perceived the world and what factors helped or hindered their work. Although there is a developing recognition of the particular strains and constrictions that pressed on women, deeper analysis is called for. What was the effect of having to write in the family living room, subject to constant interruptions? Of writing not as an established professional, but as either a dilettante or a driven hack? Of feeling it was unwomanly to reveal one's authorship of great novels? In the eighteenth century feminine modesty was a serious inhibition, as was the greater pressure on women to respect moral and literary conventions. The novel as developed by Samuel Richardson, centering on the sensibility of a marriageable young lady, provided women with a form well suited to expressing distinctively feminine feelings and experience. But, by defining what was appropriate for women to write, it could also limit an artist like Charlotte Smith, whose talents pointed toward broad social criticism. As long as these social constraints are not fully understood, it is all too easy to make disparaging generalizations about the timid conventionality of individual writers or of women in general.

It has been easier to slight women authors of the eighteenth century than those of later periods because in fact there were none of the first rank. Indisputably great women, like Jane Austen, do get treated as such. But, while minor male writers are seriously discussed and evaluated, women of the same class tend to be dismissed as hacks or to have their achievements misrepresented. Such women get recognized for extraneous reasons—Burney for her connection with the Johnson circle, Ann Radcliffe and Maria Edgeworth as the developers of new genres not considered the property of men (Gothic and local-color fiction, respectively). Since by definition women do not fit the predominant "male" pattern, they must be fitted into accepted "female" patterns. Those who do not fit are either ignored or distorted, as the gifted social critic Smith has been reduced to an undistinguished Gothic novelist. On the other hand, those who do fit are often overvalued: untalented Clara Reeve has got more than her share of attention because she was the first woman to take up the Gothic mode.

George Sherburn's discussion of the women novelists of the later eighteenth century (in his section of *A Literary History of England* [London: Routledge and Kegan Paul, 1950], the most widely used brief literary history of the period) nicely illustrates the extent to which preconceptions dominate the consideration of women writers and the disparagement to which this leads. In one brisk paragraph he dismisses the work of eight gifted and diverse women as "elegant tales of feminine distress," pausing only to quote at length a sarcastic attack on female novelists by the conspicuously antifeminist Tobias Smollett. While Bonamy Dobrée's volume on the early eighteenth century in the *Oxford History of English Literature* (New York: Oxford Univ. Press, 1959) and John Butt and Geoffrey Carnall's volume on the mid-eighteenth century (New York: Oxford Univ. Press, 1979) give fair and serious coverage to the women writers of the period, W. L. Renwick's volume in the same series (*English Literature 1789–1815* [1963]) shows the usual casual dismissive attitude toward women who do not fit an "appropriate" pattern. Renwick carelessly misreads Inchbald's *Simple Story* (1791), making its tone comic instead of tragic, its theme sectarian instead of psychological, and its heroine a mere frail vessel instead of an interesting, independent woman. He does not even mention Wollstonecraft's works in his text.

Lionel Stevenson's *English Novel* (Boston: Houghton, 1960) gives women writers special treatment by unduly emphasizing personal factors—Aphra Behn's alleged promiscuity, Reeve's spinsterhood, and Smith's rancor. *The Penguin Companion to British and Commonwealth Literature* (New York: Penguin Books, 1971) focuses on William Godwin's social theories but on Mary Wollstonecraft Godwin's emotional misadventures; it seriously discusses the literary achievement of Henry Mackenzie but dismisses Sarah Fielding as "the author of various forgotten romances," which it describes inaccurately.

Books that focus more particularly on women writers, such as

J. M. S. Tompkins' learned *Popular Novel in England* (London: Constable, 1932), have traditionally been concerned more with description than with critical appreciation. Instead of being considered on the same basis as male artists, women are used as examples to support generalizations about themes and attitudes. Similarly, in B. G. MacCarthy's *Female Pen* (Cork: Cork Univ. Press, 1946, 1947) the sheer number of women covered tends to obscure the distinction between those who were good writers (regardless of gender) and those who are of only historical interest. Again the generalization conditions the evaluation. Since Frances Brooke is seen as just one in a long line of sentimental novelists, her two better and not particularly sentimental novels are discussed solely in terms of their components of delicate distress. However, more careful readings of women authors are beginning to appear in such works as Patricia Meyer Spacks's *Female Imagination* (New York: Knopf, 1975) and *Imagining a Self* (Cambridge: Harvard Univ. Press, 1976) and in Janet Todd's *Women's Friendship in Literature* (New York: Columbia Univ. Press, 1980). The forthcoming *Dictionary of Women Writers 1660–1800,* now being edited by Todd, should contribute to a balanced picture of women's writing during this period.

Scholarship on women writers is highly uneven, largely because their biographies have attracted more interest than have their literary achievements. The colorful life of Aphra Behn has inspired much research. Generally speaking, the women who have received full-dress biographies have been connected with men: Lady Mary Wortley Montagu (Pope), Fanny Burney and Hester Thrale-Piozzi (Johnson), and even Mary Wollstonecraft (Godwin), although her most recent biographies are products of the new feminism. Books on other women writers, such as Astell and Smith, do not seriously analyze their subjects' work; now thoroughly outdated, they seem to have been inspired mainly by the need for a dissertation subject. We should have new biographies of these women, as we should of Susannah Centlivre, Sarah Fielding, Amelia Opie, and too many other interesting successful women to list here. A study of Ann Yearsley would be particularly valuable, since she was the only working-class woman in eighteenth-century England to become a professional author. Perhaps the less important women writers could best be dealt with in a series of biocritical monographs.

A survey of the Modern Language Association bibliographies from 1969 through 1980 (the latest available) shows that women authors in general get significantly less attention than men and that the coverage is disproportionate, often depending on extraneous factors. While Centlivre is represented by an article and a book and Smith and Inchbald by two articles apiece, there are nineteen articles and one book on William Collins, forty-three articles on William Godwin, and ten articles and two books on the pornographer John Cleland. Of the women who have received more adequate coverage—Burney, Edgeworth, Mary Wortley Montagu, Radcliffe, Thrale, and (only since 1972) Wollstonecraft—Burney, Montagu, and Thrale were associated with prominent men, and Radcliffe is the outstanding representative of a conventionally feminine genre, the Gothic novel.[2] In the past few years, increasing attention has been paid to women writers who have nothing to recommend them but the quality of their work, but much remains to be done with early fiction writers of respectable lives and works (such as Jane Barker), novelists who did not choose the Gothic mode (such as Smith and Sarah Fielding), and feminists other than Wollstonecraft (such as Astell and the still unidentified "Sophia").

The standard general bibliographies, supplemented by those appearing in the fall issues of *Women in Literature,* seem adequate to cover current research. But we badly need listings of eighteenth-century works by and about women. Compiling these would be an awesome task, but they would be an invaluable tool for investigating such areas as women's economic position, their general level of education, their attitudes and interests. One particularly useful work would be an annotated checklist of all novels by women (not just the well-known authors), together with a listing of the contemporary reviews. Another would be an annotated bibliography of eighteenth-century publications on the woman question, including translations of foreign works.

Women authors are better represented in reprints than in other areas of scholarship. The Oxford English Novels series includes excellent editions of the more distinguished works, such as Inchbald's *Simple Story* and Smith's *Old Manor House* (1793). The Garland Publishing Company has issued reprints of a great many less known works, usually with brief introductions bringing out feminist points not previously noticed, which do much to increase our understanding of women's attitudes and our ability to evaluate writers. Garland's reprint of *Emily Montague* (1769) shows that Brooke was not the total sentimentalist one would suppose from reading nothing but her lachrymose *Lady Julia Mandeville* (1763), the only one of her novels generally available before 1974.[3] AMS Press has reprinted nineteenth-century editions of many earlier women's works, particularly letters and journals from the Bluestocking circle. Arno's series of Gothic novels includes many women writers.

Nevertheless, important works remain to be reprinted, such as Burney's *The Wanderer* (1814), a novel that, however flawed, tells much about the condition of women. Her plays, still in manuscript at the New York Public Library, should be edited and published. There are few scholarly editions of women's works. Obvious possibilities would be the complete plays of Inchbald and Centlivre, two of the most popular dramatists of the eighteenth century. And we need a new edition of Winchilsea's poems, incorporating those discovered since Myra Reynolds' edition of 1903.

Unfortunately, there is no eighteenth-century anthology that represents women at all adequately. Of the two existing paperback anthologies, *English Prose and Poetry 1660–1800* (New York: Holt, 1961) and the eighteenth-century volume of the *Oxford Anthology of English Literature* (New York: Oxford Univ. Press, 1973), neither has any work by a woman, although the Oxford book runs to 766 closely printed pages. Volume I of the *Norton Anthology of English Literature* (New York: Norton, 1979) does a little better, with two poems by Winchilsea and two by Mary Wortley Montagu (who is represented by poems, even though her distinction is clearly as a letter writer). The new anthology *Before Their Time* (New York: Ungar, 1979), which includes Winchilsea, Astell, Montagu, Smith, Burney, and Wollstonecraft, makes it possible to treat women in an eighteenth-century course. But we need an anthology that represents writers of both sexes, to show that women were beginning to enter the mainstream of English literature. Putting the female authors side by side with male counterparts—Winchilsea with Prior, Wollstonecraft with Burke, and so forth—would be the best way to demonstrate that they should be judged on the same terms.

Women authors must be evaluated as men are—in the context of their period and the mainstream of literature—not isolated in a literary ghetto with its own separate standards. They must be considered as individuals rather than as members of a group, so that we can appreciate the distinctive gifts of each writer, as well as distinguish superior work from the ruck of hack writing or self-indulgent effusion. Only then will it be possible to make sound generalizations about the differences between women's work and men's and the particular contributions of women to the tradition. For example, we could analyze without prejudice the relationship, if any, between the faults of the later eighteenth-century novel and the increasing influence of women as writers and readers. Instead of assuming that sentimentality and an excessive emphasis on propriety are intrinsically feminine, we could examine the degree to which these qualities characterize particular women writers, compare it with the degree found in men, and inquire into the underlying reasons for any disparities.

Although we think of women predominantly as novelists, in fact they wrote copiously in all genres (partly because authorship was the only way in which a lady could make an independent living). There were more successful women dramatists in the Restoration–eighteenth-century period than in any other time up to the present. It would be interesting to investigate how women were able to break into the male-dominated field of the theater. Apart from writing imaginative literature, women produced a vast number of educational works for other women, for children, and for the poor. These works provide a rich source of everyday details, gained from women's household experience, that do not make their way into more pretentious literature; not only have they increased our knowledge of eighteenth-century life and attitudes but they may have contributed to the development of realism in the Victorian novel. We might also examine these works to find out whether women's more intimate contact with children caused them to differ from male educators and to have any beneficial influence on educational practice. It would also be useful to evaluate, on the other end of the educational scale, the scholarly achievements of women like Elizabeth Carter and Elizabeth Elstob. To what extent can the accolades bestowed on the first and the neglect of the second be attributed to their being women?

It was in the Restoration and the eighteenth century that English women first contributed significantly to literature. Yet, because they fell short of indisputable genius, they have been stereotyped and disparaged. Eighteenth-century courses, both in general literature and the novel, often ignore women writers altogether. Those who do get critical attention often get it for fortuitous reasons, such as their association with prominent men. Although traditional criticism has applied a single standard to women's working conditions, refusing to recognize the extent of their difficulties, it persists in applying a double standard to their achievements. Only by careful study of superior women artists can we divest ourselves of the prejudices that result from considering them as a group separate from "regular writers." We need to read their works with the same seriousness as we read men's and to see them as individual artists, not as examples of some stereotype, whether it be Gothic romancer, local colorist, sentimental novelist, or hack writer struggling to support her family.

Notes

1. I owe this information and other valuable suggestions to Ellen Messer-Davidow.
2. I have excluded brief notes from this count and assigned articles covering several authors to the one who is most emphasized. Unpublished dissertations, not listed here, are more likely to deal with women authors.
3. The relevant Garland series are Feminist Controversy in England, 1788–1810; The Novel in England, 1700–1775; Eighteenth-Century English Drama; and The Romantic Context: Poetry 1789–1830.

Notes on Contributors

Susan L. Cocalis is Associate Professor of German at the University of Massachusetts, Amherst. She has coedited a volume of critical essays about women in German literature (with Kay Goodman) and has written several studies on eighteenth-century German literature and on modern German drama. She is currently doing research on novels written by women in the age of Goethe.

Jean Franco is Olive H. Palmer Professor of Humanities at Stanford University. She is the author of *Modern Culture of Latin America: An Introduction to Latin American Literature* and *César Vallejo: The Dialectics of Poetry and Silence.*

H. Lee Gershuny is Professor of English at the Borough of Manhattan Community College, City University of New York. Her Ph.D. thesis (New York University 1973) was the award-winning *Sexist Semantics in the Dictionary.* She is coauthor of *Sexism and Language,* and she has published articles on semantics, linguistic sexism, and pedagogy.

Kay Goodman is Assistant Professor of German at Brown University. She is coeditor of *Beyond the Eternal Feminine: Critical Essays on Women and German Literature* (with Susan L. Cocalis), and she is currently writing a book on women's autobiography in nineteenth-century Germany.

Joan E. Hartman was a member and cochair of the MLA Commission on the Status of Women in the Profession. She is Professor of English and Chairperson of the department at the College of Staten Island, City University of New York.

Barbara Heldt teaches Russian literature at the University of British Columbia. She is Associate Editor of *Russian Literature Triquarterly.* As Barbara Heldt Monter, she is the author of *Koz'ma Prutov: The Art of Parody* and the translator of Karolina Pavlova's *A Double Life.* She has written articles on Pushkin, Pavlova, Tolstoy, Dostoevsky, Chekhov, Tsvetaeva, Nabokov, Solzhenitsyn, and Sokolov. She is currently writing a book to be called *Russian Literature: Another Image.*

Karen M. Keener has been a student of lesbian literature and culture since 1971. She has been active in the Gay Caucuses of the Modern Language Association and the National Council of Teachers of English and has participated in sessions on lesbian literature at the conventions of several professional organizations. She teaches a variety of literature and composition courses and serves as Coordinator of Literature at Parkland College.

Paul Lauter, Professor of American Studies at the State University of New York College, Old Westbury, is currently writing a book on the origins of the American literary canon. He is active in the teachers' union and on the editorial board of *Radical Teacher,* and he has been Treasurer of the Feminist Press since its inception.

Sara Lennox is Associate Professor of German at the University of Massachusetts, Amherst. She has written articles on twentieth-century East and West German literature, including studies of Uwe Johnson, Christa Wolf, East German literary theory, women in Brecht's work, and German women's writing in the 1970s.

Christiane P. Makward, who holds a D.Lit. from the Sorbonne, is Associate Professor of French at Pennsylvania State University. She has taught in higher education in Nigeria and Québec and at the University of Wisconsin, Madison. Her publications include articles in *Sub-Stance, Revue des Sciences Humaines, Poétique,* and *Women and Literature.* Her special interests include Swiss and African women writers and current feminist thought. She is a founding coeditor of *BREFF* and the general editor of *Ecrits de femmes* (forthcoming), a collective reference book and critical anthology of women writers in French. She is currently working on Swiss women novelists and contemporary women playwrights.

Elizabeth A. Meese is Assistant Dean for the Humanities and Fine Arts and Associate Professor of English at the University of Alabama. Her work has appeared in *American Literature, Criticism, Frontiers, Boundary 2,* and other journals. Her current research is directed toward a book-length study of Southern women regionalists, with an emphasis on issues of critical theory.

Ellen Messer-Davidow was a member of the MLA Commission on the Status of Women in the Profession, a founder and coordinator of the MLA Graduate Student Caucus, and Administrative Assistant to the President of the University of Cincinnati. She is currently completing a doctoral dissertation on feminist critical theory.

Katharine M. Rogers is Professor of English at Brooklyn College and a member of the Doctoral Faculty at City University of New York. She is the author of *The Troublesome Helpmate: A History of Misogyny in Literature* and *William Wycherley* and the editor of *Selected Poems of Anne Finch, Countess of Winchilsea* and *Before Their Time: Six Women Writers of the Eighteenth Century.* She discusses many early women authors in her new book, *Feminism in Eighteenth-Century England.*

Deborah S. Rosenfelt was Professor of English at California State University, Long Beach, before becoming Coordinator of Women Studies at San Francisco State University. She has edited two volumes of the Female Studies series published by the Feminist Press and coedited (with Leonore Hoffman) *Teaching Women's Literature from a Regional Perspective.* Her other work includes *Strong Women: An An-*

notated Bibliography of Literature for the High School Classroom, a commentary on Michael Wilson's *Salt of the Earth,* and various articles on women's studies and women and literature.

Erlene Stetson is Associate Professor of English at Indiana University. Her most recent work is titled *Black Sister: Black Women Poets, 1746–1980.*

Sandra M. Thomson, whose M.A. thesis is a study of women characters in a selected group of Lermontov's works and whose Ph.D. dissertation centers on Vladimir Voinovich's satirical novel *The Life and Extraordinary Adventures of Private Ivan Chonkin,* is a sessional lecturer at the University of British Columbia.

Sylvie Weil, formerly Professor of French at Bennington College, is currently a free-lance writer living in New York. She holds the Licence ès Lettres, Paris; Diplôme d'Etudes Supérieures, Paris; and Agrégation de Lettres classiques, Paris. She is coeditor of *Les Femmes en France* and a contributor to *Nineteenth-Century French Studies.*